L I V I N G   W I T H   G R I E F

ALZHEIMER'S DISEASE

EDITED BY
KENNETH J. DOKA

Foreword by Jack D. Gordon, Chairman, Hospice Foundation of America

**HOSPICE FOUNDATION
OF AMERICA**

Supported in part by the Foundation for End-of-Life Care

24.95

This book is part of HFA's *Living With Grief* ® series.

Ordering information:

Call Hospice Foundation of America: 800-854-3402

Or write:
Hospice Foundation of America
2001 S St., NW #300
Washington, DC 20009

Or visit HFA's Web site:
www.hospicefoundation.org

Managing Editor: Judith Rensberger
Assistant Managing Editor: Kate Viggiano
Cover Design: Patricia McBride
Typesetting and Design: Pam Page Cullen
Cover Photo: Photofusion Picture Library / Alamy

Library of Congress Cataloging-in-Publication Data

Alzheimer's disease / Hospice Foundation of America ;
   edited by Kenneth J. Doka ; foreword by Jack D. Gordon.
      p. cm – (Living with grief)
      Includes bibliographical references and index.
      LCCN 2003110495
      ISBN 1-893349-05-5

   1. Alzheimer's disease.   I. Doka, Kenneth J.
II. Hospice Foundation of America.   III. Series.

RC523.A374 2004   362.1'96831
                                        QBI03-200919

■ DEDICATION ■

To my new grandson,
Kenneth Hector, born June 19, 2003,
and to the hope that as he ages,
Alzheimer's disease
will become a dim memory.
—Kenneth J. Doka

Contents

■ FOREWORD ■

Jack D. Gordon
Chairman, Hospice Foundation of America

It may seem strange to some that Hospice Foundation of America has made Alzheimer's disease the subject of this year's teleconference and companion book. After all, people who are somewhat familiar with hospice are aware that Medicare specifies that a prognosis of less than six months to live is required to be eligible for the hospice benefit. While that time can be extended, most hospice referrals come in the last month or two of life.

We know Alzheimer's has a long time trajectory, with death coming eight, ten, or even 20 years after diagnosis. Long before the end, Alzheimer's patients lose their ability to communicate with others and to understand what is going on around them.

The burdens of their care fall upon their spouses and other members of their families.

This central fact about Alzheimer's disease raises a serious public policy question. Do we have any right to ask that the entire burden be placed on family members?

In my view, the answer to that question is no. It seems to me unethical. We have a health care system that pays doctors and hospitals to care for patients, but assumes that family and friends will do this work without pay, for as long as necessary, and under the most difficult and stressful conditions imaginable. With Alzheimer's disease, family caregivers put their lives on hold for years.

This "free" care may save money for our health care system. It does not take into account the direct financial costs to family caregivers, such as lost income, or the costs associated with health problems brought on or exacerbated by the stresses of caregiving. For example, studies have shown that family caregivers of dementia patients have higher rates of depression than caregivers of patients with other terminal illnesses, including cancer. Research confirms what we already knew or strongly suspected: caregiving is so stressful for caregivers, so emotionally draining and difficult, that it leads to poor health and even to premature death.

How might this burden be lessened? One approach is the expansion of hospice.

The fact is that the hospice philosophy dictates the use of an inter-disciplinary team, to care for the patient and to see that his or her wishes are followed. This is a model that is applicable to most illnesses. They do not even have to be life-threatening. But focusing on the patient's wishes and aggressively providing comfort care is a philosophy rarely found in American hospitals. In fact, it is so rare that some hospitals and physicians are attempting to create a specialty that would specifically deal with this deficiency in the hope that it could then be funded separately.

It is ironic that the medical profession, in the course of trying to make people well, should have to make a separate activity out of making them comfortable and cared for on their own terms. They have even given this activity a name, palliative care. In England, Australia, Canada, and other western countries that have a national health system, palliative care is provided along with other care because the physicians and hospitals are not entrepreneurs but, rather, healers and helpers. Their payment system does not require separate fees for each part of medical support.

What does this have to do with Alzheimer's disease? It is just to point out that the American system of entrepreneurial medicine has few answers for the management of chronic disease. Yet we are faced with a rapidly growing number of elderly who are living longer than was usual 50 years ago. This means that degenerative diseases will become much more prevalent. That, in turn, will make the creation of a solution to the problem of caring for chronically ill people an even more important public policy imperative. And this is where the expansion of hospice would provide a better life and more appropriate care for an ever-growing number of Americans.

There is another aspect of hospice care that needs to be understood as necessary for the working of the system. That is the importance of individual caregivers and their need for support. Hospice is required by Medicare to provide bereavement counseling to families of the deceased for a year after death. This is an acknowledgement of the mental health needs of the survivors. Hospice always considers the individual and his or her family as the "patient." In many cases, certainly in Alzheimer's disease, bereavement starts with the diagnosis. Families need help and support from that point forward.

The working of hospice seems so sensible and obvious that one has to consider how the health system has deviated so much from its ordained role as healer. Alzheimer's is a real test of the humanity of the system. It is that humanity, the willingness to extend a helping hand to those in need, that is pushed into the background by a system that makes ability-to-pay the first consideration in providing care.

So it is a good question to ask why we are examining the subject of Alzheimer's disease and other dementias. The answer can teach all of us more about the appropriate use of the hospice model and the relevance of hospice philosophy in situations that seem, at first glace, to be outside hospice parameters.

In this book, an important goal is to provide needed information to readers who are dealing with Alzheimer's disease either from a personal perspective or a service provider's point of view. It shows how hospice principles can make care for Alzheimer's patients and their families more humane.

■ ACKNOWLEDGMENTS ■

One of the great pleasures of editing a book is the opportunity to acknowledge and thank all those who helped along the way. First, there are those who directly contribute to the task. Jack Gordon, Chairman of Hospice Foundation of America, and David Abrams, President, can be counted upon to lend their counsel, experience, and wisdom. The very teleconference that this book supports is a testament to their vision. Judith Rensberger, Senior Program Officer, serves ably as Managing Editor, assisted by Kate Viggiano, Publications and Outreach Manager.

Others in the Hospice Foundation of America provide indirect support, assisting the foundation's work so that the book can reach fruition. Included here are Sophie Berman, Karen Higgins, Donna Hines, Robert Lee, and Bertha Ramirez. We also acknowledge Cokie Roberts, whose contribution to the annual teleconference adds to the success of the entire endeavor.

This year's program has benefited immensely from the involvement of the Alzheimer's Association. From the very beginning, the Association has been an enthusiastic participant in the development of both the teleconference and the companion book. For laying the groundwork, I want to thank Bob and Linda Mendelson. Linda serves on the Board of Directors of the national Alzheimer's Association, which is headquartered in Chicago, and Bob is immediate past president of the Association's Greater Illinois chapter.

In the Association's national office, I also want to thank Sheldon Goldberg, President and CEO; Kathleen O'Brien, Senior Vice President of Program and Community Services; Dr. William Thies, Vice President of Medical and Scientific Affairs; Patricia Pinkowski, Director of the Greenfield Library, Mary Ann Urbashich, Associate Director of Library Projects, Jeanne Heid-Grubman, Director of Education and Outreach; JoAnn Victoria Ciatto, Associate Director of Education and Outreach, and Elizabeth Heck, Associate Director of Clinical Care.

I also want to gratefully acknowledge the help of the Alzheimer's Association of Northeastern New York. In particular, I thank Marvin LeRoy, President and CEO; Trudi Cholewinski, Director of Programs and Services, and Thaddeus Rauschi, Board member and long-time volunteer. At age 57, Dr. Raushi was diagnosed with early-onset Alzheimer's disease. His first-person account appears as Chapter 7 in this book.

Across the country, other Alzheimer's Association board members and staff assisted in ways large and small with both the teleconference and this book. In this connection, I want to extend special thanks to Jennifer Owens, in Iowa; Betsy Murphy, in northern Virginia, and Sandra Wheeler, in southern Maryland.

The College of New Rochelle continues to offer a wonderfully supportive environment that allows me to write. I need to thank so many there, including Stephen Sweeny, President; Joan Bailey, Vice-President; Nancy Brown, Dean, and Marie Ribarich, Division Chair. Mary Whalen, Vera Mezzaucella, and Howard Shapiro provide critical administrative and secretarial assistance. Many others at the college, as well as my colleagues at the Association of Death Education (ADEC) and The International Work Group on Dying, Death and Bereavement, offer friendship, support, and intellectual stimulation.

I would like to thank those in my personal life who provide support and respite. This has been a year of change. My son, Michael, and his wife, Angelina, had their first child, Kenneth. My godson, Keith Whitehead, entered college. Other members of my network include Kathy Dillon, my sister Dorothy and my brother Franky, and their families. I also want to acknowledge special friends and neighbors, including Dylan Rieger, Jim and Karen Cassa, Margot and Paul Kimball, Don and Carol Ford, Allen and Gail Greenstein, Jim and Mary Millar, Linda and Russell Tellier, Terry and Herb Webber, Fred and Lisa Amore, Eric Schwarz, Lynn Miller and Larry Laterza. They are all appreciated.

Finally, I want to thank our contributing authors, all of whom met their deadlines with understanding and grace.

Kenneth J. Doka
Washington, DC
February 6, 2004

▪ PART I ▪

Alzheimer's and Other Dementias

There is a specter haunting North America and the developed world. It feeds on minds, robbing individuals of their memories, cognition, personality, and eventually their lives. It steals from families, taking their money, their time, and their relationships. It pilfers from society, businesses, and the government, costing the United States approximately $100 billion dollars a year (Ernst & Hay, 1994). The specter is dementia.

An estimated four and a half million Americans have Alzheimer's disease. That figure will likely triple when the baby boom generation reaches later life (Hebert, Scherr et al., 2003). To Kenneth Doka, in the opening chapter, this will be the coming crisis: the dreaded disease that commands the attention of a generation even as it changes society. Dr. Doka suggests that dementia will become a major social issue. Not only will there be calls and agitation for research, programs, and services to persons with dementia and their families, but the rising rates of dementia are likely to cause the reevaluation of a slew of policies including mandatory retirement, caregiving policies, insurance, and even the role of hospice. The predictability of this crisis is a saving grace, Dr. Doka concludes. There is still time to revise policies, services, and programs before rates of dementia dramatically rise.

Since much of this debate hinges on issues such as diagnosis and treatment, it is essential to review the biology of dementia. Samuel Gandy describes the biology of Alzheimer's disease. In doing so, Dr. Gandy reviews both the progress in our understanding of the disease and outlines options for prevention and treatment.

However, not all dementia is due to Alzheimer's disease. Parag Dalsania offers a description of a variety of conditions including depression, delirium, and mild cognitive impairment that may create symptoms of dementia as well as other forms of dementia that have different bases than Alzheimer's disease. Underlying Dr. Dalsania's chapter is the caution to carefully diagnose and treat dementia.

These first three chapters emphasize the critical need for research. We are at the brink of crisis as rates of dementia are likely to rise. Yet, we also are at the edge of discovery. Advances in cellular biology have the potential to answer fundamental questions that might both radically advance the understanding of the aging process as well as the processes that initiate the onset and determine the course of dementia. However, these advances provoke ambivalence in some quarters, affecting governmental support. The result is that funding is an inconsistent cycle of boom and bust, making it difficult to sustain a consistent stream of research and to attract and retain researchers. What is needed to face the coming crisis is the equivalent of a Manhattan project or Moon Shot: a long-term, well-funded plan of research unfettered by ideological or political constraints.

Dr. Dalsania's chapter provides background to Dr. Doka's chapter on ethnicity and culture. Interestingly, ethnic groups show differing prevalence rates for each type of dementia. This may be due to a variety of factors including biological, social, or environmental issues. However, it also may offer clues about the interplay between culture, biology, heredity, and environment. While the significance of differences in these rates might be argued, culture clearly affects treatment in other ways: defining how the disease is understood in distinct cultures and outlining differences in the ways each culture identifies caregiving responsibilities. It will be interesting to assess the ways that these caregiving norms may be redefined as groups continue to assimilate.

Diversity is not just about ethnicity. Philip McCallion and Mary McCarron remind us of the relationship of intellectual disabilities to Alzheimer's disease. Persons with certain intellectual disabilities such as Down's syndrome have high rates of dementia as they age. In this population, too, there will be a need to develop services, programs, and policies to effectively serve this population even as they face end-of-life issues. Drs. McCallion and McCarron note as well that there is possibility for enrichment as the two networks—the developmental disabilities system and the dementia system—interact. Both have had experiences in dealing with populations that may have difficulty in communicating both their pain and preferences.

Together these chapters reinforce a critical point. The coming crisis will leave no group or culture untouched. ■

REFERENCES

Ernst, R., & Hay, J. (1994). The US economic and social costs of Alzheimer's disease revisited. *American Journal of Public Health, 84,* 1262-1264.

Hebert, L., Scherr, P., Benias, J., Bennett, D., & Evans, D. (2003). Alzheimer's disease in the US population: Prevalence estimates using the 2000 census. *Archives of Neurology, 60,* 1119-1122.

CHAPTER 1

The Coming Crisis: Aging, Dementia, and Society

Kenneth J. Doka

INTRODUCTION

"Senator," "Senior," "Senile": these three words have very different meanings. The first is a sign of respect designating a member of a high and wise deliberative body. "Senior" is a more neutral term simply designating a person as older or an elder. Then there is "senile," a now generally discarded term that literally means "pertaining to old age" but generally is used to describe declining mental abilities in older persons.

Ironically all of these terms share the same etymological root *sene*, a Latin word designating "old man." The first two terms have obvious reference. A senior is an elder and the original Roman senators were men of age and substance, hardened by experience, chosen for their abilities to offer wise counsel. The word senile is an unfortunate connotation— a perspective of aging as inevitably leading to mental decline.

Understandings of dementia have evolved in past decades. Dementia is no longer viewed as an inevitable aspect of aging; rather it is viewed as secondary to the aging process. It is the result of a number of diseases and conditions that impair mental functioning. Clearly the incidences of these diseases are more prevalent as people age. While prevalence rates vary over a range, most estimates indicate that about four percent of persons over 65 years of age experience severe dementia and that 10-20 percent of older persons (65+) have milder forms of dementia (Geller & Reichel, 1999). Prevalence rates rise as the population ages. Current estimates suggest that only one percent of the population 65 and older exhibits dementia. However, 10 percent of those over 75 years old and 25-30 percent of those over 85 years showed signs of dementia (Geller & Reichel, 1999). One study in East Boston found a prevalence of 47 percent of those over 85 years (Evens, Funken-Staun, Albert, et al, 1989). Since the population over 85 years is the fastest growing segment of the older population, the prevalence of dementia seems destined to grow.

Alzheimer's disease is the most common cause of dementia but it is not the only one. Pick's disease, Diffuse Lewy Body disease and Supranuclear Palsy are irreversible disorders of unknown causes. In all of these cases, etiology is unknown or disputed. Other irreversible dementias may be due to vascular conditions (eg. Multi-infarct dementia), genetic disorders (eg. Huntington's disease), infections (eg. Huntington's disease or AIDS-related dementia), or trauma (eg. dementia pogilistica). In other cases, symptoms of dementia may arise from reversible conditions caused by medications or vitamin deficiency. The diagnostic and statistical manual (DSM-IV) uses the diagnosis of "delirium" to distinguish these reversible conditions from progressive dementias.

DEMENTIA AS A DREADED DISEASE

Whatever the diagnosis, whatever the cause, dementia is a dreaded disease. In an earlier work (Doka, 1977), I explored the concept of "dreaded diseases." Dreaded diseases are diseases that carry a collective opprobrium. These diseases are feared. Historically diseases have been feared for two reasons. The first types were the great epidemics such as Bubonic Plague, Influenza or diseases such as yellow fever, typhus and cholera. These diseases inspired dread by the huge number of victims left in their wake. The massive death toll radically changed their societies, overturning social structures and creating new patterns of interaction.

The other types of dreaded disease are the ones with shameful stigmas: feared not so much for their collective devastation but by the individual nature of the death. That is the horrific way that individuals die. Cancer, tuberculosis, syphilis and leprosy would, at various points in history, be included in this category. In that earlier work (Doka, 1997), I suggested that AIDS is especially dreaded since it shows characteristics of both.

So do the dementias. As the population continues to age both in North America and the world, the prevalence of dementia is likely to rise exponentially. It will be epidemic. As the baby boom generation (those people born between 1943 and 1960) ages the prevalence of the disease is expected to rise from a current 4.5 million persons to somewhere between 11.3 to 16 million by 2050 (Hebert, Scherr, et al, 2003). The disease will affect many more million such as spouses and family members.

It is a fearful way to die. One of the more frightful horror movies was "The Invasion of the Body Snatchers." Its premise is chilling. A person goes to sleep one night only to have his body taken over by an alien plant-like creature—a spore. The person looks the same, remains in the same environment yet has been altered by its invader.

In a sense, this is a cinematic metaphor for dementia. The person looks the same, even remains in the family, and yet is now different. The continuing metamorphism wrought by the disease slowly yet inescapably removes the victim from connections to family and society.

It is the very insidious nature of the disease that adds to the sense of dread. Every lapse of memory to an older person such as the inability to recall a name or face can be a frightening reminder of personal vulnerability. It sustains a fear that one may be in the world though not of it—failing to acknowledge significant others or even self, losing the memories of not only how to do things but what the things are. It suggests the possibility that one may live to the end of life fading into the shadows unaware of the world, relationships, or even self.

The course of dementia also is unpredictable. The image of dementia with later learning peeled away before earlier learning is an inadequate model. In fact, one of the difficulties in treating dementia is that the biology of memory is not well understood. In fact, the models of how memory itself works are insufficient. Therefore, patterns of decline in dementia are not so readily predictable.

As with other dreaded diseases, the very name connotates fear. The term "dementia" not only insinuates a decline in mental facilities, but also strange and aberrant behavior. A person after all, who does unspeakable acts, is described as "demented." All of these factors contribute to the sense of dread engendered by Alzheimer's disease and the other dementias.

It is highly likely then that Alzheimer's disease, which is identified in the popular mind as the cause of dementia (and in fact, a major cause), is to be the first dreaded disease of the twenty-first century. Alzheimer's disease challenges the core fears of the baby boom generation.

The baby boom generation has been resistant to the idea of aging. As they file through middle age, the boomer generation has spawned the rise of health clubs and vitamin stores—all partially attempts to stave off the ravages of aging. The ravages of dementia then are incontestable proof that one has succumbed to aging. That alone makes it fearful.

Beyond simply a sign of the loss of valued youth, dementia is an onslaught against so many of the boomer's cherished values: autonomy, independence, and control. Alzheimer's disease means the lack of control. The victim loses everything in the loss of mind. That creates a loss of autonomy and independence that the baby boom generation always has resisted.

Alzheimer's disease clearly will be the dreaded disease.

DEMENTIA AS A SOCIAL ISSUE

Because it will be their dreaded disease, Alzheimer's disease will be a public social issue for the baby boom generation. C.W. Mills, an American sociologist, distinguished between "private" troubles and "private" issues (1993). To Mills, private troubles are an individual problem, an aspect of a person's circumstances and character. For example, the fact that mom, now old, was becoming forgetful and confused was a private problem for a small number of individuals, because they had to resolve the issue perhaps by institutionalizing mother or accommodating work or home schedules so they could provide adequate supervision and support.

"Public" issues, on the other hand, merit social action. These problems transcend individual difficulties. There is an awareness that the problem does not just affect one person, but many: it is not one mother who is confused and forgetful, but millions. The problem now begs for social intervention.

Alzheimer's disease and related dementias are likely to be the social problem of the next quarter of a century. It may very well be a social issue as commanding of public attention as the Civil Rights movement was of the last half of the twentieth century. As baby boomers see their future in caring for their own parents, they are likely to agitate for increased attention to dementia. Much like the draft of an earlier era, the conquest of Alzheimer's disease has the potential to be their next generational issue.

One reason is sheer scope. The boomer generation, baring a major discontinuity as a major war, new epidemic or environmental catastrophe, is likely to live in large numbers to very old ages. For most dementias, the causes are either unknown or genetic, so they are not, with the exception of vascular dementias, preventable. Even vascular dementias are not easily preventable. Unless there are unforeseen and dramatic breakthroughs in prevention of treatment, the rate of persons affected by dementia can be expected to dramatically increase as the baby boom generation ages. Estimates suggest that well over 11 million, perhaps as many as 16 million, may have the disease (Hebert, Scherr, et al, 2003). Incremental advances in lifespan may even increase these estimates.

There also is the expense. Alzheimer's disease costs approximately a $100 billion a year (Ernst & Hay, 1994). These expenses include not only direct costs to businesses, families, and individuals, but indirect costs as well. These indirect costs may include increased costs of insurance as well as other indirect costs such as the loss of productivity and absenteeism of those shouldered with caregiving responsibilities.

Moreover, there is increased awareness of dementia. In most American subcultures, it is not a shameful stigma largely hidden from public view. Awareness generates increased awareness. The identified action of dementia in public personalities such as President Reagan or Charlton Heston focus attention on Alzheimer's disease and the problems caused by dementia. Such public identification is critical for a number of reasons. It lessens the stigma of the disease, allowing other families and individuals to come forward. The publicity personalizes the disease, placing a human face on an otherwise anonymous victim. Finally, awareness increases motivation to act.

Not that the boomer generation needs much motivation. This generation has shown considerable public savvy in dominating political debate. From their youth, their sheer numbers have instigated political debate. Their concerns have become social concerns. Their private troubles—from overcrowded schools to the draft—have transformed into social issues. As Dychwald and Flower (1988) note, the baby boom has been a tsunami wave overwhelming every social institution encountered in their life course.

They have already experienced dementia indirectly as they have cared for aging parents. These experiences have moved caregiving very much to the center of the public arena. As the boomers age and enter later life in large numbers, their experiences with friends and mates, as well as their personal fears will force public attention on Alzheimer's disease and related dementias.

They are likely to encounter a receptive society. The aging of America, as well as that of most developed societies, is likely to lead to the increased prevalence of Alzheimer's disease and related dementias. This trend will leave little untouched.

For example, schools, colleges, and other employers, in the absence of mandatory retirement, may need to develop policies regarding screening or testing. As persons stay within the work force, there are likely to be cases where employees experience early stage dementia. This in turn will raise issues once reserved for other illnesses. How far must employers accommodate such illnesses? When does dementia compromise the safety of the work place? How can one mandate that persons are tested or otherwise screened? What are the rights of employees in such situations? When can an employee be terminated?

These debates are likely to spill over into other areas. Driving licenses are a sign of both independence and adulthood. The loss of a driver's license is a symbol of declining capacity, long dreaded by older drivers. Many states already have provisions for periodic testing of older drivers. Yet, the increased prevalence of dementia suggests that states may have to reexamine this issue, perhaps by developing more sophisticated testing procedures and possibly even developing research and tracking. It very well may be that certain types of accidents or violations may be seen as early screening devices for the cognitive losses evident in early stage dementia.

These issues are likely to generate further debates about the rights of individuals versus the needs of the larger society. How early can individuals be tested and on what basis? What are the rights of individuals with cognitive declines? How will their privacy be respected and their independence nurtured? Boomers, after all, have had an historical aversion to the notion of a paternalistic government.

Health and long term care are likely to be affected as well. Research continues on early detection and treatment. Alzheimer's and perhaps other dementias are likely to be diagnosed earlier. This can exacerbate a range of ethical issues. Can a person in the early stages of the disease terminate medication even for a readily treatable infection? Are they competent to make the decision? Would earlier advance directives hold? Can Alzheimer's disease especially in the early stages be considered an untreatable disease?

The presence of a great number of persons living in the community with early stage dementia will lead to the redesign of programs and facilities. The treatment of Alzheimer's disease as well as the other dementias is likely to be a combination of medication, environmental and mental stimulation, and physical stimulation and exercise. There may be a surge of day programs that can offer such services while providing respite for the caregiver. Other respite services such as night sitters may be in demand. The provision of these services may delay more expensive alternatives such as institutionalization within a nursing home. Yet, the funding stream for such vital services is still unclear. There may be increased pressures for insurance programs, including Medicare, to cover these services.

Assisted-living facilities and nursing homes also may need to redesign policies and programs to accommodate a future population with dementia. Assisted-living facilities may need to develop services that offer more supportive care, allowing individuals with early stage dementia to stay longer. All types of facilities may need to reexamine programs to assure that these programs offer the varied stimulation that seems so critical to persons with dementia.

The policies governing hospice will need reevaluation as well. The hospice benefit that limits care to the last six months of life will be further challenged. Under the Medicare Hospice Benefit provision, persons can elect hospice care if a physician certifies that they have less than six months life expectancy. With Alzheimer's disease however, such prognostication is difficult. Furthermore, governmental efforts to investigate Medicare fraud have seemed to target patients with dementia. The result is that hospices that have provided care for Alzheimer's patients have been investigated. In some cases, care for such patients has been excluded, leaving hospices financially liable. Some hospices, then, have been reluctant to admit patients with Alzheimer's disease. This, in turn, has left individuals with the disease and their families bereft of good palliative care. The growing population with dementia should cause review of such policies that inhibit valued hospice care to dementia.

This, too, will create new challenges for hospices. Hospices were originally designed to treat late-stage cancer patients. How can one assess pain and symptom control in persons with dementia? What new services may be necessary to support patients with dementia and their families? How will staff be supported since caring with patients with dementia is not likely to bring the same satisfaction of working with persons who are aware of death? What ethical issues will arise as hospices encounter the problems of denying life-sustaining treatment to patients of perceived marginal social value—often exacerbated by the fact that these decisions may be made by family or other surrogates without the explicit wishes of the patient fully known?

There is likely to be increased pressure for funding for research and treatment. Yet, such increases carry costs. Increases in funding for research and treatment as well as for healthcare in a society already supporting a large cohort of retired persons, will either need to generate increased tax revenues or reductions in other spending. As agendas are likely to be very different for people at different stages of life, possibilities exist for provoking sharpened generational conflicts. Healthcare and other entitlements for older persons assume much of current governmental revenues. How will new services be provided? Will generational conflict develop over spending priorities?

New positions and new markets will be created for the range of services, products, and programs necessitated by an increased numbers of individuals, and their families, struggling with dementia. Day programs, medications, assisted living, and supportive care will likely grow. As legitimate opportunities increase, so do illegitimate ones. These may range from electoral fraud to miracle cures to elder abuse.

CONCLUSION: THE COMING CRISIS

Alzheimer's disease and related dementias are likely to become the crisis of the first half of the twenty-first century. The rising rates and increased prevalence of dementia will affect every aspect of the social order.

There is one saving grace. There is still time: perhaps twenty-five years before a serious problem becomes an unmanageable one.

The coming crisis of dementia merits debate, discussion, and consideration. Perhaps the most significant marker of a society is how well it treats its most fragile and vulnerable members. ■

REFERENCES

Doka, K.J. (1997). *AIDS, fear and society: Challenging the dreaded disease.* Washington, DC: Taylor & Francis.

Dychwald, K., & Flower, J. (1988). *Age wave.* Los Angeles: J.P. Teacher.

Ernst, R., & Hay, J. (1994). The US economic and social costs of Alzheimer's disease revisited. *American Journal of Public Health, 84,* 1262-1264.

Evans, D.A., Funkenstein, M.M., Arsert, M.S., Cook, N.R., Herlert, L.E., Hennekens, C.H., & Taylor, J. (1989). Prevalence of Alzheimer's disease in a coming population of older persons: Higher from previously reported. JAMA: *The Journal of the American Medical Association, 262,* 2881-2886.

Hebert, L., Scherr, P., Benias, J., Bennett, D., & Evans, D. (2003). Alzheimer's disease in the US population: Prevalence estimates using the 2000 census. *Archives of Neurology, 60,* 1119-1122.

Geller, L., & Reichel, W. (1999). Alzheimer's disease: Biological aspects. In. J. Gallow, J. Busby-Whitehead, R.V. Rabins, R.A. Sillimin, J.B. Murphy, & W. Reiche (Eds.), *Reicher's care of the elderly: Clinical aspects of aging* (5th Ed.). Philadelphia: Williams & Wilkins.

Mills, C.W. (1963). *Power, politics, and people: The collected essays of C. Wright Mills.* New York: Oxford Press.

CHAPTER 2

Alzheimer's Disease: Biology and Therapy

Sam Gandy, Ralph N. Martins, and Joseph Buxbaum

INTRODUCTION AND OVERVIEW

Alzheimer's disease is the most common cause of the clinical picture that physicians know as dementia. Literally, *de-ment* means to lose mentation, or the ability to think. Though long believed to be the inescapable consequence of advanced age, it is now known that dementias are caused instead by brain diseases. Many individuals live into their eighties, nineties and beyond, all the while maintaining their full capacity to think, reason, remember, and perform (e.g., Pablo Casals, Vladimir Horowitz). Nevertheless, Alzheimer's is very common and affects nearly half of people over age 85. The disease is named for the German psychiatrist, Dr. Alois Alzheimer, who reported the disease at a medical research meeting in 1907.

Dr. Alzheimer's first patient was a woman in her mid-fifties known as Auguste D. She was brought to his attention when she became obsessed with the notion that her husband was unfaithful. This fixation came to dominate her life to such an extent that she neglected to care for her family or for herself. She was admitted to a hospital for the mentally ill, where Dr. Alzheimer cared for her until she died. By the end of her life, the disease had robbed her of all ability to comprehend or respond to her environment.

The autopsied brain of Auguste D. was stained with silver and studied with a microscope. The nerve cells of the parts of the brain responsible for thinking, remembering, and reasoning were distorted by the presence of two types of abnormal structures: tiny round specks between nerve cells, and wiry twisted tangles inside them. These areas of the brain were also shrunken, since many nerve cells had died and dissolved. The protein deposits, known as *amyloid plaques* and *neurofibrillary tangles*, respectively, define the neuropathology of Alzheimer's disease as we know it today.

The Amyloid Hypothesis

Amyloid is a general term applied to protein clumps that spontaneously form highly ordered fibers when they stick together. Amyloids may be deposited in a general manner throughout the body (systemic amyloids) or confined to one organ (e.g., cerebral amyloid, kidney amyloid). Alzheimer's, then, is a cerebral (or brain) amyloidosis.

The word amyloid means starch-like, a property attributable to the small amounts of complex sugars that also make up the deposit. These sugars react strongly with a particular stain, which led to the misconception that the deposits were mostly sugar. In fact, they are almost entirely

FIGURE 1

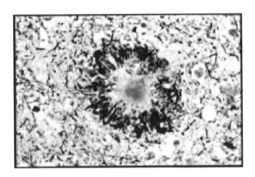

Typical amyloid plaque in the brain of a patient dying from Alzheimer's disease. The round, central area is the plaque core, formed almost entirely of amyloid, or Aβ. The black, worm-like structures radiating out from the plaque core are nerve cell fibers that contain silver-stained neurofibrillary tangles.

made up of short proteins, or peptides, specifically known as amyloid-beta peptides (abbreviated as Aß). The intracellular neurofibrillary tangles, on the other hand, are composed of a nerve cell skeleton protein called *tau*.

The question of which of these structures was most important in starting Alzheimer's disease plagued scientists for many years. A breakthrough came in 1986, when molecular biologists discovered that Aß is produced from the breakdown of a much larger protein called the *amyloid precursor protein* (abbreviated APP).

Following the discovery of the normal amyloid precursor protein, geneticists found that sometimes there were errors in the APP gene that could cause the disease to occur in several individuals in every generation. All of these errors, or mutations, lay within or near the Aß region. Cell biologists went on to show that when any mutant amyloid precursor protein breaks down, those errors cause the production of Aß peptides that are especially sticky and prone to aggregation.

Establishing Causation

The discovery of disease-causing mutations in the amyloid precursor protein established the idea that Aß accumulation could cause Alzheimer's disease. As further proof of this idea, the disease-causing human genes were put into mice. As the mice aged, their brains became clogged with Aß, just like the brains of humans who have Alzheimer's disease.

Changes in other genes can also cause Alzheimer's disease. Mutations in the gene for a protein called *presenilin* (so-named for the premature senility or dementia that it causes) can lead to disease. Presenilins control the breakdown of amyloid precursor protein, and mutations cause Aß to accumulate. Changes in a fat-carrier protein, called *apolipoprotein E*, can increase the risk for Alzheimer's.

It is worth noting that a distinct dementing illness can occur when mutations occur in the cell skeleton protein known as *tau*. These mutations cause Alzheimer-like neurofibrillary tangles. Moreover, the disease is clinically similar to Alzheimer's. But because no brain amyloid plaques form, this disease is given a different name: Pick's disease.

Toward Effective Therapies

Using the mouse model of Alzheimer's, scientists have been able to develop a number of experimental approaches that can prevent or cure the amyloid accumulation in the plaque-laden brains of these laboratory mice. These include anti-aggregation drugs, APP breakdown inhibitor drugs, and Aß vaccines (see review of new therapies below).

The hope is that one or more of these approaches (or perhaps some combination) will eventually be proven effective in delaying, slowing, stopping, or reversing the disease in humans.

Until late 2003, the only medicines available for Alzheimer's were a class of drug known as *cholinesterase inhibitors*. These drugs block the breakdown of one kind of chemical that nerve cells use to "talk" to one another; these chemicals are called neurotransmitters.

As nerve cells die in Alzheimer's disease, the neurotransmitter known as *acetylcholine* becomes particularly deficient. Most of the currently approved drugs for Alzheimer's (e.g., Aricept, Exelon, Reminyl) act to help the brain compensate for this deficiency by slowing down the breakdown of acetylcholine.

Because nerve cell death is the primary cause of the symptoms of Alzheimer's, however, the cholinesterase inhibitors do not substantially alter the course of the disease. Rather, they offer relief that is modest, transient, and symptomatic.

In October of 2003, the U.S. Food and Drug Administration approved a new drug to treat Alzheimer's (U.S. Food and Drug Administration, 2003). Memantine (trade name Namenda) is the first drug for the treatment of moderate to severe Alzheimer's. It is not a cholinesterase inhibitor; its mechanism of action is different. It is thought to work by blocking the action of the chemical glutamate. The drug's side effects appear to be few, relatively minor, and experienced by only a small percentage of patients.

The FDA announcement cautioned, however, that although memantine helps treat the symptoms of Alzheimer's in some patients, there is no evidence that it modifies the underlying pathology of the disease.

MOLECULAR NEUROPATHOLOGY OF ALZHEIMER'S

Alzheimer's disease is characterized by clinical evidence of cognitive failure. This cognitive failure is associated with cerebral amyloidosis, as well as cerebral intraneuronal neurofibrillary pathology, neuronal and synaptic loss, and neurotransmitter deficits.

The main constituent of cerebrovascular amyloid was purified and sequenced by George Glenner in 1984 (Glenner and Wong, 1984). This 40-42 amino acid polypeptide, designated *beta protein* by Glenner (or *A-4* by Masters and colleagues), has now entered standardized nomenclature as *A-beta* or Aß. It is derived from a 695-770 amino acid precursor called the amyloid precursor protein, or APP. It was discovered through molecular cloning.

Breakdown of the Amyloid Precursor Protein

Breakdown of the amyloid precusor protein is important because this is what produces Aß. It is a stepwise process that involves enzymes called *secretases*. These enzymes are major targets for the next generation of Alzheimer's drugs.

The intermediates formed during the degradation, or processing, of the amyloid precursor protein have been definitively identified by purification and sequencing. The first to be identified involves cleavage within the Aß domain. A large fragment of the amyloid precursor protein is released into the medium of cultured cells and into the cerebrospinal fluid, leaving a small non-amyloidogenic (i.e., incapable of forming or leading to formation of amyloid) fragment associated with the cell.

This pathway is designated the alpha pathway for APP, because the enzyme (or enzymes) that performs this nonamyloidogenic cleavage/release has been designated α-*secretase.* Thus, one important processing event in the biology of APP acts to preclude amyloidogenesis by proteolyzing APP within the Aß domain (Figure 2).

Aß production begins by cleavage at the Aß amino-terminus (far left end of Aß, Figures 1 and 2) by an enzyme designated ß-secretase. Cleavage of APP by ß-secretase is the rate-limiting step in Aß formation, releasing a large fragment from the cell, and retaining a fragment, or stub, with the Aß

FIGURE 2

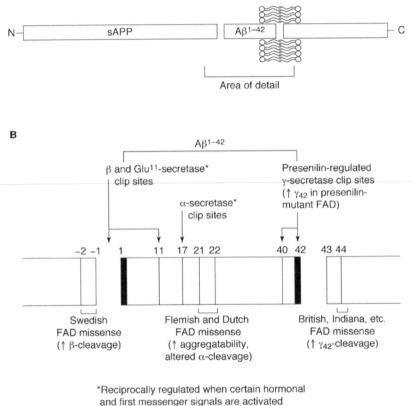

(A) Structure of the Alzheimer amyloid precursor protein (APP), including (B) the fine structure around the Aβ domain. FAD=familial Alzheimer disease. FAD missense=sites of disease-causing mutations. Secretase sites=points of enzymatic cleavage of APP to produce Aβ (beta-, Glu11-, gamma secretases) or to destroy Aβ (alpha secretase). Standard beta-secretase cleavage generates an aspartyl residue in position 1 of A-beta, i.e. [Asp1]. The alternative cleavage to yield an amino terminus at [Glu11] is also known as the beta-prime (or β') site. Presenilin is the name of another molecule that appears to contain the active site of gamma secretase; presenilin mutations are the most common cause of FAD, and presenilin mutations increase the proportion of the most aggregation-prone Aβ, known as Aβ42.

peptide intact at its amino terminus. This stub is the substrate for the final reaction in Aß generation, a reaction catalyzed by yet another enzyme, known as *gamma-secretase*.

It is important to note that the Aß carboxyl-terminus is heterogeneous (Glenner and Wong, 1984), being composed mostly of peptides terminating at residue Aß40 (see Figure 2). However, a small but important minority of peptides terminates at residue Aß42 (Figure 2), and it is these highly sticky Aß42 peptides which are believed to initiate Aß accumulation and plaque formation in all forms of the disease (Iwatsubo et al., 1994; Lemere et al., 1996).

Presenilin

Presenilin is the name of a molecule discovered by Peter Hyslop and colleagues in 1995 (Sherrington et al.). It is responsible for most early-onset, or *pre-senile*, familial Alzheimer's disease.

Presenilin plays a crucial role in gamma secretase activity. Mice deficient in presenilin cannot break down the C99 or C89 stubs. It is clear that mutations in presenilins cause Alzheimer's disease by facilitating generation of the longer, more aggregatable Aß that extends to residue 42. It is also clear that ß-secretase includes at least four components: presenilins-1, nicastrin, APH-1, PEN-2 (Fortini, 2002) and that the amyloid precursor protein is not its only target. This is important because the presence of several components offers multiple alternative therapeutic opportunities. At the same time, however, the plethora of substrates creates a daunting task when it comes to avoiding mechanism-based toxicity.

Disease-Causing Mutations

Certain mutations associated with *familial Alzheimer's disease* (abbreviated as FAD) have been identified within or near the Aß region of the APP gene. These mutations segregate perfectly with clinical disease in one or the other of two types of familial Alzheimer's disease. One is known as hereditary cerebral hemorrhage with amyloidosis, Dutch type. The other, more typical form is known as British or Indiana familial Alzheimer's disease. This provides support for the notion that aberrant APP metabolism is a key feature of Alzheimer's disease. In Dutch-type familial Alzheimer's disease, Aß molecules bearing enhanced aggregation properties are generated.

Mutations that apparently are pathogenic for the more typical form of familial Alzheimer's disease also have been discovered. In the first such mutation discovered, an isoleucine residue is substituted for a valine residue at a position two residues downstream from the carboxyl-terminus of the Aß42 species, increasing generation of Aß42. The observation that over-expressing these molecules in transgenic mice causes the mice to develop amyloidosis with human Aß plaques further attests to the importance of the mutations.

Another disease pedigree has been established involving a large Swedish family. In this instance, mutations occur just upstream of the Aß domain, resulting in the production of a six- to eight-fold excess of all species of Aß.

Regulation of APP Metabolism

Signal transduction systems involving hormones, neurotransmitters, and protein phosphorylation are important regulators of APP cleavage, acting in many cases by stimulating the relative activity of non-amyloidogenic cleavage by α-secretase. The roles of protein kinase C (PKC), PKC-linked first messengers, and ERK (extracellular signal regulated protein kinases) have received the most attention. In many types of cultured cells, activation of PKC by phorbol esters dramatically stimulates APP proteolysis by alpha secretase (Buxbaum et al., 1990, 1992, 1993, 1998; Caporaso et al., 1992; Gillespie et al., 1992; Sinha and Lieberburg, 1992). PKC-stimulated alpha-secretory cleavage of APP may also be induced by the application of neurotransmitters and other first messenger compounds whose receptors are linked to PKC (Buxbaum et al., 1992, 1993, 1998; Nitsch et al., 1992; Haring et al., 1998).

This phenomenon is sometimes referred to as "regulated cleavage of APP" or "reciprocal regulation of APP metabolism"; i.e., when certain signals are activated, ß-secretase cleavage increases and beta secretase cleavages decrease.

Steroid hormones such as 17beta-estradiol (Jaffe et al., 1994; Xu et al., 1998; Chang et al., 1997) and dihydroepiandrostenedione (Danenberg et al., 1995) are other signal transduction compounds that can apparently regulate APP metabolism in cultured cells. Several of these investigators

(Xu et al., 1998; Chang et al., 1997) have demonstrated that estradiol diminishes A-beta generation.

Clearance of Brain Aß

The levels of Aß peptide in the brain depend on balances between production and clearance. It has been suggested that a decrease in the clearance of Aß from brain and cerebrospinal fluid may be one cause of Aß accumulation and deposition in some cases of Alzheimer's disease. Many studies have focused on factors that influence production and secretion of Aß by the various cell types of the brain, and on factors that accelerate aggregation of the peptide. Although the mechanism or mechanisms for eliminating Aß from the brain are surely just as important, these remain to be elucidated.

The binding of Aß to certain proteins is thought to affect its clearance significantly. In the circulation, cerebrospinal fluid and brain interstitial fluid soluble Aß can exist as a free peptide or as a bound peptide associated with either proteins such as apolipoprotein E, apolipoprotein J, transthyretin, ß2-macroglobulin, lipoproteins, or albumin.

Blood-Brain Barrier

Several mechanisms have been suggested for the removal of extracellular Aß from the brain. Most studies have shown that the blood-brain barrier has the capability to modulate the brain's uptake and clearance of soluble Aß peptides, and that active receptor-mediated transport is involved. Interestingly, there is also evidence that Aß may be metabolized during its transport across the blood-brain barrier. Most studies appear to endorse the primary route of Aß clearance to be via transport across the blood-brain barrier followed by breakdown in peripheral organs such as the liver.

It has been found that enkephalinase (NEP, neprilysin) from brain interstitial fluid can degrade injected $Aß_{42}$ (Iwata et al., 2001).

Many studies have demonstrated that insulin-degrading enzyme can also degrade Aß. This enzyme has also been detected in the cerebrospinal fluid (Qiu et al., 1998). Overall, the half-time for total Aß efflux from the brain has been calculated to be around 25 minutes, with the blood-brain barrier efflux component measured to be around 35 minutes. A slower but still significant efflux appears to occur via the interstitial fluid.

THERAPEUTIC MANIPULATION OF Aß METABOLISM

Non-Steroidal, Anti-Inflammatory Drugs

Cole and colleagues showed that ibuprofen (Lim et al., 2000) and curcumin (Lim et al., 2001), both anti-inflammatory compounds, could lower plaque load and peri-plaque inflammation in a mouse model of Alzheimer's disease. This was soon followed by human data from a Dutch group reporting success in preventing or delaying the onset of Alzheimer's disease with non-steroidal anti-inflammatory drugs, or NSAIDs (Veld et al., 2001).

Unexpectedly, Koo and colleagues discovered that high-dose NSAIDs selectively diminish generation of Aß42. The mechanism is unknown, but it appears to be unrelated to the usual anti-inflammatory effect that acts via inhibition of cyclo-oxygenase (Weggen et al., 2001). Two recent clinical trials of non-steroidal anti-inflammatory drugs showed them to be ineffective (Aisen et al., 2003), but these particular compounds were selected for human tests based on their cyclo-oxygenase characteristics rather than their Aß42 effects. Other anti-amyloid NSAIDs are now being evaluated.

The Promise of Cholesterol-Lowering Drugs

Another discovery that has generated great interest in the academic and pharmaceutical communities is the surprising ability of cholesterol-lowering compounds (called *statins*) to activate α-secretase and lower Aß generation by cells and amyloid accumulation in mouse models (Refolo et al., 2000, 2001). Here again, an existing drug shows promise in the laboratory and is now being tested in human clinical trials.

Vaccine Approaches

Another strategy for Alzheimer prevention or treatment has been widely covered by the news media. It involves vaccination with Aß. In animal studies involving plaque-forming transgenic mice, this strategy has proven effective in reversing both plaque pathology and behavioral deficits (Janus et al., 2000; P. Hyslop, personal communication), the first such claim for an intervention that holds promise for clinical improvement.

How Aß vaccination works remains unclear. Some investigators argue for an intra-central nervous system action directly on plaques. Others suggest that circulating anti-Aß antibodies form a peripheral "sink," drawing Aß out of the central nervous system via the cerebrospinal fluid and into the bloodstream, from which it is then cleared (DeMattos et al., 2001).

In non-human primates, as well as in transgenic mice, it has been established that blood Aß concentrations rise significantly when these animals are vaccinated with Aß. Other mechanistic studies are ongoing.

Although the vaccine strategy appears very promising, trials with human subjects have revealed safety issues. One series of Phase II clinical trials was halted because some of the subjects developed acute autoimmune encephalitis. Other immunotherapies are still under investigation, however, and one preliminary study suggests that cognitive decline might be arrested in vaccinated patients with a brisk anti-amyloid immune response (Hock et al., 2003).

Signal Transduction Therapies

From a therapeutic standpoint, the modulation of APP metabolism via signal transduction pharmacology might be beneficial in individuals with, or at risk for, Alzheimer's disease (Sinha and Lieberburg, 1992; Gandy and Greengard, 1992, 1994). Such a strategy has recently been investigated in living animals. One prominent example is the ability of statins to activate α-secretase, perhaps via a signal transduction mechanism (see above).

Estrogen

The ability of estrogen to modulate Aß metabolism in the brains of living animals has been tested in two animal systems: guinea pigs and plaque-forming mice (Petanceska et al., 2000; Callahan et al., 2001; Zheng et al., 2002). Prolonged ovariectomy of guinea pigs was associated with a pronounced increase in brain Aß levels as compared to intact animals. This ovariectomy-induced increase was significantly reduced in guinea pigs receiving estrogen. Similarly, ovariectomy of transgenic, brain amyloid plaque-forming mice at an age when Aß deposition is incipient resulted in enhanced brain amyloidosis. The contributions of altered Aß generation and altered Ab clearance to the observed changes in brain Aß levels remain to be determined.

Two studies strongly infer that cessation of ovarian estrogen production in post-menopausal women might facilitate Aß deposition by increasing the local concentrations of Aß peptides in brain and that the negative correlation between hormone replacement therapy of post-menopausal women (Tang et al., 1996) and Alzheimer's disease is at least in part due to the Aß lowering effect of estrogen (Mayeux and Gandy, 2000). The guinea pig brain Aß data have been recently used as a model to test whether this phenomenon is relevant to humans.

The observation that pharmacologically-induced hormone deficiency in elderly men can cause a doubling of circulating levels of Aß (Gandy et al., 2001) suggests that hormone deficiencies in late life might play a role in the risk for, or timing of, Alzheimer's disease.

Primary prevention trials with unopposed estrogen replacement therapy should provide clear data upon which to drawn supportable conclusions regarding whether or not lowering the risk of Alzheimer's disease might be included in the decision to undertake hormone replacement in women, and perhaps in men as well. Combination estrogen/progestin replacement therapy is not effective when initiated at age 65 or older (Rapp et al., 2003).

CONCLUSION

Alzheimer genes cause buildup of the gooey Aß amyloid in the brain. Transfer of human Alzheimer genes to mice causes the mice to develop gooey amyloid buildup. We have discovered drugs and vaccines that will cure or prevent Alzheimer's in the mice, and we must now establish which of these drugs and vaccines will be most effective in man. ■

Sam Gandy, M.D., Ph.D., is Director of the Farber Institute for Neurosciences at Thomas Jefferson University, Philadelphia. He is also Professor of Neurology, Psychiatry and Biochemistry, and Molecular Pharmacology at Jefferson Medical College, and Vice Chair, National Medical and Scientific Advisory Council of the Alzheimer's Association. Dr. Gandy is an international expert in the metabolism of the sticky substance called amyloid that clogs the brain in patients with Alzheimer's. In 1989, Dr. Gandy, Dr. Buxbaum, and their team discovered the first drugs that could lower formation of amyloid. Dr. Gandy has written more than 100 original papers on this topic, and they are among the most frequently cited reports in Alzheimer's research. Dr. Gandy has received grants from the NIH totaling $10 million for studying amyloid metabolism.

For their invaluable assistance in the development of this chapter, the author wishes to acknowledge and thank Dr. Ralph N. Martins, Edith Cowan University, Perth, Australia, and Dr. Joseph Buxbaum, Laboratory of Molecular and Neuropsychiatry, Departments of Neurobiology and Psychiatry, Mt. Sinai School of Medicine, New York.

References

Aisen, P.S., Schafer, K.A., Grundman, M., Pfeiffer, E., Sano, M., Davis, K.L., et al. (2003). Alzheimer's disease cooperative study: Effects of rofecoxib or naproxen vs placebo on Alzheimer disease progression: A randomized controlled trial. *JAMA, 289*(21), 2819-2826.

Buxbaum, J.D., Gandy, S.E., Cicchetti, P., Ehrlich, M.E., Czemik, A.J., Fracasso, R.P., et al. (1990). Processing of Alzheimer beta/A4 amyloid precursor protein: Modulation by agents that regulate protein phosphorylation. *Proceedings of the National Academy of Sciences USA, 87*, 600-J-6006.

Buxbaum, J.D., Koo, E.H., & Greengard, P. (1993). Protein phosphorylation inhibits production of Alzheimer amyloid/A4 peptide. *Proceedings of the National Academy of Sciences USA, 90*, 9195-9198.

Buxbaum J.D., Liu, K.N., Lulo, Y., Slack, J.L., Stocking, K.L., Peschon, J.J., et al. (1998). Evidence that tumor necrosis factor alpha converting enzyme is involved in regulated alpha-secretase cleavage of the Alzheimer amyloid protein precursor. *Journal of Biological Chemistry, 273*(43), 27765-27767.

Buxbaum, J.D., Oishi, M., Chen, H.I., Pinkas-Kramarski, R., Jaffe, E.A., Gandy, S.E., & Greengard, P. (1992). Cholinergic agonists and interleukin I regulate processing and secretion of the Alzheimer beta A4 amyloid protein precursor. *Proceedings of the National Academy of Sciences USA, 89*, 10075-10078.

Callahan, M.J., Lipinski, W.J., Bian, F., Durham, R.A., Pack, A., & Walker, L.C. (2001). Augmented senile plaque load in aged female beta-amyloid precursor protein-transgenic mice. *American Journal of Pathology, 158*(3), 1173-1177.

Caporaso, G.L., Gandy, S.E., Buxbaum, J.D., Ramabhadran, T.V., & Greengard, P. (1992). Protein Phosphorylation Regulates Secretion of Alzheimer ß/A4 Amyloid Precursor Protein. *Proceedings of the National Academy of Sciences USA, 89*, 3055-3059.

Chang, D., Kwan, J., & Timiras, P.S. (1997.) Estrogens influence growth, maturation and amyloid beta-peptide production in neuroblastoma cells and in a beta-APP transfected kidney 293 cell line. *Advances in Experimental Medical Biology, 429*, 261-271.

Danenberg, H.D., Haring, R., Heldman, E., Gurwitz, D. Ben-Nathan, D., Pittel, Z., Zuckerman, A., & Fisher, A. (1995). Dehydroepiandrosterone augments M1-muscarinic receptor-stimulated amyloid precursor protein secretion in desensitized PC12M1 cells. *Annals of the New York Academy of Sciences, 774*, 300-303.

DeMattos, R.B., Bales, K.R., Cummins, D.J., Dodart, J.C., Paul, S.M., & Holtzman, D.M. (2001). Peripheral anti-A beta antibody alters CNS and plasma A beta clearance and decreases brain A beta burden in a mouse model of Alzheimer's disease. *Proceedings of the National Academy of Sciences USA, 98*(15), 8850-8855.

Fortini, M.E. (2002). Gamma-secretase-mediated proteolysis in cell-surface-receptor signalling. *Molecular Cell Biology: Nature Reviews 3*(9), 673-684.

Gandy, S., & Greengard, P. (1992). Amyloidogenesis in Alzheimer's disease: Some possible therapeutic opportunities. *Trends in Pharmacological Sciences, 13*, 108-113.

Gandy, S., & Greengard, P. (1994) Processing of A-beta-amyloid precursor protein: Cell biology, regulation, and role in Alzheimer disease. *International Review of Neurobiology, 36*, 29-50.

Gandy, S., Almeida, O.P., Fonte, J., Lim, D., Waterrus, A., Spry, N., et al. (2001). Chemical andropause and amyloid-beta peptide. *JAMA, 285*(17), 2195-2196.

Gillespie, S.L., Golde, T.E., & Younkin, S.G. (1992). Secretory processing of the Alzheimer amyloid beta/A4 protein precursor is increased by protein phosphorylation. *Biochemical and Biophysical Research Communications, 187*, 1285-1290.

Glenner, G.G., & Wong, C.W. (1984.) Alzheimer's disease: Initial report of the purification and characterization of a novel cerebrovascular amyloid protein. *Biochemical and Biophysical Research Communications, 120*, 885-890.

Haring, R., Fisher, A., Marciano, D., Pittel, Z., Kloog, Y., Zuckerman, A., et al. (1998). Mitogen-activated protein kinase-dependent and protein kinase C-dependent pathways link the m1 muscarinic receptor to beta-amyloid precursor protein secretion. *Journal of Neurochemistry, 71*, 2094-2103.

Hock, C., Konietzko, U., Streffer, J.R., Tracy, J., Signorell, A., Muller-Tillmanns, B., et al. (2003). Antibodies against beta-Amyloid slow cognitive decline in Alzheimer's disease. *Neuron, 38*(4), 547-554.

Iwata, N., Tsubuki, S., Takaki, Y., Shirotani, K., Lu, B., Gerard, N.P., et al. (2001). Metabolic regulation of brain Abeta by neprilysin. *Science, 292*(5521), 1550-1552.

Iwatsubo T, Odaka A, Suzuki N, Mizusawa H, Nukina N, & Ihara Y. (1994). Visualization of Aß42 (43) and Aß40 in senile plaques with end-specific Aß monoclonals: Evidence that an initially deposited species is Aß42 (43). *Neuron, 13*, 45-53.

Jaffe, A.B., Toran-Allerand, C.D., Greengard, P., & Gandy, S.E. (1994). Estrogen regulates metabolism of Alzheimer amyloid beta precursor protein. *Journal of Biological Chemistry, 269*(18), 13065-13068.

Janus, C., Pearson, J., McLaurin, J., Mathews, P.M., Jiang, Y., Schmidt, S.D., et al. (2000). A-beta peptide immunization reduces behavioural impairment and plaques in a model of Alzheimer's disease. *Nature, 408*(6815), 979-982.

Lemere, C.A., Blusztajn, J.K., Yamaguchi, H., Wisniewski, T., Saido, T.C., & Selkoe, D.J. (1996). Sequence of deposition of heterogeneous amyloid beta-peptides and APOE in Down syndrome: Implications for initial events in amyloid plaque formation. *Neurobiology of Disease, 3*(1), 16-32.

Mayeux, R., & Gandy, S. (2000). Cognitive impairment, Alzheimer's disease and other dementias. In M.B. Goldman and M.C. Hatch (Eds.), *Women and health.* San Diego, CA: Academic Press.

Nilsberth, C., Westlind-Danielsson, A., Eckman, C.B., Condron, M.M., Axelman, K., Forsell, C., et al. (2001). The 'Arctic' APP mutation (E693G) causes Alzheimer's disease by enhanced Abeta protofibril formation. *Nature Neuroscience, 4*(9), 887-893.

Nitsch, R.M., Slack, B.F., Wurtman, R.J., & Growdon, J.H. (1992). Release of Alzheimer amyloid precursor derivatives stimulated by activation of muscarinic acetylcholine receptors. *Science, 258*, 304-307.

Petanceska, S.S., Nagy, V., Frail, D., & Gandy, S. (2000). Ovariectomy and 17beta-estradiol modulate the levels of Alzheimer's amyloid beta peptides in brain. *Neurology, 54*(12), 2212-2217.

Qiu, W.Q., Walsh, D.M., Ye, Z., Vekrellis, K., Zhang, J., Podlisny, M.B., et al. (1998). Insulin-degrading enzyme regulates extracellular levels of amyloid beta-protein by degradation. *Journal of Biological Chemistry, 273*(49), 32730-32738.

Rapp, S.R., Espeland, M.A., Shumaker, S.A., Henderson, V.W., Brunner, R.L., Manson, J.E., et al. (2003). Effect of estrogen plus progestin on global cognitive function in postmenopausal women: The women's health initiative memory study: A randomized controlled trial. *JAMA, 289*(20), 2663-2672.

Refolo, L.M., Malester, B., LaFrancois, J., Bryant-Thomas, T., Wang, R., Tint, G.S., et al. (2000). Hypercholesterolemia accelerates the Alzheimer's amyloid pathology in a transgenic mouse model. *Neurobiology of Disease, 7*(4), 321-331.

Refolo, L.M., Pappolla, M.A., LaFrancois, J., Malester, B., Schmidt, S.D., Thomas-Bryant, T., et al. (2001). A cholesterol-lowering drug reduces beta-Amyloid pathology pathology in a transgenic mouse model of Alzheimer's disease. *Neurobiology of Disease, 8*(5), 890-899.

Sherrington, R., Rogaev, E., Liang, Y., Rogaeva, E.A., Levesque, G., Ikeda, M., et al. (1995). Cloning of a gene bearing missense mutations in early-onset familial Alzheimer's disease. *Nature, 375,* 754-760.

Sinha, S., & Lieberburg, I. (1992). Normal metabolism of the amyloid precursor protein (APP). *Neurodegeneration, 1,* 169-175.

Tang, M.X., Jacobs, D., Stem, Y., Marder, K., Schofield, P., Gurland, B., et al. (1996). Effect of estrogen during menopause on risk and age at onset of Alzheimer's disease. *Lancet, 348*(9025), 429-432.

U.S. Food and Drug Administration. (2003, October 17). FDA approves memantine (namenda) for Alzheimer's disease. Retrieved February 6, 2004, from http://www.fda.gov/bbs/topics/NEWS/2003/NEW00961.html

in 't Veld, B.A., Ruitenberg, A., Hofman, A., Launer, L.J., van Duijn, C.M., Stijnen, T., et al. (2001). Nonsteroidal antiinflammatory drugs and the risk of Alzheimer's disease. *New England Journal of Medicine, 345,* 1515-1521.

Weggen, S., Eriksen, J.L., Das, P., Sagi, S.A., Wang, R., Pietrzik, C.U., et al. (2001). A subset of NSAIDs lower amyloidogenic A-beta 42 independently of cyclo-oxygenase activity. *Nature, 414,* 212-216.

Xu, H., Gouras, G.K., Greenfield, J.P., Vincent, B., Naslund, J., Mazzarelli, L., et al. (1998). Estrogen reduces neuronal generation of Alzheimer beta-amyloid peptides. *Nature Medicine, 4*(4), 447-451.

Zheng, H., Xu, H., Uljon, S.N., Gross, R., Hardy, K., Gaynor, K., et al. (2002). Modulation of A-beta peptides by estrogen in mouse models. *Journal of Neurochemistry, 80,* 191-196.

CHAPTER 3

Dementias Other Than Alzheimer's

Parag Dalsania

INTRODUCTION

Dementia is an increasing health concern in the elderly population. As this population is expected to double in the next 30 years, dementia will affect a greater number of people. Recent studies indicate that at age 60, one percent of all people have dementia, and by age 85, an estimated 30-50 percent of the population will develop dementia (Evans, Funkenstein, Albert, et al; White, Cartwright, Cornoni-Huntley, & Brock, 1986). Close to 65 percent of patients who develop dementia have Alzheimer's disease, as it is the most common cause of dementia (Herbert, et al, 2003; *Dementia*, 1993). Approximately 4.5 million Americans live with Alzheimer's disease (Brookmeyer, Gray, & Kawas, 1998). However, many other conditions and diseases can also cause dementia. Studies have estimated that one third of patients can attribute their syndrome to disorders other than Alzheimer's disease. It is critical to identify the etiology of the presenting dementia. Often, there is a transient and reversible cause of cognitive dysfunction.

The clinical syndrome of dementia is defined in two critical parts. First, dementia involves cognitive impairment involving two or more of the following domains: memory (ability to learn, retain, retrieve), language, visual-spatial ability (ability to synthesize geographic and graphic information, like judging distance and orientation), and executive function (planning, organizing, sequencing, abstracting) (American Psychiatric

Association, 1994). Second, the impact of the cognitive impairment prevents affected individuals from independently carrying out tasks of daily living, such as dressing, bathing, feeding, toileting, grooming, and walking (APA, 1994). Other features may include changes in personality and behavioral abnormalities.

Dementia is a general condition, a syndrome related to a disease. Many diseases and disorders include dementia as an observable symptom. For example, symptoms of dementia can be attributed to Alzheimer's disease, Parkinson's disease, depression, head trauma, and even medications. There are more than 50 different diseases listed as causes of dementia (Mayeux, Foster, Rossor, & Whitehouse, 1993). Further, these diverse conditions have a wide range of presentation, pathology, prognosis, and treatments.

These other dementias are just as deleterious to the patient and caregivers as Alzheimer's-induced dementia because the overall effect is often the same. They have the same impact on health care systems, and utilization of resources is just as great. However, for the less common causes of dementia, there may be fewer resources, and a limited pool of medical experts who know about the correct management and treatment. Thus, for the caregivers, a relative lack of resources can frequently lead to more unanswered questions.

Accurate diagnosis in a patient presenting with cognitive impairment is critical because the labeling of their symptoms as "dementia" creates tremendous fear. Further, there are negative societal stigmas associated with this term. A common assumption is that all cognitive dysfunction is progressive and irreversible. However, for many patients, this may not be the case. Patients with cognitive impairment have a variety of presentations, ranging from behavioral changes, to loss of speech, to the ability to care for themselves. In rare cases, patients are admitted to a psychiatric unit for changes in behavior, when in fact, the patient may have a form of dementia. The first part of treatment is to accurately make the diagnosis.

Clinicians who suspect dementia must first determine the etiology by doing a comprehensive history and physical along with a series of tests and imaging studies. This comprehensive evaluation can provide the patients and families comfort and establish a foundation for the future. It is critical to first determine whether the cognitive impairment is dementia or a potentially reversible disorder. Unfortunately, "syndrome overlap" is common. Consequently, an investigation may start with one syndrome and end with more than one disease.

In addition to evaluation and diagnosis, clinicians must also educate patients and caregivers. Unfortunately, many caregivers have a limited understanding of what causes dementia, and even less understanding of the basic terminology used to describe it. Patients and families should be encouraged to have a discussion with their physician in order to answer their questions. Often there is ambiguity and confusion with regard to disease progression. Questions on the management of behavioral disturbances, especially aggressive behavior, as well as incontinence and other aspects of daily life, need to be addressed. Also, it is important to work with physicians who are experts and experienced in managing dementia. Specialized "Dementia" or "Memory" clinics may have systems in place for crisis intervention and a functioning interdisciplinary team with greater resources.

MEDICATIONS

Unfortunately, dementia goes undetected in millions of Americans. Ironically, it is inappropriately diagnosed in other conditions that can present as dementia. Certain medications and polypharmacy have been identified as the most common cause of reversible dementia symptoms (Weyting, Bossuyt, & van Crevel, 1995). "Polypharmacy" means "many drugs" and refers to problems that occur when a person is taking too many medications at inappropriate doses, or is taking duplicate (unnecessary) medication. It is well known that some medications can cause confusion, increase both functional and cognitive disability, and speed decline. Estimates suggest that 10 percent of all the reversible dementias are due to drug toxicity (Clarfield, 1988).

The most common classes of medications implicated in causing cognitive impairment are anticholinergics like diphenhydramine (Benadryl), antipsychotics, benzodiapines, central nervous system depressants such as sleeping pills (Tylenol PM), and narcotics. Some of these medications are commonly available over the counter. In patients with established cases of dementia, certain medications can lead to further confusion and agitation.

There is partial, or even full, reversal of the dementia symptoms when implicated psychoactive medications are discontinued (Weyting, et al; Schultz & Gambert, 1991). Therefore, it is absolutely mandatory that any evaluations for newly presenting symptoms of dementia include a medication review. A medical history will suggest onset of symptoms correlating with the initiating or a dosage adjustment of a medication. It may be necessary to discontinue certain medications, which have been implicated in causing the impairment (Chow & Maclean, 2001).

DELIRIUM

Delirium is a common problem with serious implications for elderly persons. Unfortunately, delirium is not recognized and often confused with dementia. In patients who develop delirium, it impacts functional recovery and survival (Francis, 1992). It is estimated that over one third of patients over 70 who are admitted to hospitals experience delirium. Approximately 25-65 percent of patients who are admitted to the hospital for a hip fracture develop delirium (Magaziner, Simonsick, Kashner, et al, 1989).

Delirium is a transient disorder, impacting the person for weeks to months. Diagnostic criteria rest on four aspects. First, there is an altered level of consciousness (alertness, inattention, awareness). Second, there is a deficit in cognition, impacting memory or language, thought, and behavior. Third, these changes occur over a short period of time (hours to days). Fourth, there has to be some evidence of physiologic disequilibrium due to a medical condition, drugs, or mixed etiology (APA, 1994).

Whether an individual will develop delirium is contingent upon the person's vulnerability. In a frail person with dementia, even mild noxious insults can tip the individual into a delirious state. Subsequently, frail patients have a lower chance of recovering fully than those with high physiologic reserve. Patients with the diagnosis of dementia have a higher prevalence of developing delirium. Some of the most common risk factors include age, cognitive impairment, sensory depravation, psychoactive medications, immobility, sleep disturbances, and dehydration.

The precipitating factors of delirium are many, including acute cardiac or pulmonary events, infections, medications, pain, and even dehydration. In many cases the cause may be multifactorial. Regardless, once delirium develops it increases the rate of complications, and is noted to have poor outcomes. After the onset of delirium, interventions by health care providers have little effect on outcomes. Therefore, the focus is on prevention and identifying high-risk persons. Studies indicate that targeting modifiable risk factors such as cognitive impairment, sleep deprivation, immobility, visual and hearing impairments, and dehydration resulted in significant reduction in onset and duration of delirium. Examples of this multidisciplinary team, multicomponent management strategies included mobilizing and orienting the person to their surroundings (Inouye, Bogardus, Charpentier, et al, 1999). Most cases of delirium resolve when the underlying causes are removed. Delirium can be prevented with a geriatric consultation, targeting a multi-component interventional strategy, in up to one third of patients admitted with hip fracture (Marcantonio, Flacker, Wright, et al, 2001). However, once delirium sets in it can last up for days to months. Utilizing a multidisciplinary team to manage cases of delirium is essential.

DEPRESSION

Depression can often present like dementia, and is often referred in medical textbooks and journals as "pseudodementia." Depression presents with poor concentration and apathy (an absence of feeling or not caring). Although appearing as failing memory, the person's symptoms are in fact due to attention deficits rather than memory deficits, as in dementia.

A person presenting with symptoms of dementia must be screened for depression (O'Hara, Hinrichs, Kohout, Wallace, & Lemke, 1986). This is usually done at the initial assessment. History will help make the diagnosis. For example, unlike Alzheimer's disease, which develops over years, cognitive impairments related to depression tend to develop rapidly. The domains that distinguish depression from dementia can only be unraveled upon screening. Significant evidence indicates that recognizing and treating depression will greatly reduce the symptoms of cognitive impairment, as well as improve chances of survival (Kunik, Graham, Snow-Turek, Molinari, Orengo, & Workman, 1998).

A diagnosis of depression does not exclude dementia. A high percentage of patients with dementia may also have depression. In patients who have dementia as well as depression, treatment with antidepressants will improve cognition and behavior (Eccles, Clarke, Livingstone, Freemantle, & Mason, 1998).

MILD COGNITIVE IMPAIRMENT

In the millions of Americans who are diagnosed with dementia, many more may have a milder form of dementia. This is clinically recognized as mild cognitive impairment, or MCI. The cognitive impairment predominately involves only memory without loss of function. Therefore, the affected persons are able to live and manage most situations independently. The loss is beyond the normal changes associated with aging, but not severe enough to meet the criteria of dementia.

Mild cognitive impairment is an intermediate stage of cognitive changes related to normal aging and dementia (Fratiglioni, Grut, Forsell, Viitanen, & Winblad, 1992). With normal aging, memory function is relatively preserved. Although there may be a slight delay in recall of newly learned material (Mitrushina, Satz, Chervinsky, & D'Elia, 1991; Petersen, Smith, Kokmen, Ivnik, & Tangalos, 1992), the typical consensus is that normal aging does not erode memory, but specific diseases can. As noted earlier, to have dementia the following criteria must be met: a decline in cognition with a significant loss of function such that affected individuals are unable to carry out the daily tasks of usual living.

Progression is along a continuum such that over a course of time a person moves from normal aging to mild cognitive impairment, and then to dementia (Petersen, Smith, Waring, Ivnik, Tangalos, & Kokmen, 1999). The pace of the progression is variable. The period of time to progress from mild cognitive impairment to dementia is dependent on the etiology of the underlying cause of dementia. In patients who suffer with dementia from cerebrovascular disease (strokes), history will suggest a stepwise progression. If the patient does not have any further cerebrovascular events, then the disease may not progress. Effective treatments of the underlying risk factors are likely to have beneficial outcomes. At a rate of 10-15 percent per year, the progression from mild cognitive impairment to dementia is much higher than normal older adults' progression to dementia. Most patients with Alzheimer's disease as the underlying cause of their mild cognitive impairment will progress to having dementia (Albert, Moss, Tanzi, & Jones, 2001).

As the name implies, the impact of mild cognitive impairment is mild and the changes are subtle. There are three different subtypes of mild cognitive impairment. The first and most common subtype of mild cognitive impairment is amnesic mild cognitive impairment, where the person has isolated memory impairment. There is subjective and objective evidence of memory impairment, with preservation in the other domains, such as speech, language, and executive function. The second subtype is single non-memory-mild cognitive impairment, where for example, the affected person may lose some ability to speak, without any other domains affected. In multiple-domain-mild cognitive impairment, the affected individual may have mild impairments in multiple regions (Peterson, Doody, et al, 2001). In all three subtypes of mild cognitive impairment, there is no impact on function to carry out the activities of daily living.

Evaluation is critical in patients with mild cognitive impairment, and should include a comprehensive history and exam, neuro-psychological testing, as well as the standard head imaging. Imaging is done to help identify the underlying cause, and to exclude vascular or brain lesions. Imaging of the brain is usually done with either a computed tomography or magnetic resonance imaging.

Neuro-psychological testing is beneficial to those patients where the diagnosis of dementia is uncertain. This is often done at specialized centers, and evaluation may take a half-day or longer. In addition to providing a baseline assessment of the cognitive function, neuro-psychological testing also confirms and identifies the specific deficiency in the cognitive dysfunction.

Although there is no current cure for mild cognitive impairment, recent studies have indicated that the use of current cholinesterase inhibitors may slow down the progression. However, just as critical as pharmacological interventions are informed families and caregivers and routine follow-ups with the treating physicians.

DEMENTIA WITH CEREBROVASCULAR DISEASE

Dementia with cerebrovascular disease is the second most common cause of dementia after Alzheimer's disease in most of the world. Although a variety of terms are still in use, including multi-infarct dementia and vascular dementia, more recently, the term dementia with cerebrovascular disease is being utilized. This more recent definition has expanded to capture patients with disease due to pure vascular disease as well as other cases that have vascular pathology and Alzheimer's disease. Estimates suggest that 11 percent of patients have pure vascular dementia, and 20 percent have a combination of Alzheimer's disease and vascular dementia (Holmes, Cairns, Lantos, & Mann, 1999).

A link exists between clinical stroke (cerebrovascular accident, or CVA) and dementia. Approximately one third of patients who sustain a cerebrovascular accident develop dementia (Vermeer, Prins, den Heijer, et al, 2003). The criteria for dementia with cerebrovascular disease involve evidence for dementia, i.e. the cognitive deficit, along with the functional loss. There has to be unequal distribution of deficits in higher cognitive functions, with some affected and others spared. Along with the changes, there must be focal brain damage that is evident by neuroimaging and with manifestation of focal neurological deficit. These deficits must have occurred within three months of a stroke (Roman, Tatemichi, Erkinjuntti, et al, 1993).

The clinical presentation in persons with dementia related to cerebrovascular accident may have a history of an abrupt onset, and often a stepwise deterioration, with or without focal neurological signs and symptoms. History of hypertension, diabetes mellitus, or even a stroke helps make the diagnosis. Depending on the location of the lesion, the clinical presentation will vary. For example, if the stroke occurred on the parietal region of the brain, then the person will have difficulty with speech (aphasia).

Factors with the greatest impact on developing dementia include age, recurrent strokes, and hypertension. Therefore, prevention is key. Following a cerebrovascular accident, emphasis shifts on secondary prevention, modifying the risk factors for another cerebrovascular accident. This involves treatment for hypertension, obesity, smoking addiction, and diabetes mellitus. These interventions have a direct effect on outcomes in developing dementia. Depending on the etiology of the stroke, patients should be treated with pharmacotherapy, which includes antiplatelets agents, such as aspirin, or anticoagulation with warfarin (Forette, Seux, Staessen, et al, 1998; Olsen, 2003).

The rate of cognitive decline is dependent on the severity of the underlying cerebrovascular disease and response to treatment. Unlike Alzheimer's disease, treating the risk factors may halt the progression. Therefore, in persons with dementia related to trauma or cerebrovascular disease, progression can be static and does not generate progressive impairment.

NORMAL PRESSURE HYDROCEPHALUS

Normal pressure hydrocephalus may occur in many as 250,000 Americans. Thus, it may affect up to 10 percent of all persons with dementia, and generally occurs in adults above 60 years of age (Vassilouthis, 1984). A triad of signs characterizes normal pressure hydrocephalus; the first is apraxic gait, which is difficulty walking due to an inability to lift their legs. When these persons attempt to walk, they seem as if their feet are stuck to the ground. This disturbance in ability to walk leads patients to fall frequently. The next preceding prominent feature of normal pressure hydrocephalus is urinary incontinence or loss of bladder function. Finally, and most importantly, normal pressure hydrocephalus causes cognitive impairment leading to dementia.

Possible risk factors for developing normal pressure hydrocephalus include brain injury, trauma, tumors, previous brain surgery, and hemorrhage (bleeding) such as subdural hematomas.

The hallmark anatomical feature of the brain in persons with normal pressure hydrocephalus is that there is an enlargement of the ventricles of the head due to excess amounts of cerebrospinal fluid within them. A normal brain has four such sacks that are filled with cerebral spinal fluid. The purpose of cerebral spinal fluid is to nourish the brain, as well as cushion the brain against injuries. In general, there is balance in the cerebral spinal fluid production, locally from the ventricles, and then absorption by the archnoid villi into blood stream (DeLand & Wagner, 1969). These fluid filled sacks occupy 25 percent of the brain. However, in patients with normal pressure hydrocephalus there is a disequilibrium where the production of cerebral spinal fluid is greater than the absorption, leading to an accumulation of fluid, and subsequently enlarging of the ventricles. With the expansion of the ventricles, there is damage to the surrounding brain tissue. In other forms of hydrocephalus, there is an increase in intracranial pressure; however, patients with normal pressure hydro-cephalus usually have normal pressures. This can be determined by measuring the pressure when doing a lumber puncture.

A thorough medical history, with proper diagnostics tests, brain imaging or lumber spinal test, and cisternogram will help guide the decision. Neuroimaging suggestive of normal pressure hydrocephalus will have ventricle dilation greater than the cortical atrophy of the brain tissues.

Treatment may include a brain shunt, where fluid from the brain ventricles is diverted into the peritoneal (abdomen) (Black, 1980; Ahlberg, Norlen, Blomstrand, & Wikkelso, 1988). The changes in improvements in cognition are higher when there is a shorter duration of the dementia.

ALCOHOL-RELATED DEMENTIA

Various environmental as well as genetic factors play a role in the acquisition of a disease. Excessive alcohol intake can result in irreversible damage to the central nervous system as well as considerable morbidity. A range of pathologies and disorders causes the cognitive impairment in persons with alcohol, not a single disorder. Alcoholics often develop personality and behavioral changes, social and personal neglect, confabulation, as well as lack of insight, empathy, and emotional control.

Korsakoff's syndrome is a form of alcohol-related dementia. It leads to cognitive disturbance where memory is impaired out of proportion to the other domains. Clinical features are characterized by both anterograde and retrograde amnesia. Persons with Korsakaff's syndrome have difficulty establishing new memory along with limited ability to recall events. Further, these persons experience disorientation with regard to their surrounding as well as time. Other aspects such as attention, social behav-ior, and alertness, are preserved. The prominent feature is confabulation. Treatment involves, first and foremost, the cessation of alcohol intake, a proper healthy diet, and vitamin supplements. Additionally, in the early periods, prolonged treatment with thiamine (vitamin B1) may slightly improve symptoms.

PARKINSON'S DISEASE

While Parkinson's disease is common in the elderly population, it is less prevalent than Alzheimer's dementia, and occurs in about one-half to one percent of persons aged 65-69, and one to three percent of persons over 80 (Tanner & Goldman, 1996). It is classically characterized by a resting pill-rolling tremor, bradykinesia (slow movement), mask-like facial expression, rigidity, shuffling gait, and postural instability (Hoehn & Yahr, 1967). In patients who have Parkinson's disease, progression leads to another concern, dementia. During an eight-year-longitudinal study, over 75 percent of the patients with Parkinson's disease developed dementia. Prevalence increased in those with a longer duration of disease. That is, the longer the person has Parkinson's disease, the greater the chance they will develop dementia (Richards, Stern, Marder, Cote, & Mayeux, 1993).

Pathological hallmarks in Parkinson's disease include the loss of dopaminergic neurons predominately in the substantia nigra and depositions of Lewy bodies (ubiquinated protein) in the cytoplasm of neurons. In persons with Parkinson's disease who develop dementia, there is non-specific loss of neurons in the cerebral cortex (Aarsland, Andersen, Larsen, Lolk, & Kraugh-Sorensen, 2003).

Fortunately, there are effective treatments to control the symptoms for early and moderate stage Parkinson disease. However, like other neruodegenerative disorders, there is no cure. Thus, the emphasis of care is based on symptom management.

DEMENTIA WITH LEWY BODIES

One of the more common disorders is dementia with Lewy bodies, possibly accounting for 10 percent of all cases with dementia (Stevens, Livingston, Kitchen, Manela, Walker, & Katona, 2002). The clinical features include progressive dementia, along with a variety of characteristic clinical features. First, is the presence of Parkinson-like symptoms, which include motor features with rigidity, tremor, stooped posture, and the characteristic slow shuffling gait (McKeith, Galasko, Kosaka, Perry, Dickson, Hansen, et al, 1996). Second are recurrent visual or auditory hallucinations. Subsequently, patients may develop delusions, usually based on recollections of hallucinations and other perceptual disturbances (Gibb, Luther, Janota, & Lanos, 1989). Third are fluctuations in cognition, where the person will be alert and then suddenly have acute episodes of confusion (Byrne, Lennox, Lowe, & Godwin-Austen, 1989). These episodes of waxing and waning may last hours or days. Some days, patients are able to think clearly and go about their daily activities quite normally. Then, in a matter of minutes to hours, someone with Lewy body dementia can become acutely confused.

Other factors that may support the diagnosis include the following: persons with Lewy body dementia, if given anti-psychotic medication, are at greater risk of severe side effects or even death than other patients. Thus, these persons have a high sensitivity to antipsychotics, where even very low dosages will have severe side effects (McKeith, Fairbairn, Perry, Thompson, & Perry, 1992). There may also be frequent falls, presenting with syncope and fainting spells, and sometimes loss of consciousness. During the early stages, however, memory is well preserved. Prominent impairment of the visual-spatial function and visual memory is also observed.

Pathologically, Lewy body dementia is a combination of Alzheimer's-type plaques and tangles, plus the Parkinson's-like deposition of Lewy bodies in the cytoplasm of neurons. These Lewy bodies occur in areas of the brain such as the cortex, places where they don't normally occur in Parkinson's disease. These persons often have a rapid rate of progression.

Every person with Lewy body dementia is different and will manifest different degrees of the above symptoms. Presently, as with most true dementias, there is no cure. However, treatments do exist for depression and behavioral issues. There may be response to the dopamine replacement drugs that are used to treat Parkinson's disease, particularly if there are Parkinson-like symptoms. There is some evidence that these impairments will respond to cholinesterase inhibitors (McKeith, Galasko, Kosaka, Perry, Dickson, Hansen, et al, 1996). The general principles of care are similar to the interventions utilized for the management of Alzheimer's disease. The main tool for diagnosing Lewy body dementia is a careful history and a routine work up, because the presence of pathologic Lewy bodies can be confirmed only at autopsy. As in Alzheimer's disease, diagnosis of Lewy body dementia is not 100 percent accurate until autopsy.

FRONTOTEMPORAL DEMENTIA

Caring for persons with dementia is more distressing when the person is younger and when the prominent features are changes in personality and behavior. This is often the case for family members and others caring for persons with frontotemporal dementia. The mean age of diagnosis is 61.5 years, much younger than the average age for diagnosis of Alzheimer's disease (Hodges, Davies, Xuereb, Kril, & Halliday, 2003).

Clinical presentation includes changes in personality, disinhibition, and inappropriate social behavior. Another aspect is language dysfunction where speech is unfocused; echo-like, with spontaneous repetition of words as well as compulsive repetition of phrases. There is disorganized executive function with impairments of goal-setting and planning and initiation. Interestingly, these patients have poor insight into their actions, exhibit apathy, and reflect a lack of concern for others with generalized passivity and lack of initiative.

Persons affected by frontotemporal dementia may not have the visiospatial dysfunction characteristic in Alzheimer's disease. Mildly impaired patients are oriented and able to keep track of recent events, but may be variable in performance on memory testing due to lack of concern or effort in the testing situation. In contrast with Alzheimer's disease, persons affected by frontotemporal dementia have an early behavioral symptom component.

Imaging of the brain is noted to show severe focal atrophy of the frontal and anterior temporal lobes of the brain. Microscopically, there may be the characteristic Pick bodies found in the neurons of the brain.

Frontotemporal dementia is a highly aggressive disorder in which the median survival is three years after the point of diagnosis. Approximately 40 percent of these patients have a family history. Treatment is mainly supportive, as in the other causes of dementia.

LESS COMMON CAUSES OF DEMENTIA

There are many infrequent disorders that cause dementia. These can be further classified into subcategories, such as metabolic and endocrine disorders. The disorders include vitamin deficiencies, hypothyroidism, chronic abnormalities of calcium and corticosteroid homeostasis, renal impairment, hepatic impairment, and others such as Whipple's disease. Classic features of disorders such as hypothyroidism include depression, irritability, and mental slowing, along with specific physical findings. The manifestations of vitamin B12 deficiency will have psychiatry symptoms, myelopathy, neuropathy, and certain hematological abnormalities (Bradley, Daroff, Fenichel, & Marsden, 2000).

Other categories include infections, drugs and toxins, trauma, neoplasms, and even Multiple Sclerosis.

The most common infections implicated include:

- AIDS-related dementia;

- Viral encephalitis;

- Spirochetal disease: Neurosyphilis, now a rare cause of dementia, which generally occurs 15-20 years after the original infection;

- Lyme disease—*Borrelia burgdorferi*;

- Chronic bacterial meningitis; and

- Creutzfeldt-Jakob disease (CJD), which is a rare, rapidly progressive dementia. CJD is caused by infection agents known as prions. It has an extremely rapid decline, and duration of disease is very short, usually one or two years. (Bradley et al, 2000)

In these rare cases, the presentations, laboratory values, and imaging will help the physician identify the cause and guide the treatment.

MENTAL RETARDATION

In persons with mental retardation, the developmental disability and impairments have occurred before adulthood, thus distinguishing these persons from those diagnosed with dementia, which usually sets in after adulthood. The extent of the impairments is significant enough to impair them in all aspects of their life, including their career, as well as their personal and financial aspects. Unfortunately, patients with Down's syndrome have a higher risk of developing Alzheimer's disease, and onset is earlier: usually between 40-50 years of age. It is staggering to note that over 65 percent of adults with Down's syndrome will have Alzheimer's disease after age 60 (The Arc of the United States, 2001).

CONCLUSION

Dementia has become an increasingly important public health problem, due to rising prevalence, long duration, and high costs of care and lack of curative treatment. Alzheimer's disease is clearly the dominant dementing disorder in the developed world. Just as important are the many other dementing disorders, which overlap Alzheimer's disease or occur independently. An important part of disease management is to have a thorough assessment, where the goal is to identify reversible and treatable factors that may cause or contribute to a dementing process. Once dementia sets in, principles of care revolve around managing specific symptoms and behavior, and reducing risk and stress on the caregiver.

The major non-Alzheimer's dementias present different obstacles and challenges, as they are complex disorders with distinct presentation. They have diverse characteristics, as well as some overlap in pathology and features. Treatment strategies need to be individualized based on the etiology of the disease. Despite the diverse etiology, some guiding principles can be utilized to help care for the individuals. They are listed below.

Universal Principles of Management:

1) Establish proper diagnosis: The first part of any treatment is an early evaluation and a correct diagnosis. An error in this initial step can have serious consequence to the affected person, and the person's family.

2) Gain knowledge: An educated caregiver is the best resource for the person affected by dementia. Being better prepared to manage behavior will delay admission into a nursing home, as well as decrease overall stress.

3) Minimize risks: Monitor safety, such as the person's ability to drive and cook, and hazards, which increase risk for injury. Remove firearms from the home. Also, when the person with dementia is hospitalized, be on guard for restraint use, as they can increase the severity of injury and development for delirium.

4) Correct sensory deficits: Evaluate and correct hearing and visual impairment. This can reduce social isolation, improve depression, and lessen the effect on cognitive dysfunction.

5) Be prepared for appointment visits:
   a. Report to health care provider any changes in sleep, personality, memory, loss of duties and tasks, ability to follow conversation, ambulation pattern, behavior in social situations, changes or additions to medications, as well as how the person with dementia reacts to and recognizes family and friends.

   b. Monitor the overall health and level of stress on the caregiver.

6) Outline goals of care: Complete advance care plans at an early stage in the course of the disease, when the person still has capacity to make health care decisions. This is critical because as the dementing disorders progresses, the individual will lose capacity to make complex decisions. At this point, a surrogate should be identified, someone who could help make health care decisions in the event that the affected person is unable to do so. During this time, the preference for, or against, Cardiopulmonary Resuscitation (CPR) should be documented. Ideally, we have preferences for everything we do throughout life; thus it is important to have some control over the end of our lives.

7) Monitor for change in behavior or conditions such as agitation or purposeless motor hyperactivity or restlessness: It may be a behavioral expression of physical discomfort, fecal impaction, pain, medical illness, change in environment, and sensory deprivation. If this is suspected, an urgent evaluation is mandated.

8) Avoid medications, which can alter cognition or level of alertness.

9) Utilize community resources: This includes adult day care centers, home health aids, respite programs and participating in caregiver support groups.

10) Focus on the person's strengths, rather than deficits.

An enormous gap exists in what the evidence-based data suggests is the ideal evaluation and treatment, and what is actually implemented in practice. In one study, over 75 percent of primary care physicians in non-academic settings missed the diagnosis of dementia. Even today, there is still a failure to recognize the existence of dementia. This lack of recognition leads to a delay in the search for potentially reversible causes, a delay in the implementation of safety issues, and to an increase in caregiver stress. There is general apathy in the community as a whole, and current medical systems of care are not capable of adequately caring for patients with chronic disease. Therefore, a well-educated caregiver making decisions based on data and factual information is essential for the complete care of persons diagnosed with dementia. ■

Parag Dalsania, MD, is director of the Geriatric Clinic for the Veterans Affairs Medical Center, Washington, DC. Serving with a faculty appointment as Assistant Professor of Medicine for the George Washington University School of Medicine and on the faculty for the fellows in Geriatric Medicine Fellowship, he has lectured widely on medical topics related to aging, including Alzheimer's disease and other dementias. Dr. Dalsania is a member of the American Geriatric Society and serves as a board member for the local chapter. He also serves as staff Geriatrician for Providence Hospital in Washington, DC.

REFERENCES

Aarsland, D., Andersen K., Larsen, J.P., Lolk, A., & Kragh-Sorensen, P. (2003). Prevalence and characteristics of dementia in Parkinson disease. *Archives of Neurology, 60*(3), 387-392.

Ahlberg, J., Norlen, L., Blomstrand, C., & Wikkelso, C. (1988). Outcome of shunt operation on urinary incontinence in normal pressure hydrocephalus predicted by lumbar puncture. *Journal of Neurology, Neurosurgery and Psychiatry, 51*, 105-108.

Albert, M.S., Moss, M.B., Tanzi, R., & Jones, K. (2001). Preclinical prediction of AD using neuropsychological tests. *Journal of the International Neuropsychological Society, 7,* 631-639.

American Psychiatric Association. [APA]. (1994). *Diagnostic and statistical manual of mental disorders* (4th ed.). Washington, DC: Author.

The Arc of the United States. (2001). *Alzheimer's disease and people with mental retardation.* Retrieved on November 18, 2003, from http://www.thearc.org/faqs/almr.html

Black, P.M. (1980). Idiopathic normal-pressure hydrocephalus: Results of shunting in 62 patients. *Journal of Neurosurgery, 52,* 371-377.

Bradley, W.G., Daroff, R.B., Fenichel, G.M., & Marsden, C.D. (Eds.). (2000). *Neurology in Clinical Practice* (3rd ed.) (Vols. I & II). Boston: Butterworth/Heinemann.

Brookmeyer, R., Gray, S., & Kawas, C. (1998). Projections of Alzheimer's disease in the United States and the public health impact of delaying disease onset. *American Journal of Public Health, 88,* 1337-1342.

Byrne, E.J., Lennox, G., Lowe, J., & Godwin-Austen, R.B. (1989). Diffuse Lewy body disease: Clinical features in 15 cases. *Journal of Neurology, Neurosurgery and Psychiatry, 52,* 709-717.

Centers for Disease Control and Prevention. (2003). *Healthy aging for older adults.* Retrieved November 17, 2003, from http://www.cdc.gov/aging/

Chow, T.W., & Maclean, C.H. (2001). Quality indicators for dementia in vulnerable community-dwelling and hospitalized elders. *Annals of Internal Medicine, 135*(8)(2), 668-676.

Clarfield, A.M. (1988). The reversible dementias: Do they reverse? *Annals of Internal Medicine, 10,* 476-486.

DeLand, F., & Wagner, H. (1969). *Atlas of nuclear medicine* (Vol 1). Philadelphia: Saunders.

Dementia. (1993). In P.J. Whitehouse (Ed.), *Contemporary Neurology: Vol. 40* (pp. 130-164). Philadelphia: F.A. Davis Company.

Eccles, M., Clarke, J., Livingstone, M., Freemantle, N., & Mason, J. (1998). North of England evidence based guidelines development project: Guideline for primary care management of dementia. *British Medical Journal, 317,* 802-808.

Evans, D.A., Funkenstein, H.H., Albert, M.S., et al. (1989). Prevalence of Alzheimer's disease in a community population of older persons: Higher than previously reported. *JAMA, 262,* 2551-2556.

Forette, F., Seux, M.L., Staessen, J.A., et al. (1998). Prevention of dementia in randomized double-blind placebo-controlled systolic hypertension in Europe. *Lancet, 352*(9137), 1347-1351.

Francis, J. (1992). Delirium in older patients. *Journal of American Geriatrics Society, 40*(8), 829-838.

Fratiglioni, L., Grut, M., Forsell, Y., Viitanen, M., & Winblad, B. (1992). Clinical diagnosis of Alzheimer's disease and other dementias in a population survey: Agreement and cause of disagreement in applying diagnostic and statistical manual of mental disorders, revised third edition, criteria. *Archives of Neurology, 49,* 927-932.

Gibb, W.R.G., Luther, P.J., Janota, I., & Lanos, P.L. (1989). Cortical Lewy body dementia: Clinical features and classification. *Journal of Neurology, Neurosurgery and Psychiatry, 52,* 185-192.

Hebert, L.E., et al. (2003). Alzheimer's disease in the US Population. *Archives of Neurology, 60,* 1119-1122.

Hodges, J.R., Davies, R., Xuereb, J., Kril, J., & Halliday, G. (2003). Survival in frontotemporal dementia. *Neurology, 61*(3), 349-354.

Hoehn, M.M., & Yahr, M.D. (1967). Parkinsonism: Onset, progression and mortality. *Neurology, 17,* 427-442.

Holmes, C., Cairns, N., Lantos, P., & Mann, A. (1999). Validity of current clinical criteria for Alzheimer's disease, vascular dementia and dementia with Lewy bodies. *British Journal of Psychiatry, 174,* 45-50.

Inouye, S.K., Bogardus Jr., S.T., Charpentier, P.A., et al. (1999). A multi-component intervention to prevent delirium in hospitalized older patients. *New England Journal of Medicine, 340*(9), 669-676.

Kunik, M.E., Graham, D.P., Snow-Turek, A., Molinari, V.A., Orengo, C.A., & Workman, R.H. (1998). Contribution of cognitive impairment, depression, and psychosis to the outcome of agitated geropsychiatric inpatients with dementia. *Journal of Nervous and Mental Disease, 186,* 299-303.

Magaziner, J., Simonsick, E.M., Kashner, T.M., et al. (1989). Survival experience of aged hip fracture patients. *American Journal of Public Health, 79,* 274-278.

Marcantonio, E.R., Flacker, J.M., Wright, R.J., et al. (2001). Reducing delirium after hip fracture: A randomized trial. *Journal of American Geriatrics Society, 49*(5), 516-522.

Mayeux R., Foster, N.L., Rossor, M., & Whitehouse, P.J. (1993). The clinical evaluation of patients with dementia. In P.J. Whitehouse (Ed.), *Contemporary Neurology: Vol. 40. Dementia* (pp. 92-129). Philadelphia: F.A. Davis Company.

McKeith, I., Fairbairn, A., Perry, R., Thompson, P., & Perry, E. (1992). Neuroleptic sensitivity in patients with senile dementia of Lewy body type. *British Medical Journal, 305,* 673-678.

McKeith, I.G., Galasko, D., Kosaka, K., Perry, E.K., Dickson, D.W., Hansen, L.A., et al. (1996). Consensus guidelines for clinical and pathologic diagnosis of dementia with Lewy bodies. *Neurology, 47*(5), 1113-1124.

Mitrushina, M., Satz, P., Chervinsky, A., & D' Elia, L. (1991). Performance of four age groups of normal elderly on the Rey auditory-verbal learning test. *Journal of Clinical Psychology, 47,* 351-357.

O'Hara, M.W., Hinrichs, J.V., Kohout, F.J., Wallace, R.B., & Lemke, J.H. (1986). Memory complaints and memory performance in the depressed elderly. *Psychology of Aging, 1,* 208-214.

Olsen, T.S. (2003). Who is at risk for post stroke dementia? *Neurology Review, 11*(2), 10-11.

Petersen, R.C., Smith, G., Kokmen, E., Ivnik, R.J., & Tangalos, E.G. (1992). Memory function in normal aging. *Neurology, 42,* 396-401.

Petersen, R.C., Smith, G.E., Waring, S.C., Ivnik, R.J., Tangalos, E.G., & Kokmen E. (1999). Mild cognitive impairment: Clinical characterization and outcomes. *Archives of Neurology, 56,* 303-308. [Published correction in *Archives of Neurology, 56,* 760.]

Peterson, R.C., Doody, R., et al. (2001). Current concepts in mild cognitive impairment. *Archives of Neurology, 58*(12), 1985-2012.

Richards, M., Stern, Y., Marder, K., Cote, L., & Mayeux, R. (1993). Relationships between extrapyramidal signs and cognitive function in a community-dwelling cohort of patients with Parkinson's disease and normal elderly individuals. *Annals of Neurology, 33,* 267-274.

Roman, G.C., Tatemichi, T.K., Erkinjuntti T., et al. (1993). Vascular dementia: Diagnostic criteria for research studies: Report of the NINDS-AIREN international workshop. *Neurology, 43*, 250-260.

Schultz, B.M., & Gambert, S.R. (1991). Minimizing the use of psychoactive medications in the institutionalized elderly. *Clinical Gerontology, 11*, 80-82.

Stevens, T., Livingston, G., Kitchen, G., Manela, M., Walker, Z., & Katona, C. (2002). Islington study of dementia subtypes in the community. *British Journal of Psychiatry, 180*, 270-276.

Tanner, C.M., & Goldman, S.M. (1996). Epidemiology of Parkinson's disease. *Clinical Neurology, 14*, 317-335.

Vassilouthis, J. (1984). Syndrome of normal pressure hydrocephalus. *Journal of Neurosurgery, 61*, 501-509.

Vermeer, S.E., Prins, N.D., den Heijer, T., et al. (2003). Silent brain infarcts and the risk of dementia and cognitive decline. *New England Journal of Medicine, 348*(13), 1215-1222.

Weyting, M.D., Bossuyt, P.M., & van Crevel, H. (1995). Reversible dementia: More than 10% or less than 1%: A quantitative review. *Journal of Neurology, 242*, 446-471.

White, L.R., Cartwright, W.S., Cornoni-Huntley, J., & Brock, D.B. (1986). Geriatric epidemiology. *Annual Review of Gerontology and Geriatrics, 6*, 215-311.

▪ CHAPTER 4 ▪

Culture, Ethnicity, and Dementia

Kenneth J. Doka

INTRODUCTION

One could possibly think that if any disease or condition were free of the influences of culture, it would be Alzheimer's disease. After all, in Alzheimer's disease and other dementias, memory and cognition deteriorate. With that decline, one could assume that connections to culture recess along with all other memories. Surely and sadly, the progressive decline of dementia should be a great leveler.

Yet, the reality of culture and dementia is very different. Culture affects dementia in dramatic ways. Culture influences the very form of dementia individuals' experience as there are significant differences in prevalence rates of different groups. The perception of the disease, of the meaning of dementia itself, differs between groups. These perceptions consequently affect treatment. For example, if the culture views dementia as a family stigma, the family may be less receptive to community-based programs. Persons with dementia may be well hid at home. In addition, each culture defines caregiving differently. Cultural norms vary on who is responsible for care as well as the limits to that responsibility. This affects a range of decisions, from whether to accept outside assistance to institutionalization in a nursing home facility, to end-of-life decisions. All of these factors interrelate to influence grief.

Culture may be described as a way of life shared among a group. Culture may be defined by a variety of factors: ethnicity, social class, spirituality, behaviors (such as the Gay/Lesbian/Bisexual/Transgendered culture), or shared condition (for example, Deaf culture). Since most of the research on culture and dementia emphasizes ethnic cultures, ethnicity will be the focus of this chapter.

Yet, there is a clear need for research that considers the ways that these other cultural groups experience and cope with dementia. This is important for a number of reasons. It is reasonable to expect that many of the differences that exist in ethnic subcultures may be mirrored in other cultural groups. In addition, such research can shed light on ethnic differences as well.

The current difficulty is that research that only looks at ethnicity is confounded by other variables. Ethnic groups, particularly in North America, have had diverse experiences. They immigrated at distinct times. They faced varied degrees of discrimination and prejudice. They are differently distributed within the social strata. Hence cultural differences may reflect distinctions not only in ethnicity but also in social class and other experiences. Differences may be less the result of ethnicity than of life-long poverty or stress influenced by patterns of discrimination.

Culture is a complex issue in dementia. Still, even with these limitations it is essential to examine the role that culture has in dementia—for both persons with dementia as well as their caregivers.

CULTURE, ETHNICITY, AND PREVALENCE

Ethnic, cultural, and demographic data always have been critical epidemiological clues—hints to the etiology of a disease or condition. The famous Broad Street pump could be said to be the birthplace of modern epidemiological science. Dr. John Snow followed demographical clues to find the source of the 1840's cholera epidemic in the polluted water of the Broad Street pump. Similarly, occupational safety regulations first began in the eighteenth century after it was noticed that London chimney sweeps had unusually high rates of testicular cancer. The laws mandated a minimum age of eight years of age for apprentice chimney sweeps and required weekly bathing to remove the suspected soot. More recently, studies of differential rates of lung and digestive system cancers among varied cultural groups added evidence to the role of smoking as a causative factor in cancer. In short, differences in the prevalence of disease amongst diverse classes, cultures, or occupational groups often yield critical clues about the causes of disease.

Are there differences in prevalence rates of Alzheimer's disease and other types of dementias? What do these differences suggest?

Clearly, there are ethnic differences. Studies have strongly indicated differences between ethnic cultures. For example, a Chinese study found that Alzheimer's disease accounted for 60 percent of all dementia while vascular disease was the identified cause of dementia in 28 percent of the cases (Zhang et al., 1990). In a Japanese study, Alzheimer's disease only accounted for 12 percent of the sample's case of dementia while vascular disease was the cause of 50 – 70 percent of the dementia cases studied (Ueda et al., 1992). In a Swedish study, the cases split—50 percent of the cases were caused by Alzheimer's disease while the other 50 percent were diagnosed as vascular (Skoog et al., 1993). This was similar to a Baltimore study that showed a similar division of cause among an African-American sample (Folstein et al., 1985). Yet, a study in Boston of a predominately Italian-American sample attributed 95 percent of the cases of dementia to Alzheimer's disease (Evans et al., 1989).

While there seem to be relatively wide differences in the causes of dementia among different ethnic groups, it is difficult to determine what these differences tell us. Larsen and Imar (1996) offer four possible explanations for these differences.

Social

This explanation stresses that the definition of Alzheimer's disease differs in varied ethnic and cultural groups. In some societies or within some subcultures, the definition of Alzheimer's disease may be extraordinarily stigmatizing. This may lead physicians to offer a more acceptable diagnosis, especially in the situations where alternative factors may be suspect. The differences in the rates may be more apparent than real, reflecting social constraints.

Methodological

This suggests that the differences found may reflect more the complexity of assessing for dementia amongst different cultural groups than actual differences in prevalence rates. The evaluation instruments for Alzheimer's disease reflect the cultures in which they are developed and tested. They may lose reliability and validity when used within other groups. There is the "Ardilla Effect": less educated individuals who are functionally illiterate can test very much like brain-injured individuals (Ardilla, 1993a, 1993b). Ardilla (1993a) cautions that any assessment has to take into account education and that in turn, engages other variables such as social class, migration, and language. In addition, test items may not have ecological relevance when applied to different cultural groups (Baker, 1996). Time orientation may mean little in cultures that do not emphasize time. Baker (1996) also notes that only one test, the Short Portable Mental Status Questionnaire, has an adjustment for race and age.

Biological

Biological factors could also account for these cultural differences. However, these biological differences are complicated. There may be clear genetic differences that increase or decrease risk for certain types of dementia. Or, these differences may be the result of differences in longevity that result from the interrelation of genetic, biological, and social factors among cultural groups. Since chances of acquiring Alzheimer's increase as a person ages, groups that live longer have more members at higher risk.

Environmental

Environmental factors also can be the cause of differences. Cultural groups differ in many aspects of their lifestyles including diet and environmental stresses. For example, the relatively high rates of dementia due to vascular disease found in the Baltimore study among African-Americans reflect the high rates of hypertension found within the African-American community. This increased hypertension may be attributed to a number of factors including diet, lifestyle, and the higher levels of stress induced by discrimination, prejudices, and consequently lower economic status of those living in the Baltimore area.

In summary, there do seem to be clear cultural differences in the prevalence rates of distinct types of dementia. However, further research will be needed to explain the significance of these differences and whether these differences will yield information about the nature of Alzheimer's disease or of the other dementias.

DEMENTIA AS A CULTURAL CONSTRUCTION

Susan Sontag in her classic work, *Illness as Metaphor* (1978), reminds us that diseases are not only biological conditions. They are social and cultural constructions. Each society attributes meaning to a disease. In early eras, for example, syphilis was not merely a venereal disease; it was a mark of depravity. Leprosy was a curse. These social constructions become reflected in the language. The very word leper became stigmatized. It referred not only to a person who had Hansen's disease but became a synonym for an outcast. Pox came to mean a curse. These meanings reflect not only on the disease. They have implications for the person with that disease. The ways cultural groups define a disease affects the ways that persons with that disease are perceived and treated.

In American culture, for example, the very term "senile dementia" carries meanings. The term *senile* associates it with older persons. Though the psychiatric definition of *dementia* merely refers to marked cognitive impairment, popular meanings of the term differ. Generally, *demented* connotes insane, even dangerous, behavior. Hence the very term *senile dementia* suggests that persons with the disease are unpredictable and to be feared. In Chinese, the word for dementia can best be translated as "silly"— a word that seems to imply less fearful attributes (Elliott, DiMinno, Lam, & Tu, 1996). It is valuable to listen to the language that individuals use to describe the condition and to explore, especially in groups where English is not the only language, the terms that are used to define the disease.

Other cultural groups may have different cultural constructions of Alzheimer's disease or other dementias. They may have distinct understandings of cause. Not every culture, for example, shares the scientific and materialistic explanations of disease evident in Western medicine. Some cultural groups may see Alzheimer's disease as retribution for family misdeeds, the result of a curse or "evil eye," God's will, an imbalance of energy, or the result of improper alignment of either the person or the environment. Alzheimer's and other dementias also can be defined as simply a mark of aging or a mental or physical illness. In some cultures it may be attributed to individual behaviors such as failure of care. In other cultures it may be considered evidence of a genetic flaw that can haunt the family for generations. It is not unusual that in many cultures, multiple meanings may abound. It is critical to explore these meanings within the family system.

The way a disease is defined within a culture has many implications for treatment. In some cultures, these definitions may inhibit treatment. It may even discourage treatment. If the culture defines the disease as an inevitable aspect of aging, there may be little belief in the efficacy of intervention. If the disease is defined as God's will, then there may be a perception that only God can change it.

Some definitions may be highly stigmatizing. For example, if the dementia is defined as retribution for family misdeeds, a mental illness, or a genetic curse, family members may hide the person, hoping that the condition remains a deep secret. The possibility of early diagnosis, treatment, or even receptiveness to the provision of services may be limited. If an affected individual fears the stigma, then he or she may make great efforts to mask his or her condition, again impeding early diagnosis and treatment. A strong belief that the disease is a genetic legacy can complicate caregiving. Family caregivers, especially adult children, may experience intense anxiety and depression, seeing in the disease their own future fate. In some cultures, the very presence of dementia may exacerbate stress. A recent study (Hinton, Haar, Geller, & Mungas, 2003) found that Hispanic caregivers experienced high levels of depression in dementia caregiving that were not apparent in other caregiving situations, even those where mild cognitive impairment was evident.

In other cultures, the disease may be taken in stride. Many African-American families who live under stressful conditions are accustomed to coping with crises, uncertainties, and changes. There is a pride of survivorship (Jackson, 1971). A person continues to be prized as long as he or she can function and relate even in the face of cognitive impairment (Lewis & Chavis-Ausberry, 1996). This may explain some of the reasons that Black families tend to find dementia care less burdensome than White families (Aranda & Knight, 1997).

Culture not only defines the disease, it suggests the type of treatment preferred. Varied folk healers—acupuncturists, herbalists, or shamans—may be consulted. Cultural sensitivity suggests that it is important not only to assess prevalent explanations of the disease but also to understand treatments that previously have been tried or are presently being utilized. It is not unusual that in many cultural groups, individuals may mix Western medicine with traditional folk remedies.

CULTURE AND CAREGIVING

Culture not only influences the perception of the disease, it frames the caregiving experience. Each culture defines caregiving responsibilities. Culture defines who is responsible and how those responsibilities are to be fulfilled. This in turn affects caregiver burden and stress.

Cultural groups may have different access to available services (Janevic & Connell, 2001). There may be cultural barriers that inhibit groups from utilizing available services. Language may be a barrier. If the group is not primarily English speaking, they may not know of the service. If the service is only offered in English, the group may be unable to benefit or even take advantage of the program. There may be economic barriers where costs or eligibility rules inhibit involvement.

Sometimes the lack of cultural sensitivity may prove to be a barrier for utilization. The service may not offer a good cultural fit. A Meals on Wheels program that does not offer kosher or halal meals may inhibit Jews or Moslems from enrolling in the program. Even where there are no clear dietary restrictions, the food offered may be unappealing to members of any given culture. Similarly, a lack of sensitivity to homosexual relationships on the part of the aging network can disempower gay clients (Kimmel & Martin, 2001).

Interaction styles also may prove a barrier. In Hispanic culture, *personalismo* is valued. That means that personal relationships take preference over professional roles. Professionals may be expected to accept food or drink and engage in personal conversation prior to offering services. The mutual discomfort that can arise when these expectations are not shared or met can inhibit utilization. Community programs and services would benefit from evaluating the utilization patterns of different groups within their communities and identifying potential barriers.

Cultures may vary in their receptiveness to services as well. Each culture differently defines who is responsible for caregiving. For example, in White families, spouses are the primary caregivers (Janevic & Connell, 2001; Connell & Gibson, 1997). In other cultures, caregiving responsibilities may be more diffused. In many Asian cultures, the concept of filial responsibility is stressed: supported in some cultures by the belief that a failure to perform obligations would bring future misfortune upon the family (Elliott, DiMinno, Lam, & Tu, 1996). In some cultures all the children share equal responsibility while in other cultures responsibility may be focused on the oldest child or the daughters. In Hispanic families, the extended family may be expected to help. In the African-American culture, quasi-family such as a church-based network may be looked upon for assistance (Lewis & Chavis-Ausberry, 1996).

The acceptance of formal services may differ among cultures. In some cultures that may be fully acceptable while in other cultures it may not. In Chinese culture, the acceptance of outside assistance reflects poorly on the family, indicating an inability to fulfill traditional and expected responsibilities (Elliott, DiMinno, Lam, & Tu, 1996).

These cultural differences can exacerbate or facilitate caregiver stress and burden. Each culture defines who is expected to help, what they are expected to do, and when and if it is acceptable to seek formal help.

WORKING ACROSS CULTURES

All of this has implications for working with different cultural groups. It suggests that any assessment of the individual client and the family system should consider cultural background. This assessment should begin with knowledge about the client. What is the cultural background? How significant is that background in the life of the client? Culture can be seen as a continuum. Some individuals are highly assimilated into the larger culture while others are immersed within their home culture. Yet, for even clients who seem highly assimilated, their own cultural roots can still subtly influence behaviors. What is the client's language? When did the client immigrate? What experiences did the client have prior to and during that immigration? This can be a critical issue as clients with Alzheimer's disease or other dementias can sometimes revisit earlier traumatic experiences.

The assessment should naturally include the client's intimate network. Who is available to the client? Who has obligation to assist? In some cultures, the network might be relatively restricted. Only immediate family may hold obligation. In other cultures, a wide range of individuals, children, extended kin, godchildren or even members of the faith community, may be looked upon for assistance. How does the family perceive or define the disease? If the disease evokes a strong sense of shame, then families may be reluctant to seek outside assistance. What is the family's view of their own caregiving responsibilities? How are decisions made within the family? Who makes those decisions?

Working with diverse cultural groups can be a challenge. Communication is inevitably complicated. Communication occurs on three levels: verbal, nonverbal, and paraverbal. Verbal communication can be difficult especially when English may not be the client or family's original tongue. The use of translators may be problematic. Translation is an art as words rarely have a direct, equivalent meaning across languages. Moreover, the ethos of translation may vary. In some cultures, it may be considered impolite or inappropriate to translate bad news or convey unseemly feelings. Even when a language is shared, there may be differences in the "universe of discourse," that is, individuals may not share, perhaps due to profession or class, a common vocabulary. In addition, communication occurs at nonverbal and paraverbal levels as well. Nonverbal use of space, gesture, and time and the paraverbal codes regarding tempo, tone, or volume may not be understood between cultures, complicating communication.

It is little wonder it may take time to develop trust between clients and helpers. This can be particularly difficult when clients are from cultures that have experienced a history of discrimination in this country or have emigrated from oppressive nations. Sometimes the simple question, "What do I need to know about your own cultural background to assist you more effectively?" can demonstrate receptiveness and a willingness to reach across the cultural divide.

Organizations as well as individuals can assess their abilities to effectively serve diverse cultures. This can begin with an environmental scan. What do people see when they enter the organization or facility? How diverse is the staff? What languages does the staff speak? What languages are evident in our materials or even the reading matter left for clients? What does the photography, art, or decorations say about this organization? What type of music is played?

A second procedure may be a process evaluation. A process evaluation asks whether an organization is delivering services to a given population. Are they meeting community needs? What groups are underrepresented? Do members of different cultures disproportionately fail or cease to utilize services? Are the services sensitive and user-friendly to the different cultural groups served? What types of training are offered that can assist staff in dealing with cultural diversity? What linkages does this organization have to ethnic or other cultural communities that are served? These questions can assist organizations in identifying and surmounting any cultural barriers that exist.

It is always useful to identify and build relationships with institutions within each culture. These relationships will have to build incrementally so that trust and communication issues can be slowly surmounted. Yet, once these ties are developed, these institutions can be sources of credibility as well as referral, advisement, and even training.

Valle (1989) once wondered whether we could ever develop either culture-free or culture-fair ways to assess Alzheimer's disease. It is still a potent challenge. Yet, a larger challenge looms for all in the field. How can we create services that are culturally sensitive to those with dementia and to their caregivers? ■

REFERENCES

Aranda, M.P., & Knight, B.G. (1997). The influence of ethnicity and culture to caregiver stress: A sociocultural review and analysis. *The Gerontologist, 37,* 342-359.

Ardillo, A. (1993a). Future directions in the research and practice of cross-cultural neuropsychology. *The Journal of Clinical and Experimental Neuropsychology, 15*(1), 19.

Ardillo, A. (1993b). Historical evaluation of special abilities. *Behavioral Neuropsycholgy, 6,* 83-87.

Baker, F. (1996). Issues in assessing dementia in African-American elders. In G. Yeo & D. Gallagher-Thompson (Eds.), *Ethnicity and the dementias.* Washington, DC: Francis & Taylor.

Elliott, K., DiMinno, M., Lau, D., & Tu, M. (1996). Working with Chinese families in the context of dementia. In G. Yeo & D. Gallagher-Thompson (Eds.), *Ethnicity and the dementias.* Washington, DC: Francis & Taylor.

Evans, D., Funkenstein, H., Albert, M., Scheer, P., Cook, N., Chown, M., Herbert, L., Hennekens, C., & Taylor, J. (1989). Prevalence of Alzheimer's disease in a community population of older persons. *The Journal of the American Medical Association, 262,* 2551-2556.

Folstein, M., Anthony, J., Parhad, I., Duffy, B., & Gruenberg, E. (1985). The meaning of cognitive impairment in the elderly. *Journal of the American Geriatric Society, 33,* 228-235.

Hinton, L., Haar, M., Gellar, S., & Mungas, D. (2003). Neuropsychiatric symptoms in Latino elders with dementia or cognitive impairment without dementia and factors that modify their association with caregiver depression. *The Gerontologist, 43,* 664-673.

Jackson, J. (1971). Negro aged: Toward research in social gerontology. *The Gerontologist, 11,* 52-57.

Janovic, M., & Connell, C. (2001). Racial, ethnic, and cultural differences in the dementia caregiver experience: Recent findings. *The Gerontologist, 41,* 334-347.

Kimmel, D., & Martin, D. (2001). *Midlife and aging in gay America.* Binghamton, NY: Harrington Park Press.

Larsen, E., & Imar, Y. (1996). Overview of dementia and ethnicity with special emphasis on the epidemiology of dementia. In G. Yeo & D. Gallagher-Thompson (Eds.), *Ethnicity and the dementias.* Washington, DC: Francis & Taylor.

Lewis, I., & Chavis-Ausberry, M. (1996). African-Americans families: Management of demented elders. In G. Yeo & D. Gallagher-Thompson (Eds.), *Ethnicity and the dementias.* Washington, DC: Francis & Taylor.

Skoog, I., Nilsson, L., Palmertz, B., Andreasson, L., & Svanborg, A. (1993). A population-based study of dementia in 85 year-olds. *New England Journal of Medicine, 328,* 153-158.

Sontag, S. (1978). *Illness as metaphor.* New York: McGraw-Hill.

Ueda, K., Kawano, H., Hasuo, Y. & Fujishima, M. (1992). Prevalence and etiology of dementia in a Japanese community. *Stroke, 23,* 798-803.

Valle, R. (1989). Cultural and ethnic issues in Alzheimer's disease family research. In G. Light and B. Lebowitz (Eds.), *Azheimer's disease, treatment and family stress: Directions for research.* Rockville, MD: NIMH.

Zhang, M., Katzman, R., Salmon, D., Jin, H., Cai, G., Wang, Z., Qu, G., Grant, I., Yu, E., & Levy, P. (1990). The prevalence of dementia and Alzheimer's disease in Shanghai, China: Impact of age, gender and education. *Annals of Neurology, 27,* 428-437.

■ CHAPTER 5 ■

Intellectual Disabilities and Dementia

Philip McCallion and Mary McCarron

INTRODUCTION

Americans with intellectual and other developmental disabilities are growing older along with the rest of the population. This aging trend reflects positively on the resilience of this population, as well as advances in medical care, advocacy and self-advocacy, and creation of quality living environments that enrich persons' lives. But advancing age also signals an increased risk for Alzheimer's disease and related dementias. The emergence of these dual diagnoses raises a whole new set of issues and dilemmas for those who are responsible for their care—family caregivers, disability service providers and hospice/end-of-life professionals.

This chapter will describe the growing population of older persons with intellectual disabilities and what a diagnosis of dementia means for this increasingly at-risk group. It also discusses where dementia and end-of-life care fit within current programming practices and philosophies for persons with intellectual disabilities and how the service system is seeking to modify its response to dementia, highlighting the specific implications of issues already familiar to end-of-life professionals, such as honoring self-determination.

There are no accurate and complete counts of people who are aging with intellectual and other developmental disabilities in the United States. Needs in later adulthood have remained hidden because families, the primary caregivers, often were able to provide lifetime care (Roberto, 1993), although that is less true as age advances. Estimates suggest that life expectancy has increased from 18.5 years in 1930 to 59.1 years in 1970 to an estimated 66.2 years in 1993 (Braddock, 1999).

Janicki and colleagues, based upon analyses of New York State data, project further advances in life expectancy paralleling the general population (Janicki, et al., 1999). Indeed, they estimate that by 2020 the number of persons with developmental disabilities over 65 years of age will have doubled from 1990 estimates (Janicki & Dalton, 2000).

Increases in life expectancy for adults with intellectual and other developmental disabilities inevitably expose more of them to age-related diseases such as Alzheimer's disease. Increased longevity thus will create a demand for services and attention that many states and localities are ill-prepared to address (Seltzer & Krauss, 1994; Braddock, 1999) and for which professionals in the disabilities, health, and aging fields have received little training (McCallion & Kolomer, 2003). A consensus conference sponsored by the World Health Organization (WHO, 2000) was a first effort to document concerns about the health and aging of persons with intellectual disabilities and to develop parameters for appropriate responses.

DEFINITIONS

Developmental Disability: As defined in Public Law 98-527, the Developmental Disabilities and Bill of Rights Act, a developmental disability is a severe, chronic disability of a person that: (1) is attributable to a mental or physical impairment or combination of mental and physical impairments; (2) is manifested before age 22; (3) is likely to continue indefinitely; (4) results in substantial functional limitations in several areas of major life activity; and (5) reflects the need for a combination and sequence of special, interdisciplinary or generic care, treatment, or other services that are of lifelong or extended duration and are individually planned and coordinated.

People with mental retardation constitute the majority of persons with developmental disabilities, with Down's syndrome considered a subset of mental retardation. They are also the primary target of publicly funded developmental disability services (Janicki & Dalton, 2001). The historic focus on this group has also resulted in greater attention to the labels used to describe such individuals. *Persons with mental retardation* has been the most common term but *persons with intellectual disabilities* now is receiving more frequent (and international) use and will be used here.

Intellectual Disability: An intellectual disability is a condition of arrested or incomplete development of the mind characterized by impairment of skills manifested during the development period contributing to the overall level of intelligence, e.g., cognitive, language, motor, and social abilities (WHO, 1992).

Down's Syndrome: Down's syndrome is a disorder in which a characteristic chromosomal aberration is associated with distinctive morphological phenotypic anomalies that are clinically recognizable at, or soon after, birth and in which cognitive deficits of a variable degree are a persistent feature (Berg et al., 1993).

Alzheimer's Disease: Alzheimer's disease is characterized by progressive deterioration of memory, cognitive functioning, and the ability for self-care (Berg et al., 1993).

DISABILITIES, DEMENTIA, HEALTH, AND END-OF-LIFE CARE

Historically, state disability systems gave more of their attention to developing educational and vocational services for children and work-age adults with intellectual disabilities, and less to the needs of those reaching old age (McCallion, 1993; Braddock, 1999). Programming for the latter has been further stymied by conflicts over which is the responsible service system: aging or developmental disabilities; who is the primary client: aging family caregivers or the person with a developmental disability; and what are appropriate service models: maintaining family living situations, planning for transitions to out-of-home placement, or promoting the person's independence (McCallion & Janicki, 1997).

A unique feature of this aging group is that about 10 percent has been in long-term out-of-home placements, in some cases since birth (Braddock, 1999). The majority of resources in the disability service system have been targeted toward out-of-home groups, and their needs have shaped service delivery philosophy for all (McCallion & McCarron, in press). Current controversy centers on whether disability service systems should "re-engineer" for the aging years—or is there a role for the aging services system to assume or assist with this care?

In cases where residential transitions have long since occurred, end-of-life care has not been a primary focus in service discussions. But it is a growing concern. Finally, those currently in family care settings may enter the out-of-home service system because of aging and chronic illness concerns (either for the person with intellectual disabilities or for his or her family caregiver).

Dementia

The incidence of Alzheimer's disease and other dementias increases with advancing age (Brookmeyer, Gray, & Kawas, 1998). An increasingly older population of persons with intellectual disabilities faces a similar risk, while responding to that risk has become a major concern of the intellectual disability service system in the United States and elsewhere (Aylward et al., 1997; Janicki et al., 1996; University of Stirling, 2001). It has been estimated that in the United States there may be 140,000 older adults with intellectual disabilities possibly affected by Alzheimer's disease, and this number will grow threefold within the next 20 years (Janicki & Dalton, 2000).

Concerns already noted about the quality of health care available to older persons with intellectual disabilities are magnified because their pre-existing disabilities often mask symptoms of dementia and make assessment difficult. Assessment instruments used with the general population are rarely effective when there is a pre-existing cognitive deficit (see Aylward et al., 1997, for recommendations). Concerns over the lack of treatment alternatives also discourage diagnosis, active treatment, and preparation for end-of-life issues (Janicki et al., 2002). Yet diagnosis, active responses and supportive end-of-life care are possible and available (Dalton, Tsiouris, & Patti, 2000; McCallion & Janicki, 2002; McCarron, 1999; Service, Lavoie, & Herlihy, 1999).

Estimates developed by Evans and colleagues (Evans et al., 1990) suggest a prevalence of Alzheimer's disease in around 10 percent for the general population over age 65, rising to more than half beyond age 85. For persons with Down's syndrome, Prasher (1995) reports a clinical presentation of Alzheimer's disease occurring at a rate of 2.0 percent in ages 30 to 39 years, 9.4 percent at 40 to 49 years, 36.1 percent at 50 to 59 years and 54.5 percent in persons aged 60 to 69 years. Onset of Alzheimer's appears to be earlier in life while its duration appears more compressed (Holland, 2000; Janicki & Dalton, 2000).

Zigman and colleagues (1997) note that differences in sampling techniques and assessment procedures, as well as lack of standardized diagnostic criteria, may contribute to the varying estimates as well as differences in age profiles. However, a higher prevalence of Alzheimer's disease among persons with Down's syndrome has been consistently reported. (See, for example, Haveman et al., 1989; Janicki & Dalton, 2000; and Tyrrell et al., 2001.)

The correspondence with Alzheimer's is less clear for persons with other intellectual disabilities. In a population survey, Cooper (1997) suggests that dementia occurs at a much higher rate among elderly people with intellectual disabilities than in the general population, with a prevalence of Alzheimer's disease at 21.6 percent, compared with an expected prevalence of 5.7 percent in a general population of the same age structure. Others have reported rates that are more comparable to the general population (see, for example, Haveman, et al., 1989; Janicki & Dalton, 2000). In all cases, the reported data tend to be drawn from clinic and residential but not family caregiving populations.

In the absence of a national database, there are few data available on families caring at home for individuals with intellectual disabilities, which constrains informed planning for future services (McCarron, 2002). Drawing upon estimates based on available state databases, we know that in the United States the population cared for at home (estimated at 2.6 million) is much larger than the number known and participating in intellectual disability service systems (approximately 400,000).

Family caregivers are aging too, with 700,000 of them now over age 60 and almost one million between 41 and 59 years of age. Therefore, by 2020, large numbers of persons with intellectual disabilities and their family caregivers both will be at the age of risk for a diagnosis of Alzheimer's disease, making them doubly at risk for the impact of dementia (Braddock, 1999; McCallion & Kolomer, 2003).

Similar to the general population, a terminal or end stage of dementia in persons with an intellectual disability has been described as marked by personality and mood changes, immobility, incontinence, and total loss of self-care skills (Prasher, 1995; Cosgrave et al., 2000). Clinical mental and physical health characteristics of persons with Down's syndrome and other intellectual disabilities, with and without Alzheimer's disease, have also received increasing attention. Moss and Patel (1997) report poorer health in persons with Alzheimer's disease compared to persons without Alzheimer's disease.

The development of new-onset epilepsy in persons who have both Down's syndrome and Alzheimer's disease has also been reported, with prevalence rates of up to 80 percent (Evenhuis, 1990), compared with 10 percent in the overall Alzheimer's population (Hauser et al., 1996).

Other studies have reported an association between depression and Alzheimer's disease in persons with Down's syndrome (Meins, 1995; Tyrrell et al., 2001), with strong recommendations for active treatment, as well as higher levels of arthritis, immobility, and gastric problems. All these conditions were found to be higher for those in end-stage versus mid-stage dementia (McCarron, 2002). Dementia-related end-of-life care therefore must also be concerned with the overall health of persons with intellectual disabilities and with responses to their actual health concerns.

Health Care

A recently completed, systematic study of the health needs of persons with intellectual disabilities aged 40 and over living in group homes in two catchment areas of New York State found them to be similar to other adults of the same age in terms of overall health status (outside of expected disability-related conditions and physical conditioning). For example psychiatric and behavioral disorders tended to decline in frequency with increasing age while cardiovascular diseases and sensory impairments increase with age (Janicki et al., 2003).

However, low rates of exercise and high rates of diet-related conditions were evident. Over half of the cohort was classified as obese according to Body Mass Index (BMI; Flegal, 1999). Obesity among these individuals was not often noted by their physicians as a concern, which suggests that health practitioners may be accepting obesity as normal among adults with intellectual disabilities and may not be aggressively addressing its health consequences.

Similarly, cardiovascular and respiratory diseases and cancers have been reported to be as prevalent causes of death for these individuals as for the general population (Evenhuis, 1997), yet there was a relatively low reported rate in the two catchment areas of symptoms of those diseases. That may be due to the relatively younger age of this group of adults (their mean age was 54). Given the risk status of this population for these diseases due to high BMIs and infrequent exercise, the results were considered surprising and may reflect under-recognition of health conditions (Janicki et al., 2003). Under-attention to end-of-life issues thus may be a symptom of the under-attention to chronic illness issues generally among adults and older adults with intellectual disabilities (McCallion & Kolomer, 2003).

Findings of inadequate health care delivery fuel an ongoing concern within the intellectual disabilities field about the mortality of persons with intellectual disabilities and its relationship to health care provided. (For a review, see Hayden 1998.) Some argue that those receiving institutional as opposed to community-based care actually have greater longevity, due to greater access to specialized and consistent health care versus the inexperience of community-based providers in meeting the needs of persons with developmental disabilities (Strauss & Kastner, 1996). For other reasons, however, the intellectual disabilities field wants to ensure that community-based care is the preferred option for persons aging with intellectual disabilities (Hayden, 1998).

A CONUNDRUM

The policy and programming framework of the intellectual disability service system places great value on ensuring continued acquisition of skills. This framework emphasizes work and day program availability and opportunities to live in the community. Intellectual disability services have also been effective in identifying supports and resources to enable people to move from institutional care to small group homes and community-based accommodations.

In many states there is a prevalent belief that no level of disability or health need precludes day-to-day community living. However, existing community care structures were not set up for people with the level of need implicit in dementia care—when different, more medically oriented staffing patterns may be needed. All staff may not have the skills to cater effectively to people with this level of need, and buildings may need to be redesigned to make them barrier-free yet safe for wanderers (Janicki et al., 2002; Udell, 1999). This conundrum has proven difficult to surmount.

A person with Alzheimer's disease will not continue to acquire or even maintain skill levels, which raises a critical question as to whether persons with intellectual disabilities who have symptoms of Alzheimer's belong in, or can be served by, the intellectual disability service system. Answers vary. In their study of Alzheimer's disease in older people with intellectual disabilities, Moss and Patel (1997) suggest that despite the magnitude of functional loss, the majority of persons with Alzheimer's disease were within the broad spectrum of ability addressed by intellectual disability services. They concluded that retaining contact with existing friends and service providers should be the overriding programming consideration.

Janicki and colleagues agree (1999); they urge drawing on the same innovative supports established for community care of persons with Alzheimer's disease generally. Using home supports, appropriate staff training and technological and environmental enhancements to help staff cope more effectively with the increasing demands of dementia care, adults with intellectual disabilities can also remain in their own homes. Operationally, however, different responses have been documented among providers and must be recognized by end-of-life specialists working with those agencies.

A recent survey of 54 group homes (Janicki et al., 2002) caring for at least one person with an intellectual disability and Alzheimer's disease found three responses to dementia: aging in place, referral to a dementia- or aging-focused unit within the provider's network, or referral to a more restrictive setting. Issues that were found to influence agency decision-making about maintaining individuals in the community included: the presentation of Alzheimer's disease symptoms, staff and home capabilities, and the resources that the agency had available to provide Alzheimer's-related care on a continuing (or long-term) basis. The survey also found that where attention was given to these issues, some service providers were able to adapt their current approaches to provide Alzheimer's care in small group living or family situation settings, irrespective of long-term disability.

What proved important were strategies to adapt physical plant (to increase safety, access, and independence); to increase administrative preparation via planning, fiscal management, and resource allocation (to provide a supportive administrative environment for clinical services); to adapt best practice models for staff training (to ensure staff readiness and capability); and to recruit and train staff for Alzheimer's-capable environments (to maintain a work force familiar with Alzheimer's-related care). Conversely, lack of attention to symptoms; inappropriate staffing, training, and programming; and poor connections to other service systems meant that decisions about the person with both intellectual disabilities and Alzheimer's disease were made in response to crises in care, often resulting in placement in more restrictive settings.

End-of-life specialists, called upon to advise intellectual disability agencies on appropriate care, should encourage changes in care early in the dementia process so that options can be genuinely considered. If end-of-life care needs are to be appropriately and sensitively met, there needs to be education about options, pre-planning, allocation of resources, and connections with end-of-life expertise. That has not yet occurred.

Another central tenet in care provision for people with intellectual disabilities has been the creation of homey, family-type care in out-of-home settings. This achievement has resulted in close, family-type relationships and bonds established between persons with intellectual disabilities, staff members and other residents. The emergence of Alzheimer's disease at a relatively young age in people with Down's syndrome, for example, has been noted to take its toll on staff (Hammond & Benedetti, 1999; Davis, 1999; Udell, 1999; Service et al., 1999).

Staff may also experience emotional conflicts, yet maintaining professional distance from the persons served often means that the emotional responses of staff are not recognized or provided for. End-of-life professionals, given their recognition of family and caregiver issues, can offer an important perspective for addressing these staff concerns. The preparation of other residents for the anticipated death of the person with Alzheimer's disease is also important.

The Edinburgh Principles

1. Adopt an operational philosophy that promotes the utmost quality of life of persons with intellectual disabilities affected by dementia and, whenever possible, base services and support practices on a person-centered approach.

2. Affirm that individual strengths, capabilities, skills, and wishes should be the overriding consideration in any decision-making for and by persons with intellectual disabilities affected by dementia.

3. Involve the individual, her or his family, and other close supports in all phases of assessment and services planning and provision for the person with an intellectual disability affected with dementia.

4. Ensure that appropriate diagnostic, assessment and intervention services and resources are available to meet the individual needs and support healthy aging of persons with intellectual disabilities affected by dementia.

5. Plan and provide supports and services that optimize remaining in the chosen home and community of adults with intellectual disabilities affected by dementia.

6. Ensure that persons with intellectual disabilities affected by dementia have the same access to appropriate services and supports as afforded to other persons in the general population affected by dementia.

7. Ensure that generic, cooperative, and proactive strategic planning across relevant policy, provider, and advocacy groups involves consideration of the current and future needs of adults with intellectual disabilities affected by dementia.

A RESPONSE TO THE CHALLENGE

The intellectual disabilities field has not been inactive in addressing dementia issues. Guidelines have been produced for more effective and responsive assessment (Aylward et al., 1997) and for care delivery (Janicki et al., 1996). A consensus conference held in Edinburgh, Scotland, produced the Edinburgh Principles (Wilkinson & Janicki, 2001) as a means for the field to shape the policy debate and encourage more planned responses for this population's needs.

There have also been efforts to operationalize the Edinburgh Principles within the tenets of quality of life driving intellectual disability service delivery. In a consensus statement, Schalock and colleagues (2002) describe subjective and objective quality of life for all persons with intellectual disabilities as comprising the same factors and relationships as for persons without identified disabilities. Quality of life occurs when major needs and wants are met, with opportunities for enrichment in all major life areas based on the individual's needs, wants, and choices; and reflecting community participation including family, intimate relationships, friends, neighbors, work, and citizenship.

For dementia care, it has been recommended (McCallion & McCarron, in press) that these concepts be combined and modified with ideas drawn from the literature on successful aging and Alzheimer's care for those without known intellectual disabilities to create a set of indicators of quality of life to guide Alzheimer's care in community homes. Specific indicators include: absence of pain, maintenance of health, psychosocial well-being, skills maintenance with support when one declines, absence of and supportive responses to problem behaviors, leisure and community participation, family and friends, dementia-focused programming, supportive environments, and alleviation of caregiver burden.

Re-conceptualization based on these indicators emphasizes the continued enjoyment of day-to-day life in the community, prepares for end-of-life concerns and highlights the resources and training needed for their achievement. Realization will require input from and collaboration among intellectual disability, dementia care and end-of-life professionals— who should familiarize themselves with the documents mentioned above.

CONCERNS FOR CARE OF PERSONS WITH INTELLECTUAL DISABILITIES AND DEMENTIA

Two issues already recognized in the end-of-life and hospice fields deserve particular attention in the care of persons with both intellectual disabilities and Alzheimer's disease: (1) understanding when end-stage dementia is present; and (2) self-determination including advance directives.

Recognizing End-Stage Dementia

In the general population, it can be a challenge to identify when a person with dementia has reached the end stage and is dying. Clues often include breakdowns in the ability to communicate, increased difficulty in independently performing activities of daily living, incontinence, and immobility. For persons with intellectual disabilities, such compromises may pre-exist, yet providers mistakenly assume that end-stage dementia is present and pursue transfer to more restrictive settings (McCarron & Lawlor, in press).

Early planning for the end stage is certainly recommended but changes in persons with both intellectual disabilities and Alzheimer's disease must always be measured and understood in comparison to the individual's previous abilities. Responses should be about maintaining connections to life as well as preparing for death. As is true for all persons with Alzheimer's disease, safe and simple activities, particularly sensory activities, encourage such connections, prompting a sense of nurturing, security, and compassionate caring in a dignified and meaningful manner. End-of-life professionals will find in the intellectual disability service system considerable experience and readiness for such approaches.

Self-Determination and Advance Directives

The intellectual disabilities services field has a history of valuing self-determination by persons with intellectual disabilities, including the capacity to choose, having one's choices determine one's actions, and having control over one's life (Duvdevany, Ben-Zur & Ambar, 2002). The pursuit of self-determination is informed by a belief that with the proper supports such self-determination is possible for almost all persons with intellectual disabilities. Even with supports, for some persons with intellectual disabilities, expression of their wishes has always been difficult. In the end stage of Alzheimer's, such expression becomes impossible.

Equally, for families and surrogate decision-makers/guardians, absence of information and rushed decisions in emotionally charged moments likely will not support decisions that are in the best interest of the person with Alzheimer's disease or that conform to his or her wishes. The maintenance of self-determination is a concern for all persons in end-stage dementia and can be achieved through living wills, advance directives, and the development of materials to support informed decision-making.

CONCLUSION

Dementia and end-of-life care historically have not been features of development and resource allocation within the intellectual disability service system but are becoming an increasing concern. Increased longevity for persons with intellectual disabilities also means increased risk for Alzheimer's disease. One group, those with Down's syndrome, raises particular issues. The intellectual disability service system currently is reorganizing itself to better respond to the challenges, developing guidelines and principles for service delivery.

There is a desire to retain the community focus on which the service system was built, yet a concern that the needs of persons with Alzheimer's disease may exceed the capacity of many providers and staff. The hospice and end-of-life care field has much to offer to the intellectual disability service system in terms of training and options for preserving community living and organizing supports for end-of-life care.

However, such assistance will only be successful if it is based on an understanding of self-determination and other core care principles of intellectual disability services. Finally, collaboration with intellectual disability providers offers hospice and end-of-life care providers a unique opportunity to experience delivery of dementia care, including end-stage care, in small, community-based settings—an experience that may improve the services they offer and advocate for other patients. ■

Philip McCallion, PhD, is Associate Professor and Director, Center for Excellence in Aging Services, State University of New York at Albany. His research and training activities have focused primarily on two broad areas. One is understanding the effectiveness of non-pharmacological interventions in addressing problem behaviors among persons with dementia. The other is investigating how residential environments might be redesigned, staff retrained, families assisted, and services redesigned to support "aging in place" for persons with intellectual disabilities. Dr. McCallion's research has been supported by grants from the John A. Hartford Foundation, the Alzheimer's Association, two federal agencies (Administration on Aging; Agency for Health Care Policy and Research), and three New York State agencies (Department of Health, Office for the Aging, and Developmental Disabilities Planning Council).

Mary McCarron, PhD, is a lecturer in the School of Nursing and Midwifery Studies at Trinity College, Dublin, where she heads a postgraduate program in specialized nursing for persons with dementia and intellectual disabilities. Dr. McCarron's research has focused on the economic and other costs of providing nursing care for persons with Down's Syndrome and Alzheimer's disease. Her current research interests also include end-of-life concerns.

REFERENCES

Aylward, E., Burt, D., Thorpe, L., Lai, F., & Dalton, A. (1997). Diagnosis of dementia in individuals with intellectual disability. *Journal of Intellectual Disability Research, 41*, 152-164.

Berg, J.M., Karlinsky, H., & Holland (Eds.). (1993). *Alzheimer's disease, Down syndrome, and their relationship.* Oxford: Oxford Medical Publications.

Braddock, D. (1999). Aging and developmental disabilities: demographic and policy issues affecting American families. *Mental Retardation, 37*, 155-161.

Brookmeyer, R., Gray, S., & Kawas, C. (1998). Projections of Alzheimer's disease in the United States and the public health impact of delaying disease onset. *American Journal of Public Health, 88*, 1337-1342.

Cooper, S.A. (1997). High prevalence of dementia among people with learning disabilities not attributable to Down's syndrome. *Psychological Medicine, 27,* 609-616.

Cosgrave, M.P., Tyrrell, J., McCarron, M., Gill, M., & Lawlor, B.A. (2000). A five year follow up study of dementia in persons with Down's syndrome: Early symptoms and patterns of deterioration. *Irish Journal of Psychological Medicine, 17*(1), 5-11.

Dalton, A.J., Tsiouris, J., & Patti, P. (2000, August). *Geriatric Training Program for the Management of Age-Associated Conditions in Persons With Intellectual Disabilities.* Paper presented at the 11th World Congress of the International Association for the Scientific Study of Intellectual Disabilities, Seattle, Washington.

Davis, D.R. (1999). A parent's experience. In M.P. Janicki & A.J. Dalton (Eds.), *Dementia, aging, and intellectual disabilities* (pp.42-48). New York: Taylor & Francis.

Duvdevany, I., Ben-Zur, H., & Ambar, A. (2002). Self-determination and mental retardation: Is there an association with living arrangement and lifestyle satisfaction. *Mental Retardation, 40,* 379-389.

Evans, D., Scherer, P. , Cook, N., Albert, M., Funkenstein, H., Smith, L., Hebert, L., Branch, L., Chown, M., Hennekens, H., & Taylor, J. (1990). Estimated prevalence of Alzheimer's disease in the United States. *The Milbank Quarterly, 68*(2), 267-289.

Evenhuis, H.M. (1990) The natural history of dementia in Down's syndrome. *Archives of Neurology, 47,* 263-267.

Flegal, K. (1999). The obesity epidemic in children and adults: Current evidence and research issues. *Medicine and Science in Sports and Exercise, 31* (Suppl. 11), S509-S514.

Hammond, B., & Benedetti, P. (1999). In M.P. Janicki, & A.J. Dalton (Eds), *Dementia, Aging, and Intellectual Disabilities* (pp 32-40). New York: Taylor & Francis.

Hauser, W.A., Morris, M.L., Heston, L.L., et al. (1986). Epilepsy in Down syndrome: Clinical aspects and possible mechanisms. *American Journal on Mental Retardation, 98,* 12-16.

Haveman, M., Maaskant, M.A., Sturmans, F. (1989). Older Dutch residents of institutions, with and without Down syndrome: Comparison of mortality and morbidity trends and motor/social functioning. *Australia and New Zealand Journal of Developmental Disabilities, 15,* 241-255.

Hayden, M.F. (1998). Mortality among people with mental retardation living in the United States: Research review and policy application. *Mental Retardation, 36,* 345-359.

Holland, A.J., Hon, J., Huppert, F.A., & Stevens, F. (2000) Incidence and course of dementia in people with Down's syndrome: Findings from a population-based study. *Journal of Intellectual Disability Research, 44,* 138-146.

Janicki, M.P., & Dalton, A.J. (1999). Dementia and public policy considerations. In M.P. Janicki & A.J. Dalton (Eds.), *Dementia, Aging, and Intellectual Disabilities* (pp. 388-414). New York: Taylor & Francis.

Janicki, M.P., & Dalton, A.J. (2000). Prevalence of dementia and impact on intellectual disability services. *Mental Retardation, 38,* 277-289.

Janicki, M.P., Dalton, A.J., Henderson, C.M., & Davidson, P.W. (1999). Mortality and morbidity among older adults with intellectual disability: Health services considerations. *Disability and Rehabilitation, 21*(5/6), 284-294.

Janicki, M.P., Heller, T., Seltzer, G., & Hogg, J. (1995). *Practice guidelines for the clinical assessment and care management of Alzheimer and other dementia among adults with mental retardation.* Washington: American Association on Mental Retardation.

Janicki, M.P., Henderson, C.M., Davidson, P.W., McCallion, P., Taets, J.D., Force, L.T., Sulkes, S.B., Frangenberg, E., & Ladrigan, P. (2002). Health characteristics and health services utilization in older adults with intellectual disabilities living in community residences. *JIDR, 46*(4), 287-298.

Janicki, M.P., McCallion, P., & Dalton, A.J. (2000). Supporting People with Dementia in Community Settings. In M.P. Janicki & A.F. Ansello (Eds.), *Community supports for aging adults with lifelong disabilities.* (pp. 387-413). Baltimore, Maryland: Paul H. Brookes Publishing.

Janicki, M.P., McCallion, P., & Dalton, A.J. (2002). Dementia-related care decision-making in group homes for persons with intellectual disabilities. *Journal of Gerontological Social Work, 38,* 179-196.

McCallion, P. (1993). *Social worker orientations to permanency planning with older parents caring at home for family members with developmental disabilities.* Unpublished dissertation, University at Albany.

McCallion, P., & Janicki, M.P. (1997). Area agencies on aging: Meeting the needs of persons with developmental disabilities and their aging caregivers. *Journal of Applied Gerontology, 16,* 270-284.

McCallion, P., & Janicki, M.P. (2002). *Intellectual disabilities and dementia: A cd-rom training package.* Albany, NY: NYS Developmental Disabilities Planning Council.

McCallion, P., & Kolomer, S.R. (2003). Aging persons with developmental disabilities and their aging caregivers. In B. Berkman & L. Harootyan (Eds.), *Social work and health care in an aging world* (pp. 201-225). New York: Springer.

McCallion, P., & McCarron, M. (in press). A perspective on quality of life in dementia care. *Mental Retardation.*

McCarron, M. (2002). The influence of Alzheimer's dementia on time spent caregiving for persons with Down's syndrome. An unpublished thesis. Dublin, Ireland: Trinity College.

McCarron, M. (1999). Some issues in caring for people with the dual disability of Down's syndrome and Alzheimer's dementia. *Journal of Learning Disabilities for Nursing, Health and Social Care, 3*(3), 123-129.

McCarron, M., & Lawlor, B.A. (in press). Responding to the challenges of ageing and dementia in intellectual disability in Ireland. *Ageing and Mental Health.*

McCarron, M., & McCallion, P. (in press). End of life care challenges for persons with intellectual disability and dementia: Making decisions about tube feeding. *Mental Retardation.*

Meins, W. (1995). Are depressive mood disturbances in adults with Down syndrome an early sign of dementia? *Journal of Nervous and Mental Disease, 183,* 663-664.

Moss, S., & Patel, P. (1997). Dementia in older people with intellectual disability: symptoms of physical and mental illness, and levels of adaptive behaviour. *Journal of Intellectual Disability Research, 41*(1), 60-69.

Prasher, V.P. (1995) End-stage dementia in adults with Down syndrome. *International Journal of Geriatric Psychiatry, 10,* 1067-1069.

Roberto, K.A. (Ed.). (1993). *The elderly caregiver: Caring for adults with developmental disabilities.* Newbury Park, CA: Sage.

Schalock, R.L., Brown, I., Cummins, R.A., Felce, D., Matikka, L., Keith, K.D., & Paramenter, T. (2002). Conceptualization, measurement, and application of quality of life for persons with intellectual disabilities: Report of an international panel of experts. *Mental Retardation, 40,* 457-470.

Seltzer, M.M., & Krauss, M.W. (1994). Aging parents with coresident adult children: The impact of lifelong caregiving. In M.M. Seltzer, M.W. Krauss, & M.P. Janicki (Eds.), *Lifecourse perspectives on adulthood and old age* (pp. 3-18).Washington, DC: American Association on Mental Retardation.

Service, K.P., Lavoie, D., & Herlihy, J.E. (1999). In M.P. Janicki, A.J. Dalton (Eds.), *Dementia, aging, and intellectual disabilities* (pp. 330-349). New York: Taylor & Francis.

Strauss, D. & Kastner, T.A. (1996). Comparative mortality of people with developmental disabilities in institutions and the community. *American Journal on Mental Retardation, 101,* 269-281.

Udell, L. (1999). Supports in small group home settings. In M.P. Janicki & A.J. Dalton (Eds.), *Dementia, aging, and intellectual disabilities* (pp. 316-329). Philadelphia: Brunner-Mazel.

University of Stirling (2001). *The Edinburgh principles: Guidelines of the Edinburgh working group on dementia care practices.* Stirling, Scotland: Centre for Social Research on Dementia, University of Stirling.

World Health Organization [WHO]. (2000). *Aging and intellectual disabilities: Improving longevity and promoting healthy aging.* Geneva, Switzerland: WHO.

WHO. (1992). *The ICD-10 classification of mental and behavioural disorders, clinical descriptions and diagnostic guidelines.* Geneva, Switzerland: WHO.

Wilkinson, H., & Janicki, M. (2002). The Edinburgh principles with accompanying guidelines and recommendations. *Journal of Intellectual Disabilities Research, 14,* 229-255.

Zigman, W., Schupf, N., Haveman, M., & Silverman, W. (1997). The epidemiology of Alzheimer's disease in intellectual disability: Results and recommendations from an international conference. *Journal of Intellectual Disability Research, 41,* 76-80.

PART II

Personal Perspectives on Alzheimer's

Alzheimer's disease is not only a neurological condition and a social and cultural problem. It is also a disease that affects individuals in profound ways.

A number of years ago, when Hospice Foundation of America published *Living With Grief: Children, Adolescents and Loss*, we believed it important to include the voices of children and adolescents. The book included not just articles by professionals explaining how children and adolescents should react, but children's own stories on how they experienced and adapted to loss.

It is no less important here. These accounts not only personalize the disease, they offer two other advantages. The personal stories provide insights for professionals on the experiences that individuals and families face and on the help they need as the disease progresses. These stories remind professionals never to lose sight of the person even as the individual with Alzheimer's disease or another dementia loses those connections to self.

Lin Noyes begins this section by sharing (with permission), the experiences of persons with early-onset Alzheimer's disease. Her chapter captures the fears and strengths of individuals who are struggling to cope even as they realize that the disease is slowly stripping them of their cognitive abilities and their memories. Her chapter is followed by Thaddeus Rauschi's first-person account, in which he describes his own painful discovery, at age 57, that he had Alzheimer's disease.

The chapters by Wayne and Terry Baltz and Elizabeth Halling show the progression of the disease. Two themes strongly emerge. The first is the frustrating struggles inherent in caregiving. Yet, even in the midst of these difficulties, the authors see glimpses of the person's prior self.

A second theme is the pervasiveness of grief. Therese Rando (1993) reminds us that anticipatory mourning is not only the grief due to the future expectation of death, but a response to all the losses encountered throughout the illness experience. The authors mourn the loss of the person they once knew even as they care for the person at hand.

These stories reinforce the critical need for professionals to learn the life histories of the clients they serve. They remind professionals, too, to stress to families the need to hear these life stories while the person can still tell them. ■

REFERENCES

Rando, T.A. (1993). *Clinical dimensions of anticipatory mourning.* Champaign, IL: Research Press.

■ CHAPTER 6 ■

Journeys Into Alzheimer's

Lin Noyes

INTRODUCTION

Alzheimer's disease can seem like a great wall that divides those with the disease from others. Only as we listen to the stories of others, can we rediscover a common humanity that truly allows effective support. After you have read this chapter, a series of vignettes sliced from the lives of people aware of their descent into Alzheimer's disease, I hope that you will know a little bit more about Alzheimer's disease from the perspective of the person diagnosed with the illness.

TOM

Tom was diagnosed with dementia of the Alzheimer's type after being referred for testing by his therapist whom he has been seeing for the last three years. He continues to go every two weeks because it is helpful and "gives him someone else to talk to." As he looks back to the past, he wonders if his trouble finding work after his retirement was because of memory loss problems that he was unaware of:

> The beginnings of this [memory loss] might have been apparent
> in the last jobs but not to me. I retired from the Air Force and
> then after a while worked in some bookstores. I was working
> at the [local university] bookstore, and I had a difficult time
> with that. And I moved to [another] bookstore and I had some

problems with that. At the time I didn't relate it to any mental problems. The job had been vacant for a year or so. It had been maintained in kind of a caretaker status and the manager was really a shithead. She was like, "You ought to be able to turn this around." I lasted there about 6-8 months, I was having some problems with memory at that time and I was aware of memory problems but it wasn't like, "Oh shit, oh dear, I'm sick;" it was more like maybe it was related to the fact that this place is in such utter chaos. We terminated under "resign in lieu of termination."

While some people are excruciatingly aware of the changes in cognitive abilities such as memory and word finding, Tom was not initially, and he blamed the problems on others until he learned of his Alzheimer's disease. He feels like he has taken care of business now and has planned for the future; but he worries about his wife who is older than he is and how his disease is affecting her. He feels bad that he is no longer able to generate income for his wife and himself.

My wife has worked with social security and that stuff is set up, it's a requirement that the money is in a certain kind of account. As far as I know the wills, living wills are set up. Bless her heart. I know this is not what she wanted to do especially. She's getting older. She really enjoys her work but she's getting to the point where she would like to cut back work, but she…I feel bad about that. Part of it [working], she wants to do, part she feels compelled to do it. We could live on my money and if worse came to worse, the kids in [another state] would help but we don't want to do that. She is very youthful and in very good health.

Tom drove to the center for the interview. I asked him how he would determine it was time to stop driving since giving up the keys is a real issue for people with Alzheimer's disease:

When it becomes a problem, when I find it confusing, I think my wife will be the best judge. Right now I don't have any problems. Getting here or there, right now I do better than she does.

That's sort of an interesting question. If I get to that point where I can't drive, will I know I'm at that point? I don't really drive a lot. I haven't noticed any problems. Is it going to be an insidious onset or rapid? So I don't know. That's a valid question. I guess I need to pose that question to my wife. But we drive together quite a bit. I usually drive. I just need to pose it to her and she can take a look.

And I'm sure when she says you can't drive anymore, I'm going to be pissed off but I mean I sort of need to be cognizant of that but right now, I don't get lost, I don't get bewildered. I know where to put the key. I have better sense of space and time but I imagine that's not going to last forever. I haven't had any problems. I impressed myself with parallel parking the other day.

I still have mental maps and if I get lost, I can usually extricate myself. Get to where I know where I am. I haven't had one of those where-am-I-who-shot-john sorts of things. I would assume that in some point in time it's inevitable that there will be that but I don't know.

While Tom knows that driving will become an issue for him, he thinks he is fine now. He knows the problems that will face him with driving (way-finding, increasing apraxia, spatial disorientation), and uses them as criteria to evaluate his own skills. He wonders if he will know when he is having problems with driving, and he is willing to place his trust in his wife to make the decision for him even though he knows he will be mad when he can no longer drive the car.

As we ended our interview I asked Tom what advice he would give to others facing memory loss problems and he responded in his usual matter-of-fact way with some very sage advice.

First off, if you feel like you have a problem is not to be in denial. If someone says it's happening, get the various tests and find out what's going on because the envelope is being expanded all the time with various remedies. So the sooner you can get help the better. Rather than wallow around, once you know, it's sort of a harsh thing to know, it's sort of like a death sentence, but once you know, you can get help and take advantage of the remedies;

at least you know what you are facing. Get all the info you can. There's a lot of information and help. Knowledge may be depressing, but it's better than being in denial, that's not going to help anything. As much as I like to be in denial of course, it doesn't work.

There's a lot being done, do what you can to prolong and protect the capabilities, stay as together as well as you can for as long as you can. Not only for yourself but for those who would be caregivers. Prepare yourself that there may be decline and not be so frustrated with those who are trying to help you. For the most part, everyone is going to try and help you hold on to what you can and protect you. So sort of accept that. It's easy to get angry and upset and mad. I think that's normal and you're going to do that but you have to come to grips with what it is and do everything you can to delay the progress, and who knows as you are delaying the progress they might come up with something that will not reverse but push things back. But if you throw up your hands, scream and holler kick your feet- hit the wall, you're not really helping anybody.

Hopefully you'll have family and friends who will be looking out for you. People are trying to help by telling you things. The whole social intercourse thing is good. The more you stay outside yourself and interact with your environment, the better off you'll be. Hopefully you like to do some of the things you need to do to slow things down or reverse things. Everybody is different but there would be threads that would be similar. The majority are going to be royally pissed at some level or another.

How long Tom will be able to follow his own advice is a question for the future. For now, he is taking care of himself as best he can, has made plans for his own future as much as he is able, and looks to his wife for guidance and leadership in his life. While angry about having Alzheimer's disease, he is doing his best to minimize the effects of the illness in his day-to-day life.

KATHY

Kathy identified herself during her first phone call as needing help with Alzheimer's disease. I assured her that she had called the right place and asked her to tell me a little about the person she was caring for. She hesitated and then said, "No, I'm not taking care of anyone, I have Alzheimer's disease and I need some help. Can you help *me*?" As we spoke, it became clear that she was serious and wanted to talk about her own journey into Alzheimer's disease.

I offered to meet her at her home, but she insisted that she could find the center. We set up a time and I gave her directions to the center, only half-heartedly expecting that she would remember when to come and be able to follow the directions I had given her—if she truly had Alzheimer's disease.

Kathy arrived at the appointed time and looked and acted more like me than the people with Alzheimer's disease in the activity room across the hall. She had to convince me that she really had been diagnosed with Alzheimer's disease because I just couldn't believe it, as she was so oriented. As she told me her story, my own denial about her Alzheimer's disease slowly melted away.

During our conversation, the boundaries that had safely separated me from "those people with Alzheimer's disease" vanished. I sat across the desk from a woman in her mid-sixties experiencing minor problems in daily activities; she could not find her keys, could not remember somebody's name, and sometimes had to take out a map to see where she was going. The only objective difference between us on that day was that she knew she had Alzheimer's disease.

The results of her neuropsychological testing had confirmed her suspicions that this highly intelligent businesswoman had areas of cognitive functioning that were significantly below normal, while other areas remained quite high. What I couldn't see was how much effort it took her to maintain her "normal" image.

What was obvious, however, was that she was struggling with the feelings and thoughts that were coming up in response to her acute awareness of having Alzheimer's disease. Not only having Alzheimer's disease today but also what it would mean for her in the future.

She had accepted that she had this illness but was not ready to give up or go gently anywhere. She wanted to learn all she could about the disease, find out what she could do to fight it, and give and receive help to and from others going through the same things. She was aware that the clock was ticking and that life as she knew it would end sooner rather than later.

She was scared of what might happen to her, angry about the little insults that forgetting brought to her on a daily basis, and distraught that she might forget the people she loved in her life. She was distressed that she would not be in control of her life. She felt lonely because people did not seem to understand what it is like to have Alzheimer's disease. Like me, they could not believe it or tried to give her lots of advice about what to try to get over it. It was easier for them, like it was for me, not to think about her illness and to deny she really had a problem. Kathy accepted that she had to go on this journey but she didn't want to go alone. I finally accepted this as well and agreed to help her as best I could.

I let Kathy lead me where she wanted me to take her. We set up a support group for people in the early stages of memory loss problems that she co-led and we began having weekly sessions of cognitive exercises. We also started a couples' dinner where people with Alzheimer's disease and their spouses could come together and enjoy a dinner out among their peers and have a chance to voice problems and solutions with one another.

There was great urgency for Kathy to get these things done. She was playing beat the clock. She knew even with the Alzheimer's medication and all the other health-oriented activities she had put in place that soon the disease would win and she would become a passenger on this journey instead of the captain at the helm.

Being with Kathy during this time was a bit like running a three-legged race with her. There were times when we were in perfect cadence and other times when the disease would trip us both up. Over the course of two and a half years, we were both falling more and more. Her once upbeat and optimistic attitude regressed into frequent tears and bouts of paranoia followed by guilt.

Once open to suggestions about symptom relief, Kathy felt I was no longer trying to help her. She did not need medication for depression, as she was not depressed. Of course she was sad and anxious. Who wouldn't be? She stopped attending the cognitive exercises and then the couples' dinner, and finally gave up on the support group after arriving late several times and blaming me for changing the time or the day the group was supposed to meet.

It became like watching individual tiles fall from a beautiful mosaic. Initially I could help her glue the tiles back in the right places but as more and more fell off, neither of us could figure out where all the falling tiles belonged. The mosaic that was once the Kathy I knew had become irrevocably destroyed. She was leaving me and herself through her loss of cognitive skills but worse leaving me because the trust and rapport we once shared had been shattered.

Two years later, I heard that she had divorced her husband after accusing him of spending her money. She had moved to rural Virginia and placed herself in the care of a foster family under very strict guidelines as to who could visit and how she was to be cared for until she died.

In retrospect, Kathy did exactly what she wanted to do. She stayed in charge of her life to the end. It was important to her. In her ferocious efforts to beat Alzheimer's disease, she brought help to many people with Alzheimer's disease in the northern Virginia area. She also left me her legacy of knowing what it was like for her to have Alzheimer's disease.

YVONNE

Yvonne and Elaine, her partner of more than fifty years, recently moved into a continuing care retirement community preemptively to have care available if and when Yvonne required it. Yvonne has had the symptoms of dementia for several years and Elaine has been doing what she can to fight it off and care for Yvonne. Yvonne, for her part, is oddly peaceful about her condition and sometimes even seems amused at how it happens: "It's kind of hard to explain. It's almost a feeling as though your brain is kind of meshed up. At other times I can be all right."

I asked her what helps to make it better and she replied, "I don't really know. I try not to think about it too much. I kind of laugh about it to myself. It's sort of scrambled, that's my own little joke." (She laughs.)

Elaine is concerned because Yvonne has very little energy and has to overcome a lot of inertia to do simple tasks. Elaine recognizes the importance of physical and mental exercise and tries to encourage Yvonne but is not very successful. Yvonne is always positive and responds, "Yes, in a minute." When Elaine repeats her question after a few minutes, she gets the same response. They kidded with each other that Yvonne never liked exercise and Yvonne laughed when Elaine said, "If she ever gets the feeling that she needs exercise, she lies down quietly until the feeling passes." When I asked Yvonne if she was tired or bored and she replied, "Tired, I think."

Yvonne's responses seem to have almost as little energy as Elaine reports her to have physically. Clearly aware that something is wrong, she seems to accept that she is now a passenger and Elaine is in the driver's seat.

I asked Yvonne if she had any advice for others who were just learning that they had Alzheimer's disease and she responded: "Just learn to live with it. There's not much else you can do."

DAVID HOLLIES

David Hollies (real name used at his request) was 42 when he was diagnosed with early onset dementia although he had been recognizing symptoms before that. When I asked him what I should say about him he wrote in an email: "You can just say that I was a many-careered, hardcore worker who took intense vacations to recoup." He now lives in a suburban home near Washington, DC, with his wife whom he married about a week before the interview took place.

David is unique in that he has the gift (or burden) of being intelligent and able to observe and reflect on the changes that are occurring in his head, body, and in his world. He has also made space for joy to occur in his life by continually bringing himself to the present and being open to what is going on right now. Because of his young age and the mental reserves he has, it has been difficult for people to accept that he has an irreversible dementia. And while he holds hope, he refuses to deny the changes and continually adjusts to the brain functioning he has at any given time.

He keeps in touch with many people through emails and has kept a collection of writings about what is going on with him and messages to his friends. In one of these missives he describes to his friends what it is like for him to answer a question on a "bad brain day."

On a bad day, if you ask me a question, I am faced with a towering challenge. I have to remember the words you say. I have to understand the meaning of those words. I have to understand that it is a question. I have to understand you are asking me to make a choice. I have to pull out or identify the options. I have to attach merits and shortcomings. And so on. There are many layers of memory and context involved. On such days, I can't handle that many layers.

It's like standing at the side of a twelve-lane freeway and crossing on foot. The cars are the random synapses of mental, emotional, sensorial and even psychic fragments or memories of any of them. Can I hang onto what I'm carrying and work my way through the lanes? Can I navigate between the speeding fragments, teetering on each broken white line with its false promise of control? Or will an 18-wheeler fragment carry me away? Will I drop my cargo of precious context?

On those days, when you see me struggling to respond, imagine me on that freeway and be patient. I just might make it across. And I might not.

Fortunately for me, when I drop my cargo of context or get carried away by an 18-wheeler fragment, I also forget that I was trying to cross the freeway. All that is left is an emotional fragment of missing something and the look of fear, confusion, or sadness on your face.

His group of friends has changed over the last few years. Some have gone because of his disease and others have come into his life through his affiliation with a chapel in Winchester and a Tantra Yoga group that he has joined. He talks about the people who have had to leave his life:

As I've gone through the changes in my life, some people have had to leave. Some people couldn't cope, couldn't have a conversation with me without telling me some new supplement I should be taking. After a while I got tired of that and said if we can't have a conversation, and some people couldn't let that go, so I wasn't interested in keeping that going.

This position was not arrived at easily and was part of David's quest to figure out who was David-with-dementia compared to who he had been without it:

> For me the hardest part of the whole thing, this loss of identity, I was a brain, it was who I was, my business cards said "for the problems nobody else can fix." So letting go of that, that's hard. If I'm not that what am I?

David prefers to spend his energy living in the day and discovering the positive things that happen in the here and now:

> In the first year or two I was more concerned about thoughts about death, I'm going to miss my daughter's marriage, one way or the other I'm not going to be around for life events. It's a source of grief and loss. There's a lot of fear around the unknown. The "I know how to do this" days are going to go. What's been surprising is getting back to my optimistic side. If you told me two years what would happen, stop speaking, stop driving, stop reading…what kind of a fucking life is that? You've taken all my joys! But you know, out of the unknown, the unexpected good things come up. It's easy to focus on the things that have gone but there's no way of knowing what the new things are coming.
>
> If I can let go, let it flow and not get too attached and tied up, the more I am open to whatever is coming.

He feels that he deals with the losses that come up. He has made a space in his life for the grief without being a slave to it and does not deny what is going on:

> Oh, everything is going to be fine! No things are completely fucked and I'm going to have a good time anyway in spite of it. I don't think you can get to a place of peace around it. I don't think you can get to a place where positive things can occur. I don't think you get there by any form of denial. I think the best thing I did was to tend to my grief.
>
> I'm not accumulating grief, I cry about once a week. Just let that part flow through.

There are so many hundreds of losses that occur day to day really all they are a trigger to the pool of losses.

I asked David what advice he would give people in similar circumstances and he answered:

> I don't have any doubt that everyone experiences the losses. It's like sadness, if you have it ingrained in you that it's not okay to express it but it is there. Give it its moment and then go on. I'm robbing the reaper, I'm living at a higher rate, and we [he and his wife] can choose to have a honeymoon every night for the next hundred days! You choose in the moment. If we allow ourselves to slip into the fear about the future, there's no present to find joy in. You really only connect to another person in the present. This is what you got right now and you have to make the most of it.

David is clear that he has a terminal disease that will end in death. Like people who have had a bout with cancer, he thinks it is important to face death squarely and then move on with life:

> And you can see it in people, walk into a room and watch how they conduct themselves in a certain event. If you can see them scooping up the joy in each moment, you can say "Ah, he had cancer." You can see it. It is self-evident: that person has had a thorough conversation with death and therefore they understand life. And there they are, picking them flowers.

CONCLUSION

It can be said that if you know one person with Alzheimer's disease, you know one person with Alzheimer's disease. We are all aware of people who have no insight into the tricks their minds are playing on them as they tumble into dementia. They have no awareness that their words are jumbled or that their judgment is impaired.

We have a gift from these people who have shared their stories. We have insights into their journeys into dementia. We see their fundamental dignity and humanity even as they descend into dementia. We appreciate their need to maintain control as their lives spiral into a personal chaos. Most importantly, we learn of the critical need to continue to respect their individuality, to hear their personal stories. Use these insights as a backdrop when you meet a person in the early stages of dementia. But keep in mind that they will want to tell you their story, too, and it will be different from the ones you read here. Stay in the moment with them and let them lead you where they need your help. ■

Lin E. Noyes, PhD, RN is the Clinical Director of the Alzheimer's Family Day Center (formerly the Family Respite Center) in Falls Church where she has worked since it opened in 1984. She has developed holistic programs for people with Alzheimer's disease and their families from the early stages of their illness to end stage care.

Lin is a founding member of the Alzheimer's Association, Northern Virginia Chapter and was a member of the Public Policy Committee of the national Alzheimer's Association from 1989 to 1994. Lin received her PhD in Administration, Health Policy, and Ethics in Nursing at the College of Nursing and Health Sciences at George Mason University in May, 2001. Lin is an adjunct faculty member at George Mason University and is a frequent lecturer for professionals and families on Alzheimer's disease.

REFERENCES

Hollies, D. (2002). *Adventures.* Unpublished Manuscript.

Further readings

Henderson, C. S. (1998). *Partial view: An Alzheimer's journal.* Dallas: Southern Methodist University Press.

Noyes, L. E., Daley, P., & French, K. (2000). Community-based services help people in the early stages of Alzheimer's disease and other cognitive impairments. *American Journal of Alzheimer's Disease, 15*(6), 309-314.

Snyder, L. (1999). *Speaking our minds.* New York: W.H. Freeman and Company

Yale, R. (1995). *Developing support groups for individuals with early-stage Alzheimer's disease.* Baltimore: Health Professions Press.

■ CHAPTER 7 ■

Something Was Not Right*

Thaddeus M. Raushi

INTRODUCTION

Symptoms of Alzheimer's slowly creep up in the night, as it were; one hardly notices that something is more than normally different. The changes may be clouded over or covered up and therefore not noticed at all by others. So it was for me. But all the time, inside, I knew something was not right. I so often heard, "Oh, why that could happen to anybody" or, "Gee, I do that all the time." But I knew that was not the norm for me. Something was not right.

WHAT'S WRONG WITH THIS PICTURE?

There was the time a car beside me at a stoplight appeared to be drifting backwards although its wheels were not turning. How could this be? I wanted to inform the other driver, but did not. And then, finally, when I realized what was happening, I broke out in a sweat. While it had appeared to me that the other car was rolling backwards, it was I who was drifting forward. I did not have my foot on the brake peddle. The light turned green and we both pulled away. All I could think was, how could I be so dumb? If I had not been first in the lane, I would have bumped the car in front of me. Fortunately, no other cars had entered the intersection for a more dangerous consequence. I realized my mind had played a trick on me. I realized the potential for a serious outcome.

"Oh, this could happen to anyone," my friends said. I still felt foolish, stupid, and unsettled. It was not like me.

Wrong Restroom

At a thruway rest stop, I followed the signs to the restrooms and after noting both door symbols, I entered, yes, the women's restroom. "Well, who hasn't misread a sign when their mind was on something else?" I heard from friends with whom I shared this incident. But for me, the distress was not simply over entering the wrong restroom, but that, once inside, I could not understand why there were no urinals. I stood there for the longest time, trying to figure out what was wrong with this picture. Then, as one woman exited a stall and two others entered the restroom, it finally clicked—I was on foreign ground. I quickly left.

What caused my sense of fright was that I stood inside the women's room for a time, not able to figure out what was wrong. How could that be? I was in no rush, I was under no particular stress, I was not tired. While I felt a moment of embarrassment in the women's room, what I could not let go of was my inability to determine what was wrong.

Reporting a Fire (Or Not)

On another day there was another judgment call, one of a more serious nature. I did not call the fire department when the situation demanded it.

I had gotten out of my car in our driveway and heard hissing and crackling sounds coming from our neighbor's house. I saw sparking at the upper bend in the main power cable leading into the house. The aluminum siding showed burnt spots around the area of the sparking, although there were no flames. The sparking continued. After knocking at the door and realizing no one was home, I decided to wait for someone to return, at which time I would inform him of the problem. A young man, my neighbor's son, soon arrived. I called his attention to the situation, and noted that the section at the base of the cable (just within a foot or so from us) was bare cable wire; the insulation had deteriorated and fallen off. I even recall pointing at the bare wire just an inch or two away from the cable. In thinking back, I had no sense of the danger of actually touching the cable.

The young man thanked me for seeing the problem, went into the house, and called his mother and the fire department. Firefighters and trucks arrived almost immediately; the utility company arrived minutes later. Power was turned off, extinguishers used, and siding removed to check for burning underneath.

It was only when the firemen and equipment arrived that I realized I had made a potentially disastrous judgment. I had not given one thought to calling the fire department. I merely waited for someone to come home.

The fact is, I should have been the one to provide direction to the less experienced young man regarding what to do. I could not understand why I had not seen the problem clearly. I was frightened. Was I becoming unable to make critical decisions? Most of the time I seemed fine, and no one else had indicated any concern. So, was I just to write this off?

Delayed Thinking

My wife Sylvia commented to me one day that sometimes my thinking appeared to her like delayed thinking. That made sense to me, an excellent description of what was happening.

There was the afternoon in the pharmacy, when I could not think of phone numbers and addresses I had known forever, and I could not decide what to do about it. I felt angry with myself for not being able to figure out what I needed to do in this simple situation, while later it all seemed so clear.

There was another afternoon, in an office supply store. I was certain I had been looking at a specific type of file folders, yet the salesperson assured me that the store did not carry such folders. I even asked the salesperson to go with me to the aisle where I had just seen them; she did, and the files were not there.

How could I be so sure and be so wrong? Never had I experienced a situation in which I was so absolutely certain about an item that, in fact, did not exist. I felt like there was some game being played on me.

There was the time in my workshop, when I plugged in a wrong cord and could not figure out why the shop vacuum would not work. I was certain the motor must have burned out or the power had been turned off. But the power was on, and only after several confused minutes did I realize I had simply plugged in the wrong cord.

Why couldn't I figure that out? It is not uncommon for me to change plugs while using the equipment in my workshop. I have done this for 20 years. I stood there, bewildered. I decided it would be better to not begin some woodworking projects until I got this straightened out, especially projects requiring the use of large power tools.

There also was the time I was using my computer and found myself unable to log onto the server to reach the Internet. I became upset and confused. I finally reached someone on the phone, explained my predicament, and described the string of garbled letters appearing on the screen at the end of the sequence for signing on. "What's wrong? What do I do? Where did this stuff come from?"

"Just click on Continue" came the calm reply. I then realized that the step he suggested was one that I had been doing for the past year. It was nothing new, nothing strange, nothing complicated. Yet I had not had a clue regarding what to do.

Or there were the times I put my briefs on backwards and didn't learn of this mis-dressing until in a public restroom, where the front and the back make a difference.

While most actions or experiences were of little consequence, they were disturbing to me. And they happened much more often than one would expect; their regularity felt like an emerging pattern in my life. These situations were causing me to be extra careful, to begin concentrating on only one thought or activity at a time, allowing little opportunity for those more automatic or spontaneous aspects of daily living. While I was coping generally, handling what I needed to handle in life, I often felt like I was being dishonest, like I was covering up the truth about handling responsibilities. I was not being me, and I did not like the feeling.

MEMORY

Remembering names had never been a strong skill for me, and it soon became even more of a challenge.

I was a college counselor, and there were many situations that highlighted my memory problem, telling me something was not right. For example: during counseling sessions, I called people by the wrong names. I could not remember information that I should have been able to remember about people I counseled. Often, I could not remember the names of my colleagues of 20 years. Often, I could not remember the information needed to advise students I saw for academic advisement, sometimes very basic information. Often, I could not follow and then remember what was happening in committee meetings.

These experiences were frustrating. I apologized often for not remembering, and sometimes I was embarrassed for not remembering someone or something. Other times I chose not to participate in an activity or to take on an assignment. I found ways of making light of situations, or getting around them. I do not recall any real problems that resulted. But this was becoming a serious concern to me. I had to work hard at what had always been automatic, taken-for-granted thinking and behaviors. These experiences did not feel good, and I found myself not wanting to go to work each morning.

In my counseling career, I had worked hard to keep up-to-date through reading and in-service training. I also earned a PhD. Instead of becoming more innovative and creative, however, I began spending increasing energy maintaining my basic work tasks and counseling relationships. Instead of performing and contributing at a high level, I felt like I was hiding under my title, my good relationships with colleagues, and my past performance. I didn't want anyone to sense what was going on; I had a professional and personal face to maintain, and I did so (I think).

My memory problems were having a significant impact on my work life and how I felt about my performance. I could not seem to change how I was performing. Resigning from my counseling position seemed to be an answer. So I took early retirement.

Being able to remember became an increasing concern. I always needed to be extra alert, to make more notes than I'd ever made before, to focus more fully on what was being said or what I was reading. And even with these tactics the problems were not resolved.

It always hurts a little bit when I cannot remember someone or something, or an event that has affected me deeply, and it is just not there. It is not just the forgetting that we all experience from time to time, but a forgetting in which there seems to be a complete void. I am not able to begin to know how to figure out the next step. It is blank.

DIAGNOSIS

The thinking and judgment and memory problems did not go away; they continued, whether under pressure of work or not. I finally decided that whatever was happening had to be faced. I spoke to my internist, who took me seriously. I then met with a neurologist; he also listened attentively to my stories and recognized the seriousness of my concerns. (I am thankful for physicians who listen.) At this point, we began the extensive testing that led ultimately to the diagnosis of probable Alzheimer's disease.

The neurologist had me go through a long series of tests. In addition to an exhaustive medical history and MRIs, I had blood tests, an EEG, and other laboratory and clinical testing.

Despite all my past medical data, all this new testing, and all the doctor's own clinical observations, no cause for my cognitive problems could be identified.

The next step was two days of comprehensive neuropsychological testing with a clinical psychologist. The psychologist identified several specific cognitive problems that seemed unrelated to age and were not psychologically based. He identified significant difficulties in "immediate and delayed recall" and holding "auditory information in working memory while performing a cognitive cooperation." He was able to put labels on cognitive difficulties that corresponded to specific problems that I had described to him. Though he could specify the types of problems, the psychologist could not pin-point the cause. He could not, though, rule out some form of dementia.

The neurologist then scheduled me for "single photon emission computed tomography." This is a relatively new imaging tool used in the analysis of brain function. This testing is often used after all other tests prove negative, yet there is good reason to believe something is not functioning correctly in the brain.

The neurologist's nurse called a few days after the test date to arrange a follow-up appointment with the neurologist. Sylvia and I both went (you have no idea how much it meant to have her with me) to discuss the test results. The neurologist wasted few words. The results revealed specific abnormalities with the brain's temporal lobe, on both sides, in a pattern consistent with Alzheimer's disease.

Based on the analysis of test results and laboratory reports, my medical history and my family's medical histories, and the neurologist's own observations, the conclusion was that the culprit was "probable Alzheimer's disease." The disease was in its early stages. I was 57 years old.

SUPPORT

Sometime after the diagnosis of Alzheimer's, Sylvia and I became part of an early-stage Alzheimer's support group. Our group is sponsored by the Alzheimer's Association of Northeastern New York. Meetings are held in a comfortable setting at the association offices, and they are facilitated by competent and compassionate professionals in dementia services.

In this group, I have had a chance to interact with several others in the early-stage experience, and Sylvia has met other spouses and families of people with Alzheimer's. It is rich and rewarding to share experiences and thoughts together. It is a chance to say things that go through your mind, sometimes get them off your chest, and then be able to put them aside without having them linger on your mind throughout the week. Here are real people who walk the same path. Here is a chance to open up, listen, share, and receive. Here is a chance to be with good people, now new friends in a world I had not known. It does not reduce or cure the disease. But to feel less alone is supportive.

GRIEVING LOSS

Grieving loss in early Alzheimer's is not unlike grieving other losses in life. For some time I had been ignoring my grief over losses, denying that I really was grieving (probably because, deep down, I was expecting to have returned what I'd been losing). But then I found that the grieving would always creep back into my life as I would experience those times in which I could not do or think as I had been able to do or think all my life.

Jury Duty

Who knew? Grieving jury duty! One Friday I received in the mail a summons for jury duty. On the following Monday I called to tell them I believed I could not serve. I do not know why I said "I believe" because I knew very well I could not serve. I have been on two juries, and a foreman of one—a three-week-long rape trial. I knew I could not keep track of what was going on in the court, retain the information, and be able to keep my mind on the trial all day long.

Not being able to do what one might expect of most any citizen, as a community service, I feel that a part of me has been lost. Many would say, "No big thing" or, "You should be glad you don't have to serve" or some such comment. Yet when some common life experience is no longer possible, a taken-for-granted capability, especially when in so many other ways I am getting along well, I feel a loss of a core part of me. And I grieve this loss.

Small Talk

It is not uncommon to be in a social situation where spontaneity is the character of the moment, and I cannot get the words to participate spontaneously. I cannot think fast enough or follow the ideas or train of thought when communicating. I then cannot get out the words I would like to get out to express myself, at least not like I have been able to do in the past. On occasion, when I have managed to express myself reasonably well, it has been a major struggle working at the process.

In conversations or discussions, I will miss the point. Sometimes jokes do not make sense to me when they clearly do make sense to others. I ask my wife to explain them. There are words I just cannot find, or people I know well I just cannot name.

I grieve being unable in these moments to be who I have been.

It would be nice if one could grieve such a loss once and be done with it. But grief keeps popping up in many ways and in many situations. So I have learned to be more careful in conversation, more intentional, more selective, less spontaneous. This helps interactions work out. It is simply a matter of learning to live with this as a change. It is learning to recognize and accept moments of grieving about the change and then letting those moments dissolve and move on.

Longing to Keep Up

I volunteer at the regional Alzheimer's office and I am very much accepted and welcomed by all of the staff members. I so often think about how much they take on in their work loads, and how quickly they are able to make decisions, and act and interact, get projects organized and completed, do training, and handle all of the phone and in-person contacts, and so on and on. I would so much like to be able to do the same, just as I have always done in my work and community service in the past. Yet I cannot even begin to keep up with just thinking about half of what they do. I was not ready in my life to give up these types of activities. I guess I am still not entirely ready to let them go.

Some projects and activities at the church to which I belong, community organization volunteer opportunities, and opportunities of teaching and counseling part-time are among other responsibilities out of my reach. To see others do them so well and so easily allows a sense of loss to creep in.

A Loved One's Burden

A friend of mine with early Alzheimer's told me that one of the important issues in his life with Alzheimer's is the feeling of becoming a burden to his wife, who is now assuming the caretaking role. I know what he is talking about. I share this feeling as well. This feeling, which runs deep, is the recognition of the increasing responsibilities being placed on your loved one by you and by the disease. It is the realization that the road ahead most likely will be far more rugged for your spouse and other loved ones than for you.

With early Alzheimer's, one knows full well and very clearly what is going on and what the implications are for the one you dearly love. No matter how much your loved one clearly makes known to you that, "We will go it together," and your life history together demonstrates a mutual partnership of caring, the feeling of burdening is not one easily put aside. Not for me. From what I understand, it is not easy for others with early Alzheimer's, either. And when you lose your patience or say things you wish you had not said, and that very special person is still by your side, and you know you are not going to be able to change these ways, and you know it can get worse, the feeling of burdening this person you love dearly weighs heavily. I know. We who have early Alzheimer's know.

CHOOSING

Early-onset, early-stage Alzheimer's can be a robber of choices. It is easy to get trapped into defining one's primary attitude toward life as one of seeing few choices. In this trap, life begins to feel as if there is little quality and worth.

I believe, instead, in the opportunity to be flexible. There is an opportunity to look at what I have, not at what I do not (and will not) have, as my primary attitude toward life. For example, I can, this very minute, think about being able to work on this book today instead of thinking about the days I cannot put the words together or even think of them, or the future when I may not be able to write at all.

As I write this, I recognize that it may sound like I have my head in the sand. It may seem like I am not facing the reality of Alzheimer's, what it can and will likely be doing to my brain and my thinking, to me and to my family. But I do face this; I am well aware of the deterioration process and end-stage realities and the pressures on the family. Yet, I cannot live with all of my future life filling today's space. This would be way too heavy a load, and most likely destructive.

Today is today. So I must shape my attitude in terms of what possibilities exist today. Tomorrow I will work on tomorrow's attitude. I also recognize that this is not always easy to do, especially as the mental changes remind me each day of their presence. But that is OK. It is part of my work. I only hope that I will be able to remain flexible, not bent out of shape. That is my hope for each of you as well, whether or not you have Alzheimer's disease. ■

■

*This chapter is excerpted with permission from Dr. Rauschi's book, *A View From Within: Living With Early-Onset Alzheimer's* (copyright 2001, Northeastern New York Chapter, Alzheimer's Association). To order, call the chapter at 1-800-303-2218.

At the age of 57, Thaddeus M. Raushi was diagnosed with Alzheimer's disease. Dr. Raushi holds a master's degree in education and a Ph.D. in social work, both from the University at Albany, New York. A former college counselor, Dr. Raushi has chosen to speak publicly in a variety of venues to raise public awareness of Alzheimer's. A longtime volunteer for the Alzheimer's Association, Dr. Raushi now serves on the Northeastern New York Chapter's Board of Directors.

CHAPTER 8

Into the Hands of Strangers*

Wayne and Terry Baltz

My mother once told me that she hoped she would die of a heart attack, quickly. She didn't. She died from Alzheimer's, slowly. I know that her illness brought her losses. I believe that it brought her gifts as well, as I know it did to Wayne and me. In caring for her and being cared for by her, in loving her and being loved by her, she was our blessing, although a fierce one. By any measure we can think of, the fiercest days of all were those in the middle of our journey, when it seemed we were all far from home, adrift, with no port in sight. . . .

September 6, Year Three. The Holly Hills Health Care social worker called this morning and told us that my mother is behaving aggressively on the Unit and that this is a matter of concern to the staff. A meeting is scheduled for the tenth to discuss options. We come to see Mom this afternoon, partly in response to this morning's call, worried about what we will see. But there is no problem during the time that we are here. Everything seems fine.

September 10. The staff describe Mom as aggressive and agitated and say that this has increased recently, although Terry and I are not aware that there has been any serious on-going problem to begin with. The main source of conflict seems to center on Mom's bowel incontinence and difficulties the staff have in working with her in relation to that. After the meeting I decide to visit Mom on the Unit. Peering through the window before opening the door, I observe her and Frances, arm in arm, walking quietly down the corridor together. Another resident, Agnes, approaches from the dining area and almost immediately a fight erupts between her and Mom. Two aides quickly appear and separate the two. Mom goes into her room. When I enter the Unit, Mom spots me immediately and greets me warmly. She clutches a bed pillow against her upper body. As we pass Agnes in the hallway, Agnes crouches, like a fighter in the ring, and wags her finger upward at Mom. "I hate you," she says. "You're hideous. I want you to be dead." The words burst from her mouth, snapping like tiny firecrackers in the space between us. The display is so unexpected and extreme, yet emanates from a body so ancient, contorted, and small, that I find myself torn between laughter and genuine, if momentary, fear. Mom pushes Agnes's arm aside and sticks her tongue out at her. Agnes swings, kicks at her, and continues her verbal assault. I step between them. Agnes strikes me in the jaw with her tiny fist. The entire exchange lasts less than fifteen seconds. Again staff appear just at the end. Mom and I take a walk outside in the courtyard and I can feel the tension in her grip on my hand. She shows me a blood blister and several scratch marks on her right forearm. They are not from the immediate scuffle, but they are fresh. They weren't there when I visited last evening. When we re-enter the building Agnes again lashes out verbally. I keep my body between them and no physical exchange takes place. At Mom's request we leave the Unit and go for a half-mile walk, long by her standards. She maintains an outwardly positive demeanor, but her conversation is more rudimentary than usual, her responses and smile forced and mechanical. She still holds her pillow like a shield across her midsection. "I need it," she says when I offer to carry it for her.

September 13. Terry's mother is sitting in the Day Area, chatting with another resident. I talk briefly with one of the nursing staff, Trish, who seems to have many good ideas about how to work with Mom. She gave her a shower last night and, while she does not suggest that it was an easy task, gives no impression that it was anything out of the ordinary in her experience with residents generally. She says positive things about Mom, both as a person and as a resident with whom she has many interactions.

I am surprised, therefore, to hear that when the doctor came today, she and the staff agreed that the problems Terry and I first heard com-plaint of on September 6 are continuing, difficult, and unimproved. They have decided, short of our flat refusal to permit it, to start her on a new medication, Inderal. Our understanding is that it will be used, along with the buspirone, which Mom has remained on since early spring, to decrease anxiety. Although our first choice would be behavioral intervention, this medication approach is the preference of doctor and staff at this time. Perhaps it will prove helpful. We decide to allow it.

September 14. One of the nurses calls to say that my mother slapped her while she was trying to get her to swallow her pills with water instead of chewing them. She is making a report of the incident as legally required, she tells me. And she is calling us, she says, also as required. She tells me she is sorry to bother me. "Is there anything I can do?" I ask. "No," she says, "she's fine now. She had a good day." This is the first such "required" call we have received since Mom's admission to the Unit more than four months ago.

■

Today I submitted for inclusion in my mother-in-law's file a write-up of my observation of the interactions between her and Agnes on September 10, followed by these reflections:

There may be circumstances entirely external to Helen . . . which directly affect her emotional state and consequent behavior. If the full precipitating event is not observed by staff, as in the above-described instances, Helen's tension or anger directed at others later on may appear irrational and unprovoked. Today, had she not been able to "take control" of her situation by getting off the Unit and getting some significant physical exercise, had she instead been required to behave in a more specific, staff-directed way, I think she may well have acted out. Perhaps this happened anyway later in the day, as it was apparent to me when I departed that there was still residual tension in her from the earlier interactions with Agnes. The truth is, I had some residual effect; I tensed a little as we re-entered the Unit and neared Agnes's door. How much more so Helen, who can feel just as much, but can comprehend, express, and influence so much less than I?

September 16. Mom has just finished supper and is sitting quietly at the table. I speak briefly with an aide, who says that she is doing much better, that her behavior is much improved. Mom herself is in a good mood. The staff seem at ease with her. A fine visit.

September 17. The social worker calls this afternoon, telling me there are "more concerns with your Mom" and that "she is very aggressive" toward other residents and staff. She describes a situation in which my mother told Cleo, while in Cleo's room—which was also Mom's room for a time—to "get out." When Cleo refused, the social worker reports, Mom "swatted the air." She calls my mother "a danger" and "unmanageable." She wants a medical evaluation.

Wayne and I are confused. With few exceptions—Wayne's experience with Mom and Agnes last week being the most notable—we've always seen neutral to positive interactions between Mom and people on the Unit. "She's different when you're here," they tell us.

Is she? And, if so, why? What is different when we are not present? Something is going on, and we want to understand what that might be. Wayne's background in psychology and education have given him experience in objective observation and recording of behavior. We decide that he will go immediately to Holly Hills to observe without interacting with my mother. To be there, as best he can, without being there.

■

I arrive at 4:30 p.m. to find Mom sitting in a common spot for her, a kind of love seat located next to the nursing station. Cleo sits next to her and they appear to be talking quietly. As soon as she sees me, Mom comes over and greets me. "I can't visit right now," I tell her. "I'm working." She accepts this readily and tells me that she's "going upstairs." It's something I've heard her, and other residents of this single-story building, say before; and it brings me an internal smile as I watch her stroll up the hall, check the Unit doors briefly and, to my surprise, key the pad, although without result.

The social worker comes onto the Unit and she and Mom share a few friendly words before Mom continues on her way. She spots Cleo again, and waves to her. Also to another resident and a staff member who are entering the Unit. She heads back to the two-seater couch, which is occupied now by Aubrey, a nurse, who appears to be doing some sort of paperwork. Mom stoops to pick up some manila folders which lie on the seat next to Aubrey. She sits down, holding the items now on her lap. With some urgency in her voice, Aubrey asks Mom for the folders, reaching for them as she speaks. "No," Mom says, just as urgently, and appears to tighten her hold. The interaction quickly intensifies, with Aubrey variously demanding ("Give it to me"), explaining ("Those are very important papers"), and coaxing ("How about we trade? You give me those papers, and I'll give you this magazine"). But Mom is not persuaded. "You are going to give them back," Aubrey says with finality and a brief tug-of-war ensues. Aubrey ends up with her papers, Mom with the magazine.

She remains seated for a minute or two, looking about the room with a pleasant expression on her face, then gets up and approaches me. "Wayne, come upstairs with me," she asks. "I can't, Mom. I'm working," I tell her again. She sticks out her tongue and blows noisy air at me in the traditional "raspberry," and goes up the hall alone. When she returns, she heads again to the love seat. Aubrey is still there, her materials again resting on the vacant seat. Mom bends to pick them up. The nurse grabs for them, and whether she gets to them first or snatches them from Mom's hands, I cannot tell. Mom swats Aubrey on the upper body/arms with the magazine Aubrey gave her a few minutes ago. "Please don't hit me, Helen," Aubrey says. There is a brief further verbal exchange which I cannot hear and Mom sits down.

By 5:10 Mom is seated alone. Soon an aide, Kristen, and Aubrey decide that Mom is "poopy" and Kristen invites Mom to "get cleaned up." Mom refuses. Now the aide asks Mom if she would like to go for a walk. "For a walk, yes," she replies. They start off down the hall, but as they approach Mom's room Kristen and another staff member physically guide her, Mom resisting, through the doorway of her room, and then, more forcibly, into the bathroom. Aubrey joins them. I move closer. The door is mostly closed but I can hear Mom cursing and demanding to be left alone. Suddenly I see her face, her eyes seeing me through the crack at the hinge side of the door. "My son-in-law is out there!" she exclaims, and I quickly move out of her line of sight. "I don't want you in there!"

she shouts at them a moment later, little doubt in my mind as to what she refers.

"Please don't hit, Helen." A staff member's voice. "I'm going to hit until you're dead," Mom tells her. Five long minutes pass, after which the nurse suggests that some staff should leave. Mom agrees. Aubrey encourages that Mom "dismiss" the two aides, which she does. "You can stay," she tells Aubrey.

As dinner approaches, several requests are made for Mom to come to the table, but she refuses. When Kristen again invites her, Mom hits at her. "No I am not going to sit down," she says. "Sit on your own ass." A few minutes later an aide brings Mom's food to her on a tray. Aubrey asks her if she is going to eat. "No." "Well, will you take your medicine, your pills?" Aubrey asks. "No." "Do you want some water?" "No. Kiss my ass."

A few minutes later Kristen invites Mom to eat or to have some juice. "No," she says, sticking out her tongue. "Here's your Jell-O, Helen," Kristen says. "I don't care what the hell it is." Hardly a minute later, Kristen says to Mom, "Helen, the nurse wanted you to come and talk to her." "Kiss my ass," Mom tells her. Aubrey says, "Helen, Terry brought you these pills." Mom says nothing, but retreats quickly to her room. Aubrey follows her, uses a similar coax, and Mom takes the medications. At 5:50 Mom still has not eaten anything. Kristen and Aubrey enter her room to get her changed into night clothes. Mom resists. "Why do you want to get your way?" she wants to know. "I'm just trying to help you," Kristen says. "I don't want them on, goddammit!" Mom tells her. Kristen leaves and Mom comes out with a pajama top and robe over slacks. The staff tell her she is only half changed and urge her to change into her pajama bottoms. Mom approaches me now, wants me to go with her. I tell her I can't. "Shit on you," she says and returns to her room. Two of the staff now enter her room and forcibly take her into the bathroom to change her slacks for pajamas. Twenty-five minutes after staff leave Mom's room she has not yet emerged.

It has been two hours since my arrival. I abandon my observer status—I have seen plenty—and go to her room. She is lying on her bed. "Well, did you get anything accomplished?" she asks, in apparent reference to my "work." "I think so," I tell her. "There's more to do, but I can finish it later."

She is wide awake, and happy for contact with me. When she asks about a commotion in the hallway I tell her, "They're playing some kind of game, I think." Mom is eager to join. Many residents and several staff are in the hall. Mom smiles at everyone and quickly becomes a part of the game. When Agnes makes a sudden face at Mom she sticks her tongue out at her in response. A male aide steps between them, facing my mother-in-law. "We have to let everyone have a turn," he tells her in a gentle yet chiding tone. Mom initiates interactions marked by affectionate touch and speech with two other residents, and is actively and positively involved with everyone she sees, staff and residents, for the better part of an hour. She goes into Cleo's room as Cleo is getting ready for bed. I stand unseen nearby, listening for five minutes to their amiable, confused conversation as they sit together on Cleo's bed. I leave for home, my pocket full of notes, my heart full of questions.

September 18. Mom's doctor called at the house while Wayne was at Holly Hills last evening. She told me that she was given an ultimatum by some unnamed—to me, at least—person at Holly Hills: my mother must either be hospitalized for an evaluation, be placed immediately on a major tranquilizer—thioridazine—or we must move her out of Holly Hills. She didn't like that they went through her rather than us. Nor did I. I think they simply don't want her. Part of me wants to go over there this minute, take Mom by the hand, walk out that door, and never come back.

■

Just before three, the Holly Hills administrator calls. Seems like suddenly we're on everybody's call list. Her name is Betty. She speaks in a casual, friendly tone, which makes me ill at ease, as we do not have a casual, friendly relationship. We have no relationship at all. I do not remember that she has ever introduced herself or spoken to Terry or to me in the four months Mom has been living at her nursing home.

On the one hand, she insists on a course of thioridazine if Mom is to stay, while on the other, she describes the severe risks of the drug and says that it's very difficult to find a therapeutic dosage. She tells me "the other families are complaining" about Mom, and that her staff is, too. "This is our first job," she says, "to make sure that people are safe." I tell her that in Mom's four months at Holly Hills neither Terry nor I have seen her attack a resident or initiate any real aggression against anyone without provocation. I mention several recent incidents with Agnes, including the one last night, as examples.

"We track all these things," she says. I tell her that in the incidents involving Mom and other residents which I have witnessed, the staff did not see the provocations but only Mom's response, and may have tracked them incorrectly. I tell her that I observed things last night that could have been handled differently. I suggest an increase in Inderal which, in addition to being more benign, seems preferable also because Mom already has an existing blood level. "It has to be thioridazine," Betty says. "We just can't experiment." But getting the dosage right, isn't that experimentation? She says that she will have to bring in extra staff to sit with Mom during an adjustment period to the thioridazine. Why not bring in extra staff to sit with her while they increase the Inderal? Better yet, why not bring in extra staff for the sake of better coverage? Maybe that will solve the problem. My sense, which has grown with each passing minute, is that Betty has called only to get Mom out of her facility or onto thioridazine. One of these two.

"My son-in law is out there!" Mom's words from yesterday haunt my memory. A simple statement of fact? Embarrassment? Or was it a call for assistance? "My son-in-law is out there. He won't let you do this to me!" If it was the latter, I'm sorry, Mom. In the interest of dispassionate, objective observation, I did. But what about today? What keeps me from telling Betty now, not about Mom and Agnes, not about things that could have been handled differently, but precisely and in detail about her own staff's behaviors? Simply this: I have no confidence that Betty and I are having a genuine discussion. We are not teammates, I fear, but adversaries, in a contest whose outcome was determined before the opening bell. And if I am right, if I should dare now to refuse all three of her options, take the offensive on Mom's behalf and fail, what then? Am I prepared to go over there and get her? As though we have another place for her to go?

"Nobody wants her," I cry into the phone, the words no sooner past my lips than I am mortified by them, embarrassed to have turned to her, of all people, for comfort. "Oh no," Betty protests. "She's so sweet." Jagged glass.

My vision just a few weeks ago was that this is the place where Mom will live out her life. All along we've been urged to let go, to live our own lives and do our work, to trust them to take care of her. I'd begun to believe it, to settle into it. I ask Betty for a few hours to consider our decision. "No," she says, "I've promised the other residents' families." Who are these families? Has any complaint actually been made? For one brief moment I fantasize sleuthing the truth out, interrogating the families and all the staff, finding out the "real" story. It's preposterous, I know. And, ultimately, what is the point? What do we gain for Mom if we succeed in forcing her on them? I can think of nothing else to do, nothing more to say. Betty's silent waiting smothers and exhausts me, and I am filled with fear. "Okay," I tell her. "Go ahead with the thioridazine." Fear, and now shame.

September 19. "Wayne!" Mom calls out immediately when I arrive, then takes me by the arm and leads me around the Unit like a manic tour guide. The drug's effect, or Mom's response to it, or some combination of the two, seems paradoxical. She appears sedated, almost stuporous, yet she is not calm. She is active, on her feet, and seems agitated, as though some part of her being realizes that her capabilities are diminished and has decided that she must make up the difference through sheer effort. Her lids droop but the eyes are scanning, searching, and when words come they pour from her mouth like wet cement, full of potential but ill-formed. "I doan like the way thozh people are lookin' at ush," she says, indicating everyone in sight and no one at all. "Like they wanna shteal somethin'." Her grip on my arm is strong. But for all her energy, her steps are small and feeble and her feet do not quite keep pace with her intentions. She doesn't have a good sense of her body in space, wobbling occasionally and leaning forward when she walks, as though she battles a head wind. I don't see any tremors but her muscle tone is poor, her voice weak.

At the dinner table she is mostly disconnected from people and circumstance, reaching for whatever food is in sight, others' as well as her own. When soup is placed in front of her, she immediately puts a fork in the bowl and tries to feed herself. I express concern about Mom's condition to the nurse. She responds by pointing out a woman unknown to me, the "extra staff person" it turns out, that Betty said they would provide. I had no idea she was present until this moment. She was not with Mom when I arrived and has not approached or introduced herself. Now, while Mom struggles with her soup and fork, she stands motionless across the room.

September 20. She's a little stronger and more alert than yesterday, though still walking in small steps, as though an invisible chain links her ankles. Her speech is still slurred. "I didn't know anythin' yeshterday," she says, clutching my arm. Moving slowly down the hall together, we approach Agnes, standing sentry just outside her room. Mom gives her a warm smile. Agnes contorts her face in reply. Mom sticks her tongue out at her. "You're ugly," Agnes tells Mom. "You're stupid." Again I am stung, but Mom seems more curious than insulted. "Why do you always . . .?" she starts, but cannot find the words to finish. "You're almost as ugly as I am!" Agnes suddenly crows. Pleased with this joke on herself, she laughs and walks away.

Terry's impression is that her mother has a lot of anger. "She may not be able to talk about it, or explain it even to herself, but she's not oblivious. She knows how she's being treated," Terry says, "and she doesn't like it. It's storing up, and it's going to come out. And when it does, it will have a lot to do with their behavior, how they've treated her. She is a person. She has feelings."

Aubrey was very positive about Mom today. She told me that she is "very manageable," as though this were a high compliment. It seems to me that manageability has lately become a major focus of the staff. "This is a Special Care Unit!" Terry says. "She should be allowed to have her dementia. She shouldn't need to be as she would out in the world." I can see the legitimacy of limits, even on a Special Care Unit. The problem I have is that the staff tend to put the burden of management on the resident, as though it's Mom's job to be manageable rather than theirs to manage. Skillfully, creatively, and lovingly.

September 23. Terry and I bring her mother to meet the Long-Term Care Ombudsman, whom we've recently contacted with our concerns about the quality of care she is receiving. I bring the lady out to the car to meet Mom and, despite her considerable limitations right now, both disease- and drug-induced, Mom is quite gracious. For her part, the ombudsman is straightforward in explaining to her the advocacy services she can provide. I'm sure Mom follows none of it. "I could come and visit with you sometime," the ombudsman offers. "Where you live." "No," Mom says quickly. The ombudsman rephrases, offers her services a second time. Mom hesitates, then smiles and tilts her head up toward this friendly, earnest stranger. "If Wayne and Terry say it's okay," she says. Standing there in the parking lot, I am touched that she falls back on us so, relies on us to make the decisions of her life, depends on us to keep her safe. Touched, and terrified, too.

September 27. "There's no excuse for blaming residents," the ombudsman tells Wayne and me in her office. As a result of her visit to the Unit several days ago she feels that there is, in fact, some identification of my mother as a problem. "Helen is a little different than most residents on the Unit," she says. "She's more direct, less passive."

October 2. Mom walks in small, wobbly steps. Terry and I have seen residents with bruises and black eyes, apparently from falls. We're afraid we'll come in some day and that will be Mom's situation.

Still unresolved, in my mind, is the question of whether the staff's issues with Mom could have been handled—whether those in the future could be still—in a more skillful, more humane, and more effective way. To a significant degree Mom has faded into the Unit. She's more like the other people there now.

October 5. Over the past month there's been a constant warring in me between guilt, anger, and reluctant acceptance that Terry and I can't make things work as well as we want them to and believe they could. It's hard to believe sometimes what is going on. All this turmoil generated by Mom's incontinence, and yet I notice again today something we have brought to the staff's attention before: there is no toilet paper in Mom's bathroom. With the ombudsman's encouragement, a Staffing has been scheduled for October 8.

October 6. Night or day, whenever I'm awake and not focused on something else, thoughts of my mother at Holly Hills dominate my consciousness. That there might be something that she wants to communicate but can't express; that someone is treating her badly; that her reaching out to others is misinterpreted. I feel so sad. I can't get past it.

October 8. On the surface there is openness and receptiveness on the part of Betty and all the staff who attend today's special Staffing on my mother-in-law. But it is a frustrating experience from the start. No one is taking real charge of the meeting. People join the discussion at will and the focus drifts from one topic to another and from one individual's perspective to another's with little organized pursuit of any single issue.

Nobody on staff seems to know how Mom got on such a large initial dose of thioridazine. Trish says that there have been a lot of recent staff changes, and that some staff from other parts of the facility seem to view the Unit and its residents in a negative light. She says she's heard my mother-in-law's name mentioned specifically in this context. "The attitude around here has got to change," she adds. Betty declares, "I don't know what we have to offer Helen." Meg, the Unit Manager, expresses frustration about the recent influx onto the Unit of residents in wheelchairs and with more severe disabilities than those admitted previously.

Terry and I both voice our feeling that we and her mother have been betrayed by the events of the past month. "We just have to have better communication," Betty says. Better communication? What Terry and I want is better care for her mother, better commitment to that goal, and a display of better skills in carrying out that commitment. When these things are in place I don't think communication will be an issue. Betty says that she wants to funnel all communications between us and Holly Hills through the Unit manager. "For consistency," she says. Better communication? More consistent communication? Fine. But the important communication is not between the staff and us. It's between the staff and Mom. We want better care.

October 9. My mother is overjoyed to see me. "I feel like I'm in a crazy house," she says. We go outside and she is talking to me the whole time. I can't make complete sense of it, but it's about how she has been trying to tell the staff here about something that upsets her. But what? For all her effort to tell me and to request my help, for all my burning desire to intercede for her, I cannot decode the specifics of her plea. But could it be that the specifics are not the heart of her message? Could it be that she is simply telling me, "I'm upset," that what she is asking for is nothing more than to be comforted?

"Don't worry, Mom," I tell her finally. "Let me tell them." "Oh, good," she says, and real relief settles in her eyes and soothes her face.

At Kentucky Fried Chicken she moves slowly and seems sedated but has a good time anyway. She uses the toilet paper-equipped bathroom with no problem. We go to the grocery store and then to a friend's house to see her and her baby. Mom glows in their presence.

October 10. Mom awakens and smiles at me and I sit next to her in the dining area. She clutches a newspaper and several magazines in her arms, which are crossed and tight against her upper body. Mom abruptly rises from her seat and skillfully navigates the tight spaces between chairs, tables, wheelchairs, residents, and staff. As she passes Mary, a nurse, Mary asks, "Do you need to go to the bathroom, Helen?" I neither hear nor see any response. "Do you need to go to the bathroom?" she says again, in an interested but otherwise neutral tone. "Yes," Mom says. "I'll come with you," she offers. Mom accepts, and they walk off arm in arm toward her room. I follow Mom and Mary's path, pausing outside Mom's bathroom door. I can hear both Mary's quiet voice, giving brief explanations and offers of assistance, and Mom's occasional responses. Although I cannot make out the words very well, I don't detect any trauma or upset in either voice. It sounds remarkably like a conversation. I return to the dining room. Mom returns in a minute or two and sits down again, apparently relaxed and in a level mood.

"How did that go?" I ask Mary. She looks at me with a puzzled expression. I mention the tales of woe I have heard over the past weeks.

"I've never had any problem with Helen," she says quietly. "You just have to be respectful. "First of all," she explains, "I notice when Helen has a sudden change of behavior, such as getting up and walking with purpose. That means something. And she is very sensitive about her mastectomies, and about her body being exposed and observed. She's very modest. I respect that by, in dressing, for instance, helping her with her shirt or blouse from behind, rather than facing her. Taking time is very important and helpful, too. I don't rush. And I explain what I'm doing, or about to do.

I ask permission." She says again that she has no trouble with Mom in toileting. She just feels that it has to do with respecting her and giving her dignity. The words fall on my ears like blessings. "I need to stop," Mary says. "I don't want to be seen talking to you when the nurse comes in." I return and visit with Mom a while longer, replaying the conversation in my head, recalling what Mary says Mom told her when they were finished in the bathroom: "I'm glad you were here." Not more than I, Mary.

October 12. I find my mother outside, sitting alone on a bench in the cool autumn sun. "I don't feel good," she tells me. Her face is puffy. Congestion rattles in her throat. Her legs are covered with rash up to the knee. Her feet are swollen. "Do you think you should be outside, Mom? Maybe you'd be more comfortable indoors." "No, I feel safer out here." I discover that she has had diarrhea. Did she know or sense this, and retreat out here alone? I go looking for help, and am glad to find Mary. She and I work together to clean Mom up. Mary is very calm, very good with Mom. I could learn from her. She tells Mom everything that is happening, what she is doing and why. Mom, too, is patient with this unpleasant task. She doesn't swat. Nothing like that. When we're finished, Mary thanks me for being there. I thank Mary. Mom thanks Mary. "That's what I like about Helen," Mary says. "She always says thank you."

I take Mom out to lunch. She looks and seems to feel much better. But as soon as we're back and in her room she shoots me a long, penetrating look. "I'll be back tomorrow," I promise. "No. I'm not staying," she tells me. "It's like West Side Story here." She gets up off the bed and goes to the window. She looks out for long seconds, her back to me. She doesn't want to accept the fact that I am leaving, and that I am leaving her here. She has decided to leave me first. I go out quietly.

October 15. At this second special Staffing in a week, Betty makes an opening statement about the importance of communication, echoing her emphasis of seven days ago. The first topic on the agenda is toileting.

Terry and I share our positive observations of Mary in her interactions with Mom—her alertness to behavioral cues, her careful patience, her respectful demeanor, her explaining to Mom what she's doing. "My mother doesn't swat at Mary," Terry says. "She doesn't fight her, she thanks her."

"So the toileting is all much better now, right?" Betty says. "No, not really," Meg says. "Sometimes better, sometimes not." Does Betty not grasp that our intention was to provide an example of a skilled and successful approach to the problem at hand? Is she blind to the notion that outcomes can be influenced by her staff?

Near the end of the meeting Betty says that it's necessary to weigh Mom's best interest against everybody else's best interest. I don't see those interests as mutually exclusive. ■

■

*Excerpted from *Fierce Blessing: A Journey into Alzheimer's, Compassion, and the Joy of Being* (Prairie Divide Productions, April 2003), by permission of the authors. See www.fierceblessing.com

Wayne and Terry Baltz, married for 35 years, have co-authored four children's books and shared the writer's life with 60,000 elementary school students nationwide. When Terry's mother developed Alzheimer's disease, they cared for her—first at home and later in long-term care facilities— until her death. Over the next few years they wrote Fierce Blessing: a Journey into Alzheimer's, Compassion, and the Joy of Being *(Prairie Divide Productions, April 2003), from which this chapter is excerpted with permission. Wayne Baltz has a master's degree in counseling psychology. Terry Baltz has a master's in human development and family studies. They speak to professional and lay groups on caregiving and end-of-life issues, challenging Alzheimer's stereotypes and offering hope, validation, and tools for enhancing relationships under difficult circumstances. Their website is www.fierceblessing.com*

CHAPTER 9

Still Here, Wherever Here Is

Elizabeth Halling

It's best to keep the washcloth away from Grandma. If she gets hold of it, sitting on her bath chair, she'll dab the washcloth around her arms and legs and consider herself done. She is not done. I have to wash her armpits, hidden in folds of skin like layers of soft dough, her horny feet with their hard yellow toenails, and her bottom and crotch.

At first I expected her to be embarrassed that her granddaughter, whose diapers she once changed, is now washing her private parts. But she is unfazed, even cooperative. She has always been a genial person, acquiescent, happy to please. A photo from her honeymoon trip to Yellowstone shows an old-fashioned car with her on one side and a bear on the other, its nose through the window. My grandmother has a naughty, gleeful look on her face, but the bear just looks hungry. I imagine my grandfather holding the camera and pointing ("Go on up there, Mabel! He won't hurt you!"), and my grand-mother, oblivious to the dismay this photo would cause her descendants some 60 years hence, mincing across the road to stand by the car, giggling. Like I said, she's acquiescent.

So besides maintaining control of the washcloth, the only other bathtime problem is the obvious one: friction, and its absence. I watch her lean and reach and try not to imagine what would happen to that mottled, tentative flesh if it hit porcelain suddenly, at high speed.

My grandmother is 98 years old. She doesn't use a wheelchair, walker, cane, or even orthopedic shoes. Her daily meds consist of a vitamin pill and an aspirin, to guard against stroke. She's healthy as a horse except for her mind. More than a decade now since her Alzheimer's diagnosis, her memory, both short-term and long-term, is almost gone. I picture her memory as a slowly self-erasing blackboard containing names, images, references, and lots of shadowy words and phrases in a language that's increasingly foreign to her.

I bathe my grandmother and do other caregiving chores when my parents, with whom she lives, go out of town or out for an evening. This arrangement allows me to feel good that I'm helping out in the family without getting grossed-out or bogged down in the thanklessness of caregiving. I don't know if I'd still be able to treat Grandma gently and with love if I had to be with her every hour of every day. Everyone tells my mom they don't know how she does it. I don't know, either.

I always think I will be serene and helpful when I stay with my grandmother, and I usually end up wanting to spank her. It's like Chinese water torture, the pointless questions and commentaries, the same ones over and over. It's like running a marathon on a quarter-mile track, round and round and nobody even wins.

Grandma often uncannily remembers the things you wish she'd forget. She cannot remember whose house this is, but she can remember that my mom, Marilyn, is supposed to return in two hours. These spots of clarity make for screamingly frustrating conversations. "Now, they're coming for me tonight?" she'll say.

"No, nobody's coming for you."

"But you brought me here, this afternoon."

"No, I didn't bring you, Grandma. You've been here the whole time."

A pause, painful and confused. She tries again. "Who's coming?"

"Marilyn and Jerry are coming."

"And they'll come here?"

"Yes."

"You're sure?"

"Yes, I'm sure."

"Because maybe, do you think they might think we're at your house and go over there?"

"No, Grandma, they know we're here."

"Oh. You told them we're here?"

"No, Marilyn asked me to be here. She asked me to stay here with you, so I'm here."

"So Marilyn's coming?"

"Yes."

"And then she and I'll go home."

"No, Grandma, you'll stay here. This is your home."

"Oh, I don't know." A wry shake of her head. "We'll have to talk about that."

A longish pause. "So you're sure they're coming?"

"Yes, Grandma."

"Did they tell you they'd be coming here?"

"They live here. This is their house. They'll come back here."

"Oh. And then I'll go home with you."

"No, Grandma, you live here. This is your home."

A benevolent smile, to humor me. "Oh, no, that can't be right." Another pause. "When will they be here?"

"Soon." I try to smile at her.

"Now, you're sure they know we're here? Because maybe they'll think you and I are over at your house and then go over there."

"No, Grandma, I'm sure they'll come here."

"You're sure?"

This can go on for hours if I let it. The amazing part is, after rounds and rounds of questions and answers, after the fretting, the anxiety, the growing conviction that she's been improperly left here, wherever *here is*— after all this, you'd think the glorious arrival of my parents would be a cause for celebration and relief. But when they arrive, Grandma usually sits passively in her chair. She might not even smile.

It's situations like this that push caregiving beyond difficult to corrosive. The boring, repetitive, and often distasteful physical tasks (scrubbing dentures, wrestling with seat belts, wheedling her into clothes) are hard enough without the constant nagging questions. You try everything you can think of to reassure her and make her comfortable, but it's never enough.

I have a few coping strategies. I often pretend my conversations with Grandma are being broadcast live on NPR. I imagine Grandma's querulous, repetitive questions coming out of somebody's car stereo, and try to fashion the kind of replies that will impress listeners with my sublime patience and loving faithfulness.

When the NPR thing seems stupid, I think of the episode of "E.R." where the earnest doctor dying of a brain tumor tells his teenaged daughter that the most important thing is generosity. Be generous with your time, your talent, yourself, he says, and I try to remember how little that generosity costs me, remembering that I'm big enough and calm enough to smile at Grandma instead of blowing her off or yelling at her. I try to remember that I have a choice.

When NPR and generosity both fail, I think about the yoga mantra that I sometimes apply, like a heating pad, when I'm feeling stressed: Be in the now moment. It's not about being able to do this for two weeks or two months or the rest of my life; it's about being able to do this right now, this moment.

And, since none of these strategies works 100 percent of the time, I buy myself a lot of chocolate.

■

On one long stay with Grandma, I moved my family into my parents' house, the house I grew up in, where Grandma now lives. I remember flying through one busy morning, trying to get the baby girl dressed on the bed in the guest room. She hid in the sheets, playing peek-a-boo. She looked up at me, crinkling her nose, and I suddenly saw that my hurry— my need to get all this stuff done and out of the way—was almost brutal, or at least unnecessary. So I stopped and blew a raspberry on her springy, taffy-colored tummy. She squealed with delight, and I remembered a moment years ago when Grandma and I stood in this same room. We were supposed to be polishing the furniture or putting things away, but I had found a book of song lyrics—show tunes and war songs, old songs from her times—which we leafed through, standing at the dresser in front of the big mirror. Grandma sang the ones she knew, her trombone-y old voice slooping up to the high notes and sliding down the low ones. She sang "Abba Dabba" and "Five Foot Two" and "Moon River." It made her laugh, and she turned the page to find the next one, playing hooky from the day, with me her accomplice, her partner in mischief.

I felt that same joy with the baby on the bed that morning—a stolen piece of fun plucked from the grinding gears of the morning's relentless time clock. And I realized something: Grandma would have liked to play with this baby. Grandma should be here.

But she isn't here, in any but the most superficial sense. She is lost.

My grandmother usually seems little and fragile, her steps like a bird's, her movements tentative and deflective. But sometimes, like when I give her a bath or when I wake her up, she seems huge: flesh hanging off arms and collarbones, unending folds of belly and thigh.

■

Caring for an Alzheimer's patient is a lot like caring for a baby: you monitor her meals, you tie her shoelaces. But the soul of the task is different. While my baby girl always knows who's in charge—me—my grandmother has her doubts. To her I am still a whippersnapper. She can never quite believe I'm old enough or smart enough to get us all through the day. Her lingering belief in herself as the competent one compels me to keep up the slight fiction that I'm helping her, not controlling her. Besides, when I pretend I'm only giving her advice and guidance, then I can believe she's still fundamentally okay. I don't want her to be helpless, I want her to be help-able.

Caring for Grandma always makes me think about her death. When I stay overnight with her, I mount the stairs in the morning to wake her up imagining I might find a dead body instead of a grandmother in the bed. It would be terrible and it would be a terrible relief. I must correct myself: It *will* be terrible when it happens in the coming months or years. And it *will* be a terrible relief.

Of course, she might not go easy, in her sleep. She might put up a fight. People can lose almost everything and still continue to live, bedridden, incontinent, incapable of speech. My grandmother might end up like that. The fact that there's nothing wrong with her 98-year-old body seems like a miracle except when it seems like a curse.

I often wonder how aware Grandma is of her mind's creeping deterioration. If at some point you began to perceive that the you-ness of you were disappearing, wouldn't you panic? I don't see panic in Grandma—not anymore. Once several years ago, when she was supposed to be asleep, I overheard her reciting, in the darkness of the bedroom, a litany of self-identity: "My husband is Archie. My children are Bob, Marilyn, and Jim. We live in New Salem." She may have been battling back the fear of losing those names and places, or she may have just been putting herself to sleep. I don't know.

For awhile at the beginning of her dementia it was obvious when she knew or suspected something wasn't right, like when nobody would allow her to help with the dinner dishes or hold the baby. Those limits frustrated her, but she was too polite to complain. Nowadays she seems more and more oblivious, and for that I'm frankly grateful. If she is going to cling to her life this tenaciously, I would like for her to find a way to absent herself from its indignities and pain. I hope the spark of selfness that makes Grandma Grandma burns out before her body does, so that the final days and hours of suffering are just a biological end-game, just a brute process that works itself out the way it needs to. I hope she doesn't have to stick around for all that.

■

One morning Grandma was particularly agitated as I drove her to the Club, the adult day-care facility she attends three days a week. She wouldn't have been so upset if she hadn't been amazingly in command of a few important facts: I was taking her there—to this slightly familiar place—but I wasn't staying, and after a certain amount of time I would come pick her up. All of this could only mean it was some kind of holding-pen or way-station or, worse, school. (Grandma started school not knowing a word of English with a teacher who, according to the family stories, was just plain mean.)

"Well, am I supposed to—" She made a vague gesture. "…supposed to *learn* something there?"

"Well, you'll play bingo and have a nice lunch—"

"What?"

"Bingo," I said loudly. "And a nice lunch."

This only confirmed her fears. She shook her head. "Well, I'm sorry to put you through this. I'm sorry you have to do all this."

And there it was, the glimpse, ever so small, of my old grandma, the one who paid her own way, who made herself small, who wouldn't trouble anyone to open a tight jar or give her a ride to the store in the snow. My old grandma, the one I knew, would apologize that I had to wash her and dress her and take her to day care. She would feel bad that she was such an inconvenience to me.

I found nothing to say in reply, none of the jolly stock phrases or mollifying comments or veiled cajolings that take up most of our conversation nowadays. We drove in silence over a bridge, past a hedge. It wasn't until days later that I thought of an appropriate reply, and then, of course, it was too late to say it. But what I would have liked to say to her is, "I'm sorry too, Grandma." ■

Elizabeth Halling is a writer living in Overland Park, Kansas. Her essays and poems have appeared in Good Housekeeping, salon.com, Brain, Child, The Kansas City Star, Potpourri, *and in various Hospice Foundation publications. She has a BA in English from Carleton College. She is currently working on a memoir.*

PART III

Helping Patients and Caregivers Adapt

The themes of the previous section of loss and caregiving are further explored within this section. Kenneth Doka begins with a broad overview of the grief issues experienced by persons with dementia and their caregivers. He explores the concepts of anticipatory grief and mourning, noting that these processes are experienced throughout the illness by both persons with dementia as well as by their families as they cope with continuing loss. He also reminds us that grief at the time of death, even if mixed with a sense of relief, is still present. Often that grief may be discounted or disenfranchised by others who see only the easing of responsibility and the loss of an impaired and hence devalued individual. Dr. Doka notes the grief reactions of persons with dementia as they cope not only with ongoing loss of self but also other losses within their environment. The chapter reinforces another basic theme that even though persons with dementia may have difficulty in communicating their understanding, it does not mean that they do not understand.

These themes are developed even further in the next two chapters. Larry Force offers approaches for offering grief counseling to populations that are cognitively impaired. To Dr. Force, knowing the person—his or her degree of impairment, relationships, and abilities—is key. One might also add that it is important to know the modality or modalities that may work with each individual. Effective counseling should be eclectic, using varied modalities based on the individual's past. The expressive arts, or even play therapy, have a long history of success with populations that may not be verbal. Dr. Force reemphasizes that acknowledging and dealing with loss may diminish some of the agitation or other negative behaviors observed in individuals with dementia.

Samuel Marwit, Thomas Meuser, and Sara Sanders make a similar point in their discussion of family caregivers. To these authors, sensitivity to caregiver stress must acknowledge the losses that caregivers experience. Validating grief is a key element in mitigating caregiver stress. The authors also offer a practical tool to assess that loss.

Mary Corcoran continues the discussion about caregiving. Dr. Corcoran reminds us that the caregivers' styles, that is their perceptions of their roles, is a critical variable in understanding caregiver strengths, stress, grief, and even the ability to access and accept outside help. Her line of research provides interesting ideas for future work. It would be valuable, for example, to assess ethnic and generational differences in caregiver styles.

Moreover, both of these chapters reinforce the difficulties for family caregivers in caring for a person with dementia. This raises an interesting ethical question. Families provide close to 75 percent of all care for persons with dementia (US Congress, 1987). If this care were provided professionally, it would increase health expenditures greatly. Yet, this care not only costs caregivers financially and emotionally, it even affects the caregivers' health (Sherman, 2001). It seems that there is an ethical responsibility, then, to offer services to support caregivers.

It also seems that there is an ethical responsibility to know when that burden should be shifted. Families need to be advised that there may come a point where it may no longer be appropriate to care for the person at home. It may be useful to raise this question early on in care, assisting the caregiver to delineate conditions that may no longer make it possible to offer home-based care. This has value for a number of reasons. It introduces the idea that institutionalization within a long-term care facility may someday be necessary. It assists caregivers in assessing their own limits. In addition, most caregivers decide to institutionalize far later than they originally planned. Institutionalization can offer significant comfort at a painful time. It also is important to reaffirm that one still remains a caregiver, albeit in a different way, even when settings change.

This illustrates as well the importance of advance directives. Caregivers are assisted when there are clear determinants of how far treatments should go. Knowing the person's prior wishes mitigates both caregiver stress and grief.

Earl Grollman concludes this section with a discussion of the spiritual issues raised by Alzheimer's disease and other dementias. This, too, reflects the holistic focus of hospice. Every disease raises medical, psychological, social, familial, and spiritual issues. All must be addressed. Rabbi Grollman's paradigm of reaching up, in, and out to acknowledge spiritual strengths is not only a reminder to individuals with dementia and their families. It offers a model of care to faith communities as well. That, too, is a mark of hospice. Care is best provided in cooperation with and in the context of each individual's family, however defined, and the communities, including the faith community, where those individuals belong. ■

References

Sherman, D. (2001). The reciprocal suffering of caregivers. In K. Doka & J. Davidson (Eds.), *Loss and caregiving: Family needs, professional responses*. Washington, DC: Hospice Foundation of America.

US Congress (Office of Technology Assessment). (1987). *Losing a million minds: Confronting the tragedy of Alzheimer's disease and the other dementias*. Washington, DC: US Government Printing Office.

■ CHAPTER 10 ■

Grief and Dementia

Kenneth J. Doka

INTRODUCTION

Grief is the constant yet hidden companion of Alzheimer's disease and other related dementias. Grief can arise when an individual in the early stages of the disease fearfully encounters the symptoms and anticipates the losses that the disease entails. Grief will certainly be experienced by family members as they view the slow deterioration in the memory and even the being of the person they love. Grief will increase as family members see, from that decline, a stranger emerge: a stranger who needs unceasing care.

That grief will be experienced even after the death—complicated by all the feelings that arose in the course of caregiving, such as the caregiver's own losses and discomfort, guilt about institutionalization, and perhaps even troubling feelings of relief and emancipation at the death. Professional caregivers, who in moments of intimate care, saw in their patient a glimpse of a former self and developed a caring connection, may also share that grief.

This chapter explores the grief both in the disease as well as in the mourning that follows the death. At all levels of the experience, grief can be disenfranchised by the shame, secrecy, and stigma that are companions of Alzheimer's disease. The chapter also seeks to enfranchise this grief by discussing strategies that can be used to support and validate all the grief throughout the course of the disease.

GRIEF AND ALZHEIMER'S DISEASE

Therese A. Rando (1986, 2000) reminds us that the term, "anticipatory grief" or as she prefers, "anticipatory mourning," is useful yet paradoxically misunderstood. It is misunderstood when the term simply is seen as a reaction to an anticipated or future loss. Here "anticipatory grief" is conceived as limited—a person reacts to the foreknowledge of an impending loss.

Rando's redefinition of anticipatory mourning is useful. To Rando (2000), "anticipatory mourning" is a reaction and response to all losses encountered in the past, present, or future of a life-threatening illness. These losses and the grief reactions they evoke are part of the daily experience of those who experience Alzheimer's disease or other dementias. Patients, families, and even professional caregivers can experience these losses.

In Alzheimer's disease and in many dementias these losses can be profound. First, there is the very loss of the past as memory deteriorates. As one ceases to remember, the links to the past are severed. One no longer recalls experiences or relationships from memory. This type of loss was poignantly expressed by one Alzheimer's patient who, struggling to recount an incident from childhood, cried, "I used to remember!"

The deterioration of memory also affects the present. Memory links one to another, allowing one to recall the relationships and histories that bind a person to another. Those affected may no longer remember the individuals around them—unable to recall or to express the relationship. One woman with Alzheimer's disease had a long, close relationship with her daughter-in-law. Yet, as the disease progressed, she could only express the relationship as "the woman who married my son"—a term that caused a great deal of grief to the younger woman as it seemingly invalidated their long, positive relationship.

As memory lapses, other losses follow. One may no longer be able to effectively function in other roles. Work and other cherished tasks may have to be relinquished. There may be a gradual loss of independence.

In the early stages of dementia both the patient and the family may experience these losses. As the disease progresses, the patient may no longer have the ability to cognitively experience loss and grief. Also as the disease progresses, the sense of specific loss and deterioration may be replaced by a generalized feeling of "wrong–being," a vague sense that something is not right. Moreover, this generalized sense may be manifested in behaviors that indicate inner pain, such as expressing agitation. For though cognition declines, feelings and states of emotional stress remain (Rando, 1993).

Eventually it may be that the patient experiences "psychological death": the loss of individual consciousness. The person ceases to be aware of self. "Not only does he not know who he is—he does not know that he is" (Kalish, 1966, p. 247). Naturally others can only infer this state.

There is one other issue as well. Even as individuals struggle with dementia, they may experience additional significant losses apart from the illness. A loved one, for example may become ill, be hospitalized or institutionalized, or die.

Unfortunately, there is little research that considers how an individual with dementia copes with loss. As noted earlier, Rando (1993) emphasizes that the loss of cognition should not be compared with the absence of emotion. Grief in dementia may be evident in changes of behaviors such as unusual or increased manifestations of agitation or restlessness.

However, persons with dementia may not be able to be aware of the loss. They may, as mentioned earlier, have a vague sense that something is not right, or that some significant individual, perhaps one they cannot even identify, is missing. Persons with dementia may confuse the present loss with earlier losses. For example, Herrmann and Grek (1988) documented two cases where bereaved spouses with dementia delusively believed that a parent rather than a spouse had died. They may retain a constant delusion that the person is still alive (Vennen, Shanks, Staff & Sala, 2000).

In other situations, persons with dementia may be unable to retain the information that an individual has died. They may ask repeatedly what has occurred to that person. They may even mourn the loss only to later reiterate the question. In such cases, caregivers may need to acknowledge their own frustration and be reassured that such behaviors are normal in the disease and are not indications of an inadequacy of explanations. It might be useful to return to a picture or memory each time the person with dementia questions the loss or expresses a sense of grief. Naturally, in individuals with Alzheimer's or other dementias, expressions of grief will be affected by a variety of factors, including the extent of disease and loss of awareness, the immediacy of the lost relationship, and the affected persons' abilities to communicate their loss. It is critical, however, to be sensitive to that loss. It has even been hypothesized that significant losses, as well as the inherent changes that occur as a secondary effect of loss may exacerbate the dementia (Rando, 1993; Kastenbaum, 1969).

The family, however, experiences a continuous and profound sense of loss and subsequent grief—a grief that becomes more intense as the patient's symptoms increase (Ponder & Pomeroy, 1996). The family may experience a deep sense of "psychological loss"; that is the persona of the person, or the psychological essence of an individual's personality is now perceived as lost even though the person is physically alive. The sense of individual identity is so changed now that family members experience the death of the person who once was. (Doka & Aber, 2002)

Spouses may become "crypto widows"—married in name but not in fact. They may grieve the losses associated with that role—losses of intimacy, companionship, and sexuality (Doka & Aber, 2002; Teri & Reifler, 1986).

The very experience of caregiving may complicate grief. Caregivers may experience secondary losses such as the loss of social and recreational roles, work roles, and relationships with others. These losses and the increased demands of caring for someone with a progressive illness as well as the experience of psychosocial loss may generate an unceasing state of grief sometimes identified as "chronic sorrow" (Mayer, 2001; Burke, Hainsworth, Eakes & Lindgren, 1992; Loos & Bowd, 1998) and a reactive depression (Walker & Pomeroy, 1996).

Progressive dementia also diffuses caregiver grief in another way. As individuals deteriorate, their ability to monitor and regulate their behaviors diminishes. They may exhibit a range of bizarre and unusual behaviors such as foul language or indecent and inappropriate actions. They may relive earlier traumas. For example, some holocaust survivors, as they experienced Alzheimer's disease, began to hoard food and experience troubling flashbacks or heightened anxiety (McCann, 2003). Others may express attitudes that were once self-censored, engaging for example in racial or personal diatribes. All of this behavior can humiliate, embarrass and isolate caregivers—increasing ambivalence and discomfort that subsequently can complicate grief. There also may be ethical decisions, such as withholding treatment, which may generate guilt, complicating grief. Moreover, the deleterious affects of caregiving may diminish coping abilities and the constant demands of care may limit social support (Bodnar & Kiecolt-Glaser, 1994).

Grief changes focus as the patient dies. For some the death may be a "liberating loss," (Jones & Martinson, 1992; Elison & McGonigle, 2003) characterized by feelings of relief and emancipation that caregiving responsibilities and the suffering of both the patient and family have ended.

Yet, others may actually grieve the loss of the caregiving role. They may now feel a lack of focus and meaninglessness in their present activities. For others, though, these feelings may be accompanied by guilt and sadness. Survivors may reminisce about the caregiving experience, reflecting on times that they might have shown more patience or empathy. There might be considerable work, unfinished business, believing that there was more that could have been said or done. Such memories, while common and understandable, are related to greater depression, stress, and social isolation (Bodnar & Kiecolt-Glaser, 1994).

This grief may not only be manifested in affect but in cognition, behavior, and spirituality. It also may be experienced physically. Health consequences do not end with the transition of the caregiving role. In fact, increased medical symptoms in caregivers are associated with transitions from the caregiving role such as the nursing home placement or death of the person with Alzheimer's disease (Grant, Adler, Patterson, Dimsdale, Ziegler & Irwin, 2002).

Others may disenfranchise the grief that patients and survivors experience. Disenfranchised grief refers to losses that are not appreciated by others. In effect the individual has no perceived "right" to mourn. The loss is not openly acknowledged or socially sanctioned and publicly shared. Others simply do not understand why this loss is mourned and they may fail to validate and support grief (Doka, 1989, 2002).

Grief resulting from dementia can be disenfranchised for a number of reasons. Often the person with Alzheimer's disease or another form of dementia is devalued. They are seen as old, confused, and a burden. Death may be seen as a release—for both the caregiver and the person who died. Survivors may be expected to have already grieved in the course of the illness and to be relieved about the death. Even the customary statements of sympathy and support may be tinged with ambivalent sentiments like "this is a blessing," or "it must be a great relief." There may be little understanding of the impact of the loss and the depth of grief of survivors. And for persons with Alzheimer's disease or other dementias, grief may also be disenfranchised as they may be perceived as incapable of sustaining grief.

Naturally a wide range of factors that can include the nature of the relationship will affect the nature and extent of grief: the circumstances surrounding the loss, individuals' coping capacities, and grieving styles as well as other social and psychological variables (Worden, 2002; Rando, 1993; Martin & Doka, 1999). Ethnicity and culture certainly play a role. For example, Owen, Goode, and Haley (2001) found that African American caregivers compared with White caregivers were more likely to experience higher levels of grief.

Other research notes that manifestations of grief are different between those who cared for their partners with dementia at home compared to those who placed their spouse within a nursing home. Those who cared for the patient in the home reported exhaustion, stress, anxiety, and anger while spouses of individuals placed within nursing homes indicated higher levels of guilt and sadness (Rudd, Viney, & Presten, 1999; Collins, Liken, Kirz & Kokinakis, 1993).

While many factors may mediate the experience of grief, one fact remains. Grief is a companion to Alzheimer's disease at all phases of the disease and following death. The goal of support, then, is to acknowledge and validate the loss—to enfranchise grief.

ENFRANCHISING GRIEF

In validating grief, it is critical to revisit two points. First, grief is experienced by the person with Alzheimer's or other form of dementia, as well as by family members and professional caregivers. Second, grief is encountered throughout the illness as well as after the death. Assistance and support, then, should be offered to all that are involved throughout the illness and after the death.

For persons with dementia, two considerations are essential in offering support: validation and control. When an individual experiences dementia, there can be a tendency to invalidate that person's emotional expression. Often expressions of anxiety, anger, or other manifestations of grief are discounted and denied. Often this is done to protect the person—to offer glib reassurance that everything is fine even though the individual with dementia is aware and fearful of the manifestations of the disease.

This is unhelpful. Persons in the early stage of dementia have very clear awareness of symptoms of decline. Even later in the progression of the illness, individuals may have vague feelings of loss of capabilities. Empathetic listening, expressions of support, reassurances of remembrance by reaffirming relationships, and when appropriate, physical touch, are ways to validate and show support.

It also is important to respect the affected individual's sense of control. As persons feel abilities slip away, they may be determined to maintain as much control of their environment as possible. In the early phases of the disease, there may be expressions of anticipatory bereavement (Gerser, 1974) or actions where the persons clearly need to plan for impending losses. Individuals may need to finish business—contacting associates, giving instructions and then reviewing or creating advance directives. This too should be supported. However, not every person will choose to confront feelings, or plan for the future. That, too, is a way to cope.

There are a number of strategies that may assist family members as they cope with the loss both prior to and following the death (Doka & Aber, 2002).

PROVIDE EDUCATION ABOUT THE UNDERLYING CONDITION

It is important to assess each family member's perception of the affected individual's underlying condition. Often, the family's understanding of that condition can be faulty. In asking families to describe the underlying cause, counselors can determine whether the client's theories of causation sustain false hopes or unrealistic beliefs (e.g., that the person can control behavior or will get better).

Exploring family members' beliefs gives counselors the opportunity to provide education at each client's level. Counselors should be aware of and suggest resources to families. Associations, self-help groups, and nonprint and print media—particularly books by people who have experienced similar losses—can all be useful in the educational process. Such education not only provides realistic information about the nature and course of the condition, it also enhances a sense of coping and control by allowing family members a meaningful sense of activity and by providing them with opportunities to anticipate and plan for future contingencies.

ASSIST PERSONS IN DEALING WITH THE EMOTIONAL ISSUES RELATED TO LOSS

Often family members feel constrained in recognizing and expressing their emotions. Because the affected person is alive, perhaps living in the same environment, and in some cases defined as not responsible for his or her state, individuals may lack the opportunity for emotional expression, feel personally inhibited from expressing negative emotions, or even face social sanction from friends and relatives who consider such expression disloyal or unfeeling. Moreover family members, especially caregivers, may have considerate emotional issues related to the caregiving experience. They may feel angry and resentful towards the person with dementia or at others who they feel are unsympathetic or unsupportive. They may feel guilty about their ambivalence in caregiving or any feelings of relief and emancipation they might experience at the time of death. Family members may add unnecessary guilt by comparing their reactions to the person with dementia to others. With all of these emotions, counselors can assist by creating a nonjudgmental atmosphere where individuals can express and explore these complicated emotions. In addition to reassurance that such feelings are normal, counselors can offer strategies such as journal writing, ritual, or addressing an empty chair, that assist individuals in acknowledging their emotional needs.

ASSISTING FAMILY MEMBERS IN RECOGNIZING AND RESPONDING TO CHANGES IN THEIR OWN LIVES AND IN THE LIFE OF THE SIGNIFICANT OTHER

When people experience significant loss in their lives, they are likely to find that their lives subsequently change. Thus in dementia, people will often experience many modifications in the daily course of their lives. They may lack the prior companionship; cease to engage in previously enjoyable activities; take on new responsibilities; lose contact with friends or relatives; experience loss of dreams and expectations; and have unmet psychological, social, sexual, and financial needs. After the death, they may experience other changes such as the loss of a meaningful role. These changes can occur so quickly that persons may not realize just how profoundly their own lives have been altered or have the time to develop effective coping strategies. In response, counselors may wish to try several approaches.

First, they may want to review with the individual ways in which life has changed. Often the simple question, "In what ways has your life changed since ____?" can release a flood of responses. Counselors can assist individuals in determining these secondary losses that are most significant and what aspects of loss can be regained (perhaps in a modified way). They can explore responses and strategies for dealing with such losses.

Next, counselors may want to discuss the nature of the family members' support systems. Here family members can consider such issues as assessing the extent and nature of the support system (which may provide strategies for respite and resumption of missed activity), the use of that support system (which may allow further discussion of coping styles and problem-solving abilities), and "surprises" in the support system (e.g., people who individuals were surprised to find were there for them, as well as people who individuals felt were not supportive). This last issue is partic-ularly significant because it may provide further opportunity for the coun-selor to discuss emotional responses such as anger and resentment and to help persons develop their problem-solving skills and coping strategies. Upon assessment, individuals may recognize that they did not adequately communicate their needs or feelings to others in their support system or that they used others in inappropriate ways. In one case, a woman was very angry that her daughter seemed unable to listen to her complaints about the demands placed on her by her spouse's dementia. Upon reflection, the woman realized that her daughter's strengths were always in active doing rather than passive listening. Once the woman realized that, she modified her expectations of her daughter and found that her daughter was extremely supportive as long as the mother confined her requests to asking for help in active tasks, such as providing rides for her father or doing chores.

Counselors can also assist families in finding additional sources of support, such as self-help groups, day care and respite programs, and, if necessary, institutional care. Often this approach has additional value because it allows clients to reduce stress and to take direct actions that may diminish guilt and reaffirm control. Support groups have been particularly successful for both caregivers as well as persons newly diagnosed with Alzheimer's disease (Wasow & Coons, 1987; Simank & Strickland, 1986; Yale, 1989). These groups can decrease isolation, facilitate grief, and exchange information and resources. But counselors must do more than simply have clients identify needs and sources of support. In some cases, counselors may need to explore resistance and ambivalence toward such support. As Quayhagen and Quayhagen (1988) note, some caregivers may experience considerable guilt over leaving the care of the person to others; and accepting help from formal agencies may no longer allow the defense of denial.

With families, a counselor can explore role problems, dilemmas, and ambiguities. One of the most significant problems of dementia, especially for spouses, is that it creates considerable role strain and generates additional burdens. For example, the spouse may remain legally married but effectively be widowed because the companionship and sexuality that were part of the prior relationship no longer exist. Often in these situations it is helpful for persons to explore the tensions, ambiguities, burdens, and difficulties that accompany the state of crypto widowhood. It is also helpful to explore all possible options because, even if an option is precluded for moral or practical reasons, the very consideration of that option reaffirms a sense of control and reduces the feeling that the future is totally constrained. In one case, a woman whose husband was institutionalized with Alzheimer's disease became involved in a relationship with another man, but she decided at this time she would neither divorce her demented spouse nor cohabit with her new love. Exploring those options, however, allowed her to affirm that she did have some control over events and that the decisions she made now were not necessarily final.

Counselors may wish to discuss the ways in which individuals generally cope with change and the ways in which they are coping with it now. They can help individuals assess which of their strategies are effective (reaffirming and reinforcing such skills) and which are not (providing opportunity to assess and develop better strategies). They may also want to explore current ways in which persons deal with stress and when necessary, teach clients effective stress-reduction techniques. They can explore clients' caregiving role. Clients are often very willing to take on caregiving responsibilities, but they may make decisions that do not adequately take into account their own or the other's role. For example, an individual's decision to quit work to take care of a spouse with Alzheimer's disease may remove him or her from a support system, may eliminate necessary respite, and may create financial problems. One might try to find other ways to resolve the issue. Thus counselors need to assist individuals periodically in assessing their caregiving plans and roles and in reviewing alternative plans. Finally, counselors can legitimize the needs of family members to help them recognize and balance their own needs with the demands of care.

HELPING FAMILIES PLAN REALISTICALLY FOR THE FUTURE

The nature of dementia often encourages an attitude of "one day at a time." In many ways such a perspective is functional. With irreversible syndromes, the future can be dismal. Nevertheless, it is important for individuals to plan for the future. Such planning allows clients a sense of control and permits them to rehearse problem-solving skills, anticipate future issues, and conduct necessary research within sufficient lead-time. In such sessions, it is important for counselors to reaffirm confidence in the individual's abilities, coping skills, and realistic hopes and to allow family members to explore the effects of change in their own sense of self, the sense of others, and their beliefs.

Dementias such as Alzheimer's disease can profoundly alter views of self or others as well as fundamental beliefs about faith and meaning. Individuals may be fearful of their own future—worrying about future dementia. They may question their feelings and beliefs about other family members—perhaps experiencing a profound sense of disappointment in the reactions or support of others.

They may even have troubling memories of the person with dementia—uncovering heretofore-unseen behaviors or attitudes. For example, in one case a woman was clearly discomforted by her mother's reactions to persons of a different race. Prior to dementia, her mother had been a strong supporter of the civil rights movement and had never expressed such attitudes. Such individuals will need space and opportunity to confront their beliefs and reconstruct meaning. Asking questions such as "How does this affect your beliefs about yourself and your family or your beliefs about the world?" can offer a beginning. Assignments in which clients seek out information or enter into discussion with others, including members of their own faith community, can facilitate this process. Tasks such as putting together videotapes or photo albums can reconnect individuals to earlier memories.

In addition to family members, it also is important to offer support to professional caregivers. Since many dementias progress over a long period of time, it is not unusual for nursing home aides, home companions and home-health aides to develop long-standing relationships with family members and the individual with dementia. When that person dies, the aide not only terminates a relationship with the individual but often with the family members as well. Here health aides may lose a position and income. They may need to develop another relationship almost immediately. In cases of advanced dementia, where decisions may have been made to terminate treatment, the aide's perspective may be unasked and unwelcome. Yet, professional caregivers mourn too. Their grief needs to be acknowledged and supported by the agencies that employ them. Empathetic debriefings following an assignment, notes from the family and agency, and policies encouraging participation in rituals offer tangible ways to support staff.

CONCLUSION

Grief is a constant companion to Alzheimer's disease and related dementia. It accompanies the patient and family. It journeys with professional caregivers. It is ever present—throughout the illness and after death.

It does not, however, have to be the only companion. As others—family and friends, counselors, and supportive others—travel together, the journey through grief continues. It is, though, now less lonely and not quite as frightening. ■

REFERENCES

Bodnar, J.C. & Kiecolt-Glaser, J.K. (1994). Caregiver depression after bereavement: Chronic stress isn't over when it's over. *Psychology & Aging, 9*, 372-380.

Burke, M.L., Hainsworth, M.A., Eakes, G.G. & Lindgren, C.L. (1992). Current knowledge and research in chronic sorrow: A foundation for inquiry. *Death Studies, 16*, 231-245.

Collins, C., Liken, M., King, S.O. & Kolinakas, C. (1993). Loss and grief among family caregivers or relatives with dementia. *Qualitative Health Research, 3*, 236-253.

Doka, K.J. (Ed.) (1989). *Disenfranchised grief: Recognizing hidden sorrow.* Lexington, MA: Lexington Books.

Doka, K.J. (Ed.). (2002). *Disenfranchised grief: New directions, challenges and strategies for practice.* Champaign, IL: Research Press.

Doka, K.J. & Aber, R. (2002). Psychological loss and grief. In K. Doka (Ed.), *Disenfranchised grief: New directions, challenges and strategies for practice.* Champaign, IL: Research Press.

Elison, J. & McGonigle, C. (2003). *Liberating losses: When death brings relief.* Cambridge, MA: Perseus Publishing.

Gerber, I. (1976). Anticipating Bereavement. In B. Schoenberg, A. Carr, A. Kurscher, D. Peretz, & I. Goldberg (Eds.), *Anticipating grief.* New York: Columbia University Press.

Grant, I., Adler, K., Patterson, T.L., Dimsdale, J.E., Ziegler, M.G. & Irwin, M.R. (2002). Health consequences & Alzheimer's caregiving transitions: Effects of placement and bereavement. *Psychosomatic Medicine, 64*, 477-486.

Herrmann, N. & Grek, A. (1988). Delusional double mourning: A complication of bereavement in dementia. *Canadian Journal of Psychiatry, 33,* 851-852.

Jones, P.S. & Martinson, I. (1992). The experience of bereavement in caregiving of family members with Alzheimer's disease. *IMAGE: Journal of Nursing Scholarship, 214,* 172-176.

Kalish, R.A. (1966). A continuum of subjectively perceived death. *The Gerontologist, 6,* 73-76.

Kastembaum, R. (1969). Death and bereavement in later life. In A. Kutscher (Ed.), *Death and the elderly.* Springfield, IL: Thomas.

Loos, C. & Bowd, A. (1997). Caregivers of persons with Alzheimer's disease: Some neglected implications of the experience of personal loss and grief. *Death Studies, 21,* 501-514.

Mayer, M. (2001). Chronic sorrow in caregiving spouses of patients with Alzheimer's disease. *Journal of Aging and Identity, 6,* 49-60.

McCann, T. (2003). *Holocaust survivors with Alzheimer's can relive old horrors.* Retrieved on July 20, 2003 from http://www.serlvisobispo.com/ mrd/sanlvisobispo/news/nation/por690.btm

Owen, J.E., Goode, K.T. & Haley, W.E. (2001). End-of-life care and reactions to death in African-American and White family caregivers of relatives with Alzheimer's disease. *Omega: Journal of Death and Dying, 43,* 348-361.

Quaghagan, M.P. & Quaghagan, M. (1988). Alzheimer's stress: Coping with the caregiver role. *The Gerontologist, 28,* 391-396.

Ponder, R.J. & Pomeroy, E.C. (1966). The grief of caregivers: How pervasive is it? *Journal of Gerontological Social Work, 27,* 3-21.

Rando, T.A. (1986). *Loss and anticipatory grief.* Lexington, MA: Lexington Books.

Rando, T.A. (1993). *The treatment of complicated mourning.* Champaign, IL: Research Press.

Rando, T.A. (2000). *Clinical dimensions of anticipatory mourning: Theory and practice in working with the dying, their loved ones and their caregivers.* Champaign, IL: Research Press.

Rudd, M.G., Viney, L.L. & Presten, C.A. (1999). The grief expressed by spousal caregivers of dementia patients: The role of place of care of patient and gender of the patient. *International Journal of Aging & Human Development, 48,* 217-240.

Simank, M.H. & Strickland, K.J. (1986). Assisting families in coping with Alzheimer's disease and other related dementias with the establishment of a mutual support group. *The Journal of Gerontological Social Work, 9* (2), 49-58.

Teri, L.V. & Reifler, B.V. (1986). Sexual issues of patients with Alzheimer's disease. *Medical Aspects of Human Sexuality, 20,* 86-91.

Vennen, A., Shanks, M.F., Staff, M.F. & Sala, S.D. (2000). Nurturing syndrome: A form of pathological bereavement with delusions in Alzheimer's disease. *Neuropsychological, 38,* 213-224.

Walker, R.J. & Pomeroy, F.C. (1986). Depression or grief?: The experience of caregivers of people with dementia. *Health & Social Work, 21,* 247-254.

Wasow, M. & Coons, D.M. (1987). Widows and widowers of Alzheimer's victims: Their survival after spouse's deaths. *Journal of Independent Social Work, 2,* 21-32.

Worden, T.W. (2002). *Grief counseling and grief therapy.* (3rd ed.). New York: Springer.

Yale, R. (1989). Support groups for newly diagnosed Alzheimer's clients. *Clinical Gerontologist, 8,* 86-89.

CHAPTER 11

Grief Therapy for Cognitively Impaired Individuals

Lawrence T. Force

*Dad, I am so sorry to be the one to tell you. I really
don't know how to say this, but Mom has died.
Dad, do you understand what I mean?*
—42-year-old son of an Alzheimer's patient

When an adult child presents his father with the news that his wife, companion, and friend of 53 years has died, it is an overwhelmingly sad event. When Alzheimer's disease is present, however, the task becomes even more difficult, unpredictable, and complex. The purpose of this chapter is to review the issue of grief therapy for individuals with cognitive impairment, specifically Alzheimer's disease, and to provide a framework for intervention strategies.

COGNITIVE IMPAIRMENT: DEFINITION

Cognitive development begins at birth. Throughout the lifespan there is an increase in the mastery and complexity associated with the process of thinking, i.e., cognition moves from an overarching general perspective to one where the individual is able to master complex tasks. Individuals move through cognitive stages of development beginning with sensory development and transitioning to formal operational stages where one is able to deal with higher-order skills such as abstraction, meta-cognition, or "thinking about thinking" (Piaget, 1972).

The Piagetian construct of cognitive development presents a parallel between the increase in age and the increase in the organization of behavior. Therefore, it is expected that as people age, they are able to process more complex information, manifesting in the outcome of good judgment and socially acceptable behavior. However, there are times based upon reactive situations (head trauma), life-long disabilities (mental retardation), and disease models (Alzheimer's disease) that cognition is impaired. Regardless of the etiology, cognitive impairment impacts the ability to think, concentrate, reason, remember, formulate ideas, and make good judgments. The behavioral manifestations of cognitive impairment present as behaviors that are outside the range of what are expected or accepted as appropriate behaviors.

ALZHEIMER'S DISEASE YESTERDAY AND TODAY

Over 100 years ago, Alois Alzheimer, a neuropathologist, provided the first description of a cluster of behaviors that would later become known as Alzheimer's disease. In 1901, Dr. Alzheimer, working at a hospital for the mentally ill in Frankfort, Germany, was caring for a 51-year-old female patient named Auguste D. Clinically, this woman presented a profile of "confusion, language loss, paranoia, and unpredictable behaviors." Her behavioral patterns and clinical profile did not fit into any existing disease model of the day. In 1906, Auguste D. died. At autopsy, the distinctive findings were a "tangled bundle of fibrils" and "pathological metabolic produce know as plaques" (Snowdon, 2001). Today, the presence of "plaques and tangles" is the hallmark of what has become known as Alzheimer's disease.

Over the last century, Alzheimer's disease has become one of the most widely recognized yet misdiagnosed disorders in modern medicine. We now know that Alzheimer's disease is one of a number of dementias. Researchers have made great strides in characterizing the neurodegenerative profile of the disease. There is strong evidence to suggest that a familial form of the disease exists. Unfortunately, there is also strong evidence, supported by individual and family anguish, that the manifestation of this disease is commonly misdiagnosed. In fact, it is not uncommon that the presence of Alzheimer's disease is mistaken for Lyme disease, depression, or alcohol abuse. In addition, there are perhaps thousands of cases each year of over-diagnosis, resulting in an increased percentage of pseudo-dementia.

Historically, the common picture of Alzheimer's disease portrays an elderly person experiencing memory loss and confusion. However, we now know that the onset of the disease is not dictated by age. (Ironically, it was the diagnosis of a 51-year-old woman that was the beginning of the identification and treatment of a disease that would become a household name.) Regardless of the age of onset, a proper diagnosis is required. The diagnosis of Alzheimer's disease demands more than a cursory conversation between a practitioner and a person presenting evidence of confusion. A trained eye is required.

A proper diagnosis continues to be a major quest for individuals with Alzheimer's disease. Advances in medical interventions have been accompanied by greater accuracy in identifying the markers of Alzheimer's disease, thereby extending the life expectancies and experiences of Alzheimer's patients. This, in turn, has created a need for additional areas of specialization. One such area of specialization focuses on the psychological and emotional needs of individuals with Alzheimer's disease. For example: how does one provide emotional care, psychological support, and therapeutic intervention to Alzheimer's patients who are experiencing loss and grief?

TREATMENT REALITIES

Individuals with Alzheimer's disease, their family members, and practitioners need to understand that grief is a multi-stage continuum. The level of the individual's cognitive impairment will dictate the receptive, expressive, and reasoning abilities of the person, including how the individual internalizes and expresses a grief response. Therefore, intervention and supportive strategies need to reflect an understanding of this knowledge-base.

Practitioners and family members will require sensitivity in order to meet the need-level of the individual with Alzheimer's disease. Realizing that the level of cognitive impairment of the individual with Alzheimer's disease will be reflected in language deficits, as well as in reasoning and memory difficulties, the practitioner and/or family members must be aware of the uniqueness of this grieving process. This awareness is vitally important to ensure the development of accurate treatment approaches. Therefore, prior to introducing loss and grief strategies that will assist the person who is cognitively impaired, family members and practitioners need to develop a holistic perspective, encompassing an understanding of the developmental context of person and place.

STAGES OF DISEASE

Beginning in the early-stage of Alzheimer's disease, anxiety associated with pre-diagnostic concerns usually becomes evident. The individual may begin to realize that something is wrong. Generally, this occurs without the knowledge of any family members. The individual may begin to sense changes in perception and concept formation. At this point, the individual may be experiencing mild-to-moderate episodes of memory lapse, poor judgment, and gaps in receptive or expressive language. Self-monitoring and an internal dialogue laced with themes of denial, doubt, and second-guessing begin to increase. This stage of Alzheimer's disease typically evolves to a mid-stage.

In this mid-stage, individuals with Alzheimer's and their support systems (family, friends, colleagues at work) are aware of memory concerns and behavioral changes. The mild-to-moderate lapses of memory, errors in judgment, and difficulties with language start to become more frequent and more severe. At this point, independent living arrangements, driving, and working may need to be modified. It is not uncommon to find evidence of forced retirements, enrollment in social model adult day health services, and changes in residential settings as markers within this stage. Overall, cognitive impairment is beginning to increase. Finally, in the late-stage of Alzheimer's disease, the severity of the impairment may require full-time supervision and oversight. It is here where we typically find individuals in medical model adult day health services, structured assisted living programs, and nursing homes. Overall, intervention techniques need to be built upon a knowledge-base that is in tune to the specific needs, strengths, and deficits of the individual. A multi-dimensional understanding, including the history of the individual coupled with the knowledge of the severity of impairment, is required.

ALZHEIMER'S DIAGNOSIS AND GRIEF

When the presumptive diagnosis of Alzheimer's disease is made, the result can be an emotional roller-coaster. Patient and family are flooded with a multitude of feelings (Force, 2003). Alzheimer's disease, with its associated loss, is an example of a "living-grief." Patients and family members grieve for the lives and the identities they once knew.

An underlying characteristic of the grieving process, one that is commonly experienced by individuals with Alzheimer's disease, is disenfranchised grief: "grief that is experienced when a loss cannot be openly acknowledged, socially sanctioned, or publicly mourned" (Doka, 1989). Therefore, family members and practitioners cannot expect individuals with cognitive impairments to process and respond in the same fashion as individuals without cognitive impairments. In the presence of Alzheimer's disease, reasoning and judgment are diminished and predictability is absent. This does not mean that the history of the individual or the expressed desires of the person can be discounted. Rather, it becomes the responsibility of the family members and practitioners to appreciate the uniqueness of the connection between Alzheimer's disease and grief.

Loss and grief are not associated exclusively with the absence of a significant other. Individual grief can be enmeshed with loss of independence, loss of home, and loss of reference points as the person struggles to maintain a sense of self, a sense of identity. For individuals with Alzheimer's disease, the focus is on decreasing the speed of a changing world. At the same time, this effort to maintain a sense of stability is being bombarded with frustration, denial, anger, rage, sadness, and grief.

However, the reality of the relationship between Alzheimer's disease and grief is not confined to just the individual going through the disease process, but the impact overflows into the family system. Examples of this dynamic are found in the words of Susan, a 57-year-old daughter, questioning a social worker about her father with Alzheimer's disease: "How do you reason with somebody who doesn't remember what you are talking about?" Or the words of Mary, a 67-year-old wife, as she speaks to members of an Alzheimer's disease caregiver support group about her 74-year-old husband with Alzheimer's disease: "I feel that my life is like a perpetual grieving process. First, when Walter was diagnosed I cried and felt like the floor had fallen out beneath me. I felt as though he had died. But now two years later I am OK with it, but I realize that Walter is still alive and that sooner or later I will have to go through this grieving process again."

The words of Susan and Mary provide us with a glimpse of the anguish associated with episodes of memory loss and Alzheimer's disease. Both women profess a sense of sadness and loss that permeates their thinking. Susan and Mary show us that the reality of the relationship between Alzheimer's disease and grief is not confined to just the individual; it impacts everyone in the family in a unique way.

The question is what now? What steps can be taken to help individuals with Alzheimer's disease as they move through the grieving and loss process?

TREATMENT MODALITIES: LOSS, GRIEF, AND ALZHEIMER'S DISEASE

Grief, a response to loss, can be found in the physical, emotional, and cognitive realm of the person. The process of grieving is individualized and complex. For Alzheimer's patients, however, the unpredictability of the grieving process is magnified. In developing intervention approaches, one must rely on good judgment, common sense, and a wealth of empathy.

For both family members and practitioners, the important first step is to recognize the complexity and magnitude of the situation. The newly-diagnosed Alzheimer's patient not only is grieving, but also struggling with an assault on memory, reasoning and language skills. Still, practitioners and family members need to move beyond overgeneralizations and stereotypes about how Alzheimer's patients will address issues of grief. Just as grieving is an individualized process, so too, is the experience of Alzheimer's disease. Treatment approaches and supportive interventions need to reflect the skill level and personal history of the patient. That is why the value of "knowing where the person is" is extremely important.

Based upon their years of contact with the individual, family members are expected to possess greater knowledge of the individual in question. However, this wealth of information may overshadow the reality of recognizing present deficits. Practitioners, depending upon their history with the individual, may possess a limited knowledge of the person prior to the onset of the disease. A practitioner's information may be gathered from a review of medical records, a review of a psycho-social history or from a discussion with staff members. It helps to have additional information from the family, as well as a dialogue with the individual. In the ideal world, the best approach would involve the individual expressing his or her own needs, as the family member provides historical information to the trained practitioner. Depending on the severity of the impairment, however, this is not always the case.

FRAMEWORK FOR PRACTITIONERS

Know the Person

This point cannot be overemphasized. Information from the individual, family members and record reviews is not enough; it is also essential to understand the developmental context of the person. Age, health factors, and temperament will influence outcome. The severity of the impairment will dictate the treatment approach. If the person is in the early stage of Alzheimer's disease, then the use of language, symbols, and metaphors may be an effective way to address the individual. If the person is in late-stage Alzheimer's, then the use of touch and tactile stimulation may be the preferred approach. However, regardless of the level of severity, a reassuring voice combined with active listening, the strength of "presence" and the power of empathy may be the most effective tools.

Emphasize Safety and Security

The practitioner needs to make certain that the basic needs of safety and security are met. It is important to try to create a situation or setting that is predictable and familiar for the Alzheimer's patient.

Understand Connections

The nature of the loss may influence the severity and outcome of the grieving process. Factors that may influence grief include the temperament of the individual, the emotional nature of the relationship, and the severity of the disease. An understanding of the complexity of the relationship is important. Not all relationships are built upon a foundation of respect and loyalty; in some instances, the loss of the person will not be mourned. It is important to listen carefully to the grieving individual's insights, recollections, verbal, and non-verbal cues as they relate to the loss. Collaterals (family, friends, and staff) may be able to provide a deeper understanding of the dynamics of the relationship.

Use Environmental Cues

The use of pictures, personal items, familiar names, and reference points (names of family pets, friends, favorite vacation spots, hobbies, interests, etc.) can be useful as the practitioner begins to develop a dialogue with the affected individual. It is useful to build upon the person's history and experiences. If the person was a nurse or an educator, then medical references or academic themes might be integrated into the discussion. If the person was employed as a carpenter or electrician, then references specific to those trades might be used. If the individual is over the age of 80, then memories of World War II and the Great Depression can be useful reference points.

Rely on a Theoretical Framework

A good theory, like a compass, will show the way. A theory allows us to recognize, explain, and understand new situations. There are a variety of intervention approaches that can be employed. However, as one reviews the theoretical landscape, it becomes apparent that some perspectives would not be helpful or appropriate. For example, utilizing a psycho-analytical perspective, i.e., encouraging the extensive review of the past, analysis of language or symbols, and the examination of dreamwork would not be a good fit. Similarly, a traditional behavioral approach that deals with rewarding appropriate behaviors and does not focus on cognition and insight might also generate its own shortcomings.

COGNITIVE-BEHAVIORAL APPROACH

Due to the presence of a cognitive impairment, which might impede the processing of grief, the use of a cognitive-behavioral approach might make the most sense. There are a number of models that are grounded in the cognitive-behavioral school. One is the task-centered approach, a short-term practice intervention with a focus on the here-and-now.

General Concepts of the Task-Centered Approach

- *Empirical orientation.* Hypotheses and concepts about the client system need to be grounded in case data; speculative theorizing about client's problems and behavior is avoided; assessment, process, and outcome data are systematically collected in each case.

- *Integrative stance.* The model draws from compatible approaches, e.g. problem-solving, cognitive-behavioral, cognitive, and family-structural.

- *Focus on client-acknowledged problems.* The focus of service is on specific problems clients acknowledge as being of concern to them.

- *Systems and contexts.* Problems occur in a context of multiple systems; contextual change may be needed for problem resolution.

- *Planned brevity.* The service is generally planned short-term (six to twelve sessions within a four month period).

- *Collaborative relationship.* Relationships with clients emphasize a caring but collaborative effort; the practitioner shares assessment information and avoids hidden agendas; extensive use of client's input in developing treatment strategies not only to devise more effective interventions, but to develop the client's problem-solving abilities.

- *Structure.* The intervention program, including treatment sessions, is structured into well-defined sequences of activities.

- *Basic assumptions of the model.* Guided by the foregoing theory, the practitioner helps the client identify specific problems and move forward with solutions to psycho-social problems. (Reid, 1996)

Case Illustration

Edna, a 79-year-old woman in late-stage Alzheimer's disease, resides in a nursing home. Her family members are very concerned about her. Two months ago, Edna's husband died; they were married for 48 years. Until the death of her husband, Edna lived at home. She has resided in this nursing home for the last six weeks. Family members and staff are concerned because she is becoming more agitated and upset. Edna states:

I don't know what kind of illness this is supposed to be. My
family is afraid of what I will do. They are afraid I will not
remember my name. I told them I will wear a bracelet. I want to
be home. What do I have to do? For how long? Will it get worse?
The things I forget are not important. I can't believe I can't go
home. I have had this brain all my life. I know my husband is
dead, but I don't remember that. In a way, it would be better
for me to remain here, rather than going home and creating
difficulties. But I want to go home. I am not having any
problems. I have lost a lot, Mister.

Edna has expressed a multitude of concerns, including despair, grief,
and confusion. Each of these dimensions could require extensive work.
However, based upon the severity of the concerns and Edna's potential
for increased agitation, the immediacy of a treatment approach is evident.
For the practitioner, the first question is where to begin.

In working with Edna, it is important to develop the intervention
from the five points previously outlined: knowing the person, emphasizing
safety and security, understanding connections, utilizing environmental
cues, and relying on a theory.

It is helpful to partialize, i.e., listen to Edna's concerns and then
develop them into areas that can be worked upon. Based on Edna's
concerns, the practitioner can work with her to develop two or three
problem areas or goals that can be explored.

It is also helpful to focus on the reality of the moment and answer
Edna's questions directly. Edna is an adult, and entitled to an adult
exchange. Because she may experience difficulty in expressing her feelings,
it is important to maintain the dignity of the interaction and to listen
closely for significant words and meanings.

It is important to talk openly with Edna about her concern about her
memory loss and the fact that she is experiencing episodes of confusion.
It helps to let her know that she is very important to many people, and that
her family is concerned about her. Admittedly, this part of the dialogue may
be difficult initially. It helps to refer to events from her earlier life,
the importance of her role in the family, and the reality that her present
behaviors are creating legitimate concerns.

Because Edna is experiencing late-stage Alzheimer's disease, words may need to be repeated in a low voice, and the use of a supportive touch may be required. Edna might ask the same questions over and over. She might dwell on the idea of going home, for example, or of not remembering her husband. It may be necessary to develop a phrase or standard response if this occurs, for example, "Edna, we know that you want to go home, but this is a safe place for you. Your family is concerned about your safety and you did say that it would be better for you to remain here."

If the issue is the loss of her husband, the response might be, "Edna, we know you are having difficulty with the loss of your husband. Who wouldn't? It is such a difficult time. But from what we hear from your family, you are a good woman going through a difficult time."

It may be helpful to spend time working with families or training support staff on the overarching themes and response techniques being developed. A consistent approach will increase the power and effectiveness of the intervention.

MENTAL RETARDATION AND ALZHEIMER'S DISEASE

Although information about the natural history of Alzheimer's disease among adults with mild and moderate mental retardation is sparse, indications are that the clinical progression is similar to that seen among adults without mental retardation. Most research has focused upon the association between Alzheimer's disease and Down's syndrome, the most common genetic disorder associated with mental retardation (Janicki et al., 1995). A person's intellectual level influences how he or she expresses loss and grief. It does not influence the fact that he or she feels the loss and suffers ensuing grief (Botsford & Force, 2000). Loss and grief are universal experiences and Alzheimer's disease is the greatest equalizer that we know.

Case Illustration

Tom is a 71-year-old man who has lived in a group home for the last 17 years. Prior to moving into this home, he lived in a state developmental center. Tom suffers from Alzheimer's disease, shows signs of depression, and benefits from anti-depressant medication. Recently, Tom was informed that his 93-year-old mother Lillian passed away. The staff at the group home is concerned about Tom's emotional state. He is withdrawn and refuses to eat.

It is not uncommon to find this type of grief reaction (increased evidence of depression) to the experience of loss. Individuals with Alzheimer's disease and mental retardation express grief in the same individualized and unique way as individuals with Alzheimer's without the presence of mental retardation. The treatment modality for individuals with mental retardation and Alzheimer's disease is similar to the approach utilized for individuals with Alzheimer's disease without the presence of mental retardation. The practitioner's treatment response should be drawn from a foundation of knowledge, caring, empathy, and understanding. Recommendations for therapeutic strategies appear in the treatment modalities section of this chapter.

FUTURE DIRECTIONS AND SUMMARY

Worldwide population profiles indicate that life expectancy is increasing. This change in longevity has implications for individuals with Alzheimer's disease, their family members, and those who provide services to them.

As people continue to experience an extension in lifespan, theoretical models and practice interventions that demonstrate an understanding of the intersection between age, disease, and emotion will be required. Students of medicine, social work, and psychology will need exposure to these specialized interventions early in their training. In addition, seasoned practitioners will need advance training in order to maintain their commitment to professional standards.

We have developed sophisticated names and terminology that allow us to take an emotional snapshot of people in distress. Our diagnostic perspectives provide us with the opportunity to categorize and identify diagnostic codes that begin to explain the experience of individuals in need. The irony of our ever-increasing sophistication in identifying and classifying mental disorders is that the words "loss" and "grief" are not found in the index section of the Diagnostic and Statistical Manual of Mental Disorders (DSM-IV TR, 2000). These words are buried within the lexicon of a psychiatric vocabulary. However, it is the loss and grief that provide the momentum for what is really happening. A true understanding of this dynamic will increase the sensitivity for all involved. ■

Lawrence T. Force, Ph.D., a gerontologist, is Professor of Psychology at Mount St. Mary College. For 25 years, he has worked in the field as a practitioner, teacher, program developer, and researcher. Dr. Force completed his graduate training in psychology at the New School for Social Research and he holds a doctorate in social welfare from the Rockefeller College at SUNY/Albany. He has published articles, book chapters, monographs, and technical reports that address topics of developmental models of aging, life-long disabilities, adult day services, Alzheimer's disease, end-of-life care, and family caregiving. He was sponsored as a Summer Institute Fellow at the National Institute on Aging (NIA) and the RAND Corporation, and he has presented his work at national and international conferences.

REFERENCES

Botsford, A.L., & Force, L.T. (2000). *End-of-life care: A guide for supporting older people with intellectual disabilities and their families.* Albany, New York: NYS ARC.

Doka, K. (1989). *Disenfranchised grief: Recognizing hidden sorrow.* Lexington, MA: Lexington Press.

Force, L.T. (2003). ACTION: *The voice of early-onset Alzheimer's disease.* Newburgh, New York: Mount Saint Mary College.

Janicki, M.P., Heller, T., Seltzer, G.B., & Hogg, J. (1996). Practice guidelines for the clinical assessment and care management of Alzheimer's disease
and other dementias among adults with intellectual disability. *Journal of Intellectual Disability Research, 40,* 374-382.

Piaget, J. (1972) Intellectual evolution from adolescence to adulthood. *Human Development, 15,* 1-12.

Reid, W.J. (1996). Task-centered social work. In F.J.Turner (Ed.), *Social work treatment* (pp. 617- 641). New York: Free Press.

Snowdon, D. (2001). *Aging with grace.* New York: Bantam Books.

■ CHAPTER 12 ■

Assessing Grief in Family Caregivers

Thomas M. Meuser, Samuel J. Marwit, and Sara Sanders

INTRODUCTION

Grief is a universal human experience. We all suffer personally significant losses and feel the anguish that follows. The universality of grief stems from the fact that human beings form close, intimate bonds with one another. When such bonds are broken, either by death, disease, or other circumstances of life, a process of grief necessarily follows (Bowlby, 1977). Grief is our innate adjustment process to loss and, when ignored or downplayed, can result in complications such as depression and other co-morbidities (Parkes, 1992; Worden, 2002).

Long recognized as part of the dementia caregiving experience (Rabins, 1984), grief is only now emerging as an important target for study, assessment, and therapeutic intervention (Boss, 1999; Doka, 2000; Liken & Collins, 1993; Lindgren, Connelly, & Gaspar, 1999; Meuser & Marwit, 2001; Marwit & Meuser, 2002; Walker & Pomeroy, 1996). Family caregivers witness robust, active loved ones change gradually over years into restricted, dependent shadows of their former selves. "The persona of the individual is so changed that others experience the loss of that person as he or she previously existed" (Doka, 2000, p. 478). Over the past ten years, numerous studies have examined the impact of this loss experience on caregivers (see Table 1).

TABLE 1: OTHER LITERATURE ON GRIEF IN DEMENTIA CAREGIVERS

Author(s)	Design	Caregiver Sample	Measurement
Almberg (2000)	Qualitative	N = 30, 21 females, 9 males; combination of spousal and adults children	Series of open-ended questions
Dubois (2002)	Qualitative	N = 61 38 females, 23 males, all respondents were daughters or sons	Series of open-ended questions
Collins, Liken, King, & Koki-nakis (1993)	Qualitative	N = 82, 57 spouses, 14 adult children, 11 other	Open-ended questions
Jones & Martin (1992)	Qualitative	N = 14, 9 females, 5 males; combination of spouses and adult children	Open-ended questions
Lindgren & Connely (1999)	Ex-post facto quantitative design	N = 33; 29 females, 4 males; combinations of spouses and daughters	Grief Experience Inventory (Sanders, et al., 1985); Family Caregiver Background Inventory (developed for study)
Loos & Bowd (1997)	Qualitative	N = 68, combination of spouses, adult children, and other relatives and friends	Open-ended question; written comments, letters, poems
Meuser & Marwit (2001)	Qualitative	N = 87, 67 females, 20 males; combination of spouses and adult children	Questionnaire; semi-structured focus group
Marwit & Meuser (2002)	Quantitative/ qualitative	N = 166, 135 females, 31 males; 83 spouses, 83 adult children	Caregiver grief items, Beck Depression Inventory, Anticipatory Grief Scale, Well-being Scale, Perceived Support Scale

Key findings

21 caregivers reported feelings of grief prior to death of care recipient; Grief was expressed in combination with pleasant memories; Grief varied based on the experiences of the caregivers

Findings demonstrated that ambiguous loss is a "process" involving multiple stages, not a single event for caregivers; Ambiguous loss was found to progress through a series of stages including 1. anticipatory loss, 2. progressive loss, and 3. acknowledged loss

Six themes related to grief and loss emerged: 1. Loss of familiarity and intimacy, 2. Loss of hope, 3. Grief before death, 4. Expectancy of death, 5. Post-death relief, and 6. Post-death reflection

Caregivers reported grief reactions, including crying and sadness; more common in caregivers whose loved ones did not recognize them, were less affectionate, and experienced difficulty communicating; many caregivers anticipated the death of their loved one. Post death findings were also identified.

Grief reactions were found to be part of the caregiving experience. Individuals who had higher levels of grief reported less emotional health. Grief reactions were not related to progression of care recipient's condition and did not differ between spousal or adult child caregivers. Levels of grief, except as measured by "guilt," remained stable throughout the caregiving experience. Grief was impacted by prior relationship closeness.

Four themes related to grief emerged from data: 1. Loss of social and recreational interaction, 2. Loss of control over life events, 3. Loss of well-being, and 4. Loss of occupation

Grief varied by caregiver type (spouse, adult child) and by stage of disease progression. Dimensions explored and analyzed include degree of emotion, quality of emotion, focus (self vs. other), anticipatory grief. Presented is a model useful for assessment and intervention.

Factor analysis resulted in a 50-item caregiver grief index containing three factors: personal sacrifice burden, heartfelt sadness and longing, worry and felt isolation. Relationship to standardized measures indicated that caregiver grief is a definable entity which overlaps with, yet is sufficiently dissimilar, from caregiver depression, stress, and burden.

(continued on next page)

TABLE 1: OTHER LITERATURE ON GRIEF IN DEMENTIA CAREGIVERS *(continued)*

Author(s)	Design	Caregiver Sample	Measurement
Morgan & Laing (1991)	Qualitative/ Descriptive	N = 9; gender not specified; all spouses	Series of open-ended questions
Ponder & Pomeroy (1996)	Quantitative, cross sectional	N = 100, 83 females, 17 males; 31 spouses, 53 adult children, 16 other relationship	Stages of Grief Inventory (authors of study); Grief Experience Inventory (Sanders, et al, 1985)
Rudd, Viney, & Preston (1999)	Quantitative, cross sectional	N = 60, 30 females, 30 males; 30 wives and 30 husbands	Grief measured through the combination of a variety of other scales for guilt, anxiety, hostility, and affect
Sanders & Corely (2003)	Qualitative	N = 253, 178 females, 71 males, 100 spouses, 112 adult children, 31 other relative, 10 unknown	Grief measured through one open ended question at end of survey
Sanders, Morano, & Corely (in press)	Qualitative	N = 71, all males; 43 husbands, 21 sons, 7 other relationships	Grief measured through one open ended question at end of survey
Walker & Pomeroy (1996)	Exploratory, cross sectional	N = 100, 83 women, 17 men, 31 spouses, 53 adult children, 16 other relationship	Grief Experience Inventory (Sanders, et al, 1986); Beck Depression Inventory (Beck, et al., 1961)
Walker, Pomeroy, McNeil, & Franklin (1994)	Descriptions of intervention techniques	N/A	N/A

Key findings

Four of nine spouses were in the "grief group." This group was characterized as having close friendships and relationships with spouses, which were jeopardized by disease process. As this group was "coming to terms" with the disease, they went through a grief process of accepting the diagnosis, adjusting to life with the disease, trying to normalize situation, preparing themselves for disease related changes, and beginning the process of letting go.

Intensity of grief changed at different stages of the disease. Majority of caregivers were in the "acceptance phase" of anticipatory grief; however, others experienced denial, over involvement, anger, and guilt. Intensity of feelings of grief was the highest in caregivers who exhibited the anticipatory grief symptoms of anger and guilt. On average, 7.23 anticipatory grief behaviors were exhibited.

Spousal caregivers of individuals in nursing homes experienced higher levels of anxiety, sadness, anger, and guilt than at-home caregivers. Similarly, wives experienced higher levels of anxiety, sadness, anger, and guilt than husbands.

Grief of caregivers was characterized by a sense of ambiguity, multiple losses, and feelings of losing control. Caregivers expressed a great deal of self-awareness about their grief. Caregivers who indicated that they were not grieving reported feeling relief, had increased faith in a spiritual being, or experienced conflict with the care recipient.

The themes associated with grief responses included: Grief turned into crisis, insight into the grieving journey, and a range of multiple losses with loss of communication and intimacy being the most prevalent answers. Even if the men did not report grief reactions, there were elements of loss within their statements.

No significant differences in GEI scores between caregiver responses and normative sample data; Significant positive correlation between grief scores and depression scores; Grief scores (as well as other control variables) accounted for 67% of variance in depression scores

Examined a variety of variables, such as social stigma, ambiguous loss, and multiple losses that impact the grieving process of caregivers. Authors argue that caregivers have different needs throughout the disease process, which will facilitate the grieving process: information, expression of emotions, communication, acceptance of new roles, and saying goodbye.

FAMILY CAREGIVERS, DEMENTIA, AND GRIEF

While bodily death may be the eventual endpoint, it is not necessarily the focus of grief and affective disturbance for this caregiver population. From our own research with caregivers (Marwit & Meuser, 2002; Meuser & Marwit, 2001) and the work of others (Gilhooly, Sweeting, Whittick, & McKee, 1994), we have learned that the progressive "psychosocial death" of persons with dementia (i.e., the inability to maintain meaningful interpersonal and emotional bonds with others) is far more challenging to caregivers' emotional health than is distant bodily death. From our perspective, the grief that dementia caregivers experience over the course of disease progression is true grief and relatively indistinguishable from post-death grief in personal impact and meaning.

The reality of grief in the face of dementia-related decline has tremendous face validity for family caregivers. They know the grief experience well, yearn to talk about it, and often choose to write about it (e.g., Peterson, in press; Haugse, 1999). Our experience in running caregiver focus groups (Meuser & Marwit, 2001) has taught us that these individuals do not just experience grief in anticipation of future death, but rather they experience tangible anguish in response to felt loss in the present. This is a subtle yet important distinction, and forms the foundation for our theoretical contention that pre-death grief is a true experience for family caregivers of individuals with dementia and, as such, is unique among those providing care for terminally ill persons (i.e., in contrast with caregivers of terminal disorder where psychosocial death does not precede physical death and where anticipatory grief may be a more relevant concept).

Pre-death grief in response to dementia is not socially sanctioned, however, and caregivers and those that support them may misattribute grief manifestations to other affective etiologies. This misattribution can disrupt emotional coping and healing when loss-related grief is the primary cause of felt distress. Sensitizing caregivers to the normal range of grief reactions should be a component of all supportive and therapeutic interventions in this population.

GRIEF AS A CAUSAL FACTOR IN CAREGIVER DISTRESS

Depression, burden, stress, and other related constructs have been studied extensively in the caregiver literature over the past three decades. It is generally accepted that the stresses of caregiving are associated with the emergence of emotional and physical health problems (Connell, Janevic, & Gallant, 2001; Gwyther, 1998; Pinquart & Sorensen, 2003). Given how progressive loss and consequent grief form such a strong undercurrent in the caregiving experience, we believe it is time to give grief its due as a distinct experiential construct along with the better-known depression-stress-burden constellation. To this end, we propose that grief, which is conceptualized as the caregiver's emotional, cognitive, and behavioral reactions to the recognition of personally significant loss, be considered as a causal factor contributing to many affective responses in family caregivers of persons with dementia.

Although all human beings are subject to grief, the construct remains a challenging one to study from a research perspective. The expression of grief is multiply determined and varies as a function of individual personality, culture, loss circumstance, and a number of other personal and social factors. Yet, at least in western culture, there are a number of reactions common enough to the grief response—sadness, pining, regret, guilt, anger—to be considered normative (Raphael, 1983; Worden, 2002). Despite a growing literature on the nature of grief and bereavement in general, it is interesting how little attention has been paid in the caregiver literature to this core experience. In fact, grief, when attended to at all in the caregiving literature, is generally subsumed under the construct of depression. Of 78 controlled intervention studies for dementia caregivers prior to 2002, for example, not a single study included grief as a primary intervention or outcome variable, whereas depression received frequent attention (Sorensen, Pinquart, & Duberstein, 2002). We would argue that to focus only on depression is to miss the larger context of loss and grief that defines most caregivers' daily experience. This viewpoint corresponds well with literature emphasizing the importance of a grief perspective for understanding the full range of affective responses to loss in general (Neimeyer & Hogan, 2001) and to loss from dementia specifically (Walker & Pomeroy, 1996).

FIGURE 1: A PROPOSED CAUSAL PATHWAY FOR GRIEF IN DEMENTIA CAREGIVING

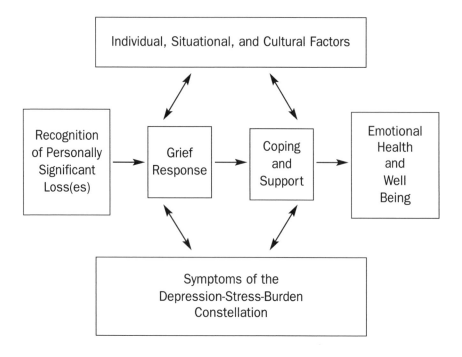

ROADMAP FOR ASSESSMENT AND INTERVENTION

A grief perspective can also provide a roadmap for assessment and supportive intervention. Figure 1 presents our emerging conceptualization of how grief may influence emotional health and well-being in dementia caregivers. It starts with the individual and his or her felt experience. By definition, grief occurs only in response to the recognition of personally significant loss (Rando, 2001). Factors associated with the individual, the loss situation, and cultural practices influence how grief is expressed. We further posit that causal influences run in both directions, from grief to the depression-stress-burden constellation and back. Caregivers with signs of clinical depression, for example, may respond to dementia-related losses based on qualitatively different personality and/or coping resources (or the influences of different instrumental/physical circumstances) in comparison to those showing more typical grief-related distress. In other words, normal grief may turn "pathological" based on the presence of certain individual difference variables (Meuser & Marwit, 2000; Meuser, Davies, & Marwit, 1995).

Understanding the interplay of the factors summarized in Figure 1 can be a challenge for those charged with offering supportive assistance. While many areas are potential targets for intervention, the only universal target in this conceptualization is grief itself. As a common and expected experience, grief can be readily discussed and normalized in the context of loss that is dementia. It is a place to meet, communicate, and gain leverage to attack the depression-stress-burden constellation, enhance coping, and promote well-being all at once.

For those in a position to offer coping-related support to dementia caregivers, it is important to understand how grief is manifested in this population, how to assess it, and what might be reasonable strategies for intervention. The rest of this chapter is devoted to these issues.

UNDERSTANDING AND ASSESSING CAREGIVER GRIEF

When it comes to grief, nonjudgmental listening and open discussion may be the best tools for discovering what a person is truly experiencing and for offering meaningful emotional support. Although grief is universal among human beings, the expression of grief can vary quite a bit. Groups of individuals sharing a similar loss experience (e.g., dementia caregiving) may have more in common in terms of grief than those experiencing other losses. It is important to know what is typical for a certain group before reaching out to offer support. Our grief model was developed with this objective in mind: build an awareness of the factors involved in the grief experiences of caregivers in order to apply this information to individual assessment and intervention.

Our model of caregiver grief is based on 32 hours of focus group interviews involving 87 current and former family caregivers. We interviewed adult child and spouse caregivers at each stage of dementia progression (mild, moderate, severe, post-death). We analyzed our data with assistance from a committee of dementia care specialists from various fields, including psychology, social work, and pastoral care. Questionnaire-derived quantitative data supplemented this effort (Marwit & Meuser, 2002; Meuser & Marwit, 2001). Our findings suggest that grief related to any loss situation can be understood in at least three ways:

- Intensity of grief-related distress or involvement;
- Reaction pattern; and
- Focus of loss.

Intensity refers to the degree to which an individual's psychological make-up is affected or otherwise disturbed by the loss experience. Depending upon individual characteristics and circumstances, intensity may be assessed as high, moderate, or low; appropriate, inordinately excessive, or unnecessarily repressed; normal or abnormal; warranting intervention or not. Pattern refers to the range of reactions (sadness, anger, guilt, etc.), their interplay, and their relative importance for the individual in question. Finally, focus of loss addresses the target(s) of the grief response. What aspects of the loss situation appear to drive the dominant symptoms of grief? Is the individual grieving a loss that is highly personal or internal in nature (e.g., targeted focus being loss of time with family or career), or a loss that is more external or relational in nature (e.g., targeted focus being loss of relationship)?

In the case of dementia caregivers, these three aspects of grief appear to change in group-specific ways as a function of caregiver type (spouse

TABLE 2: DEMENTIA OF THE ALZHEIMER'S TYPE— DESCRIPTION OF STAGES[1]

Ella has very mild Alzheimer's. To others she seems perfectly normal. She is a little more forgetful than others her age and this worries her. Ella functions well in her established routines, but sometimes needs help when handling new or complex problems. Persons at this stage need general support and encouragement, but little formalized care.

Ella has mild Alzheimer's. She generally looks and acts normal. She has difficulty remembering conversations and repeats herself frequently. Her son supervises her checkbook and helps to arrange home repairs, but otherwise she manages reasonably well in her established routines. She uses a weekly pillbox to remember her medications and relies on her son to take her to appointments. She still tends her garden and attends church, but activities involving new learning are a real challenge for her.

Ella has moderate Alzheimer's. Although her social graces remain intact, others definitely notice a problem when they interact with her for more than a few minutes. She sometimes forgets to eat and she has difficulty recalling her address and phone number. She cannot take care of her house alone and her son thinks she should move to a supervised setting. He must now check on his mother multiple times per day and has hired an in-home aid for the evenings.

Ella now has severe Alzheimer's. She relies on others for all her care including dressing and bathing. She sometimes has urine accidents. Her memory of her own life is mostly a blur. Ella requires more care than her son can provide, so she now resides in a nursing home. She knows her son as a familiar person when he visits, but his name and identity are lost to her memory.

---

[1]Based on the Clinical Dementia Rating (Morris, 1993).

versus adult-child) and dementia stage (see Table 2). For example, adult children caring for parents with dementia appear to experience peak intensity of grief-related distress, both qualitatively and quantitatively, at the moderate stage of impairment when care demands and personal losses are mounting. This peak may appear more pronounced for women because of their tendency to be more expressive of emotion. The reaction pattern appears to favor the emergence of anger. The focus of loss for adult children at this point is primarily their own personal/individual losses (loss of time, career, family, etc.) rather than loss of the parent per se. In contrast, spouse caregivers at the same moderate stage display a lower intensity of grief, accepting their spousal obligations with grace and compassion. The predominant feelings in the grief pattern are those of concern and caring, and the focus of grief is on the loss of shared activities. More complete descriptions of the caregiver grief response as a function of caregiver type and stage of disease are found in Meuser and Marwit (2001).

Development of Caregiver Grief Inventory

The grief experiences reported by our focus group participants were used to develop the Marwit-Meuser Caregiver Grief Inventory. This is a 50-item questionnaire to assess caregiver grief. The details of the derivation of this instrument can be found in Marwit and Meuser (2002). Psychometrically, our caregiver grief inventory divides into three components, which we believe are useful for assessment and intervention:

- *Personal sacrifice burden,* which addresses what the caregiver must give up to function in the caregiving role;

- *Heartfelt sadness and longing,* which refers to personal sadness and separation pain traditionally understood as grief in western culture; and

- *Worry and felt isolation,* which represents a more pervasive depression-like sense of uncertainty and withdrawal from others.

We believe that identifying the intensity, pattern, and focus of these three components is important for determining intervention approach (discussed in more detail later). A 16-item short form of the Marwit-Meuser Caregiver Grief Inventory has also been developed. Readers are welcome to copy and distribute this short form for use in assessment and support of family caregivers and others.

MARWIT-MEUSER CAREGIVER GRIEF INVENTORY (SHORT FORM)

Instructions: This inventory is designed to measure the grief experience of family caregivers of persons living with a progressive dementia, such as Alzheimer's disease. Read each statement to the right carefully, then decide how much you agree or disagree. Circle the number 1-5 that reflects your response (1 = Strongly Disagree, 5 = Strongly Agree).

Self-Scoring Procedure: Add the numbers you circled to derive the following sub-scale and total grief scores. Use the letters to the right of each score to guide you as indicated below.

Personal Sacrifice Burden *(A Items)*   =   _____ (High > 25)
(6 Items, M = 20.2, SD = 5.3, Alpha = .83)

Heartfelt Sadness & Longing *(B Items)*   =   _____ (High > 25)
(6 Items, M = 20.2, SD = 5.0, Alpha = .80)

Worry & Felt Isolation *(C Items)*   =   _____ (High > 23)
(6 Items, M = 16.6, SD = 5.2, Alpha = .80)

Total Grief Level (Sum A + B + C)   =   _____ (High > 70)
(18 Items, M = 57, SD = 12.9, Alpha = .90)

Plot your scores using the grid to below. Make an "X" nearest to your numeric score for each sub-scale heading. Connect the X's. This is your grief profile. Discuss this with your support group leader or counselor.

MM CGI-SF Personal Grief Profile

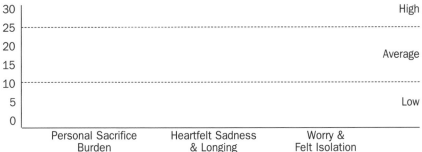

What do these scores mean?

Scores in the top area are one standard deviation (SD) higher than average based on responses of other family caregivers (n = 292). High scores may indicate a need for formal intervention or support assistance to enhance coping. Low scores (one SD below the mean) may indicate denial or a downplaying of distress. Low scores may also indicate positive adaptation if the individual is not showing other signs of suppressed grief or psychological disturbance. Average scores in the center indicate common reactions. These are general guides for discussion and support only— more research is needed on specific interpretation issues.

MARWIT-MEUSER CAREGIVER GRIEF INVENTORY (SHORT FORM)

1 = Strongly Disagree   //   2 = Disagree
3 = Somewhat Agree   //   4 = Agree   //   5 = Strongly Agree

1	I've had to give up a great deal to be a caregiver.	1	2	3	4	5	A
2	I feel I am losing my freedom.	1	2	3	4	5	A
3	I have nobody to communicate with.	1	2	3	4	5	C
4	I have this empty, sick feeling knowing that my loved one is "gone".	1	2	3	4	5	B
5	I spend a lot of time worrying about the bad things to come.	1	2	3	4	5	C
6	Dementia is like a double loss...I've lost the closeness with my loved one and connectedness with my family.	1	2	3	4	5	C
7	My friends simply don't understand what I'm going through.	1	2	3	4	5	C
8	I long for what was, what we had and shared in the past.	1	2	3	4	5	B
9	I could deal with other serious disabilities better than with this.	1	2	3	4	5	B
10	I will be tied up with this for who knows how long.	1	2	3	4	5	A
11	It hurts to put her/him to bed at night and realize that she/he is "gone"	1	2	3	4	5	B
12	I feel very sad about what this disease has done.	1	2	3	4	5	B
13	I lay awake most nights worrying about what's happening and how I'll manage tomorrow.	1	2	3	4	5	C
14	The people closest to me do not understand what I'm going through.	1	2	3	4	5	C
15	I've lost other people close to me, but the losses I'm experiencing now are much more troubling.	1	2	3	4	5	B
16	Independence is what I've lost...I don't have the freedom to go and do what I want.	1	2	3	4	5	A
17	I wish I had an hour or two to myself each day to pursue personal interests.	1	2	3	4	5	A
18	I'm stuck in this caregiving world and there's nothing I can do about it.	1	2	3	4	5	A

MM-CGI Short Form to be published as an appendix in this chapter in early 2004:

Meuser, T.M., Marwit, S.J., & Sanders, S. (2002). Grief in Dementia Caregivers: A Model for Assessment and Intervention. *In Living with Grief: Alzheimer's Disease.* Kenneth Doka (Ed.). Hospice Foundation of America.

GRIEF BY DEMENTIA STAGE

The following descriptions address normative issues in grieving for adult child and spousal caregivers at each stage of dementia progression. These descriptions are not intended to be exhaustive or otherwise proscriptive. They do, however, have an empirical base (Meuser & Marwit, 2001). Normal grief reactions can vary widely among individuals. These descriptions are intended to sensitize the reader to potential differences in grief expression and support needs among caregiver subgroups.

Mild Dementia

Adult children caring for a parent in the mild stage of dementia tend to have low grief intensity and few prominent manifestations of grief. Their loss focus is mainly on the personal sacrifices of caregiving (i.e., an "own" focus rather than an "other" focus). The parent shows obvious impairment in memory and higher order thinking skills, but social graces, personality, and personal interests remain largely intact. Caregiving at this stage involves assisting with instrumental tasks of living (e.g., help in tracking appointments, reminders to take medication, assistance in paying bills), while continuing to enjoy relative normalcy in the child-parent relationship. In talking with adult children at this stage, we found them to be intellectualized, task-oriented, and emotionally avoidant. Their emphasis was primarily on the present, handling immediate care needs, and helping the parent to remain as independent and competent as possible. Grief is present, but subtle. Scores on the caregiver grief inventory's subscales are likely to be low to moderate at this stage.

For spouse caregivers at the mild stage, grief intensity is also likely to be low, but tangible sadness may be evident upon questioning. The spouse caregivers we interviewed were quite open about their feelings and acknowledged undergoing an early grief process. Focus of loss at this stage is mainly on the patient spouse (i.e., competencies that the patient spouse is losing) and changes in shared activity and relationship (i.e., a predominantly "other" focus). Those we interviewed reported a strong sense of mutual determination and togetherness in facing dementia. Not nearly as avoidant as the adult child caregivers, these spousal caregivers spoke openly about the dementia diagnosis, its impact on their daily lives, the various losses involved, and the likelihood of future decline. Dementia is not viewed as a good thing, but its onset is accepted as an eventuality of older age and as something to be dealt with head on. On our caregiver grief inventory, scores on the *personal sacrifice burden* and *worry and felt isolation* subscales are likely to be low to moderate, whereas the *heartfelt sadness and longing* score may be somewhat higher.

Moderate Dementia

Adult children providing care at the moderate stage of dementia demonstrate high grief intensity and a number of dominant reactions, often including anger, guilt, and resentment. Focus of loss is still primarily on the self—what the caregiver him/herself has given up. The defensive attitude witnessed at the mild stage now gives way to a powerful recognition of personal loss and the harsh reality of parental decline. The true impact of dementia can no longer be avoided as care demands shift from discrete tasks to a round-the-clock exercise. Emotions that were reasonably well-contained in the mild stage now erupt in raw bouts of feeling. Escapist thoughts are common, and increasing amounts of energy are focused on just making it through the day. Although some established parent-child patterns continue, a clear shift in roles now places the child in a decision-making posture over the parent. Losses are many, and adult child caregivers now readily acknowledge that grief is part of their daily experience. On the caregiver grief inventory, scores are expected to be moderate to high on all dimensions.

For spouse caregivers at the moderate stage of dementia, grief intensity is growing, but still reasonably contained. Dominant reactions include compassion, frustration (but not anger or resentment per se), sadness, and a loving redefinition of the relationship (i.e., as the caregiver takes on increasing responsibility for the welfare of the patient spouse and their partnership). Focus of loss remains on the patient spouse and the impact of dementia on shared activities, but caregiver-related sacrifices are starting to be a source of upset. The spouse caregivers we interviewed expressed determination to provide high quality care and maintain as many established patterns of relating as possible. They resisted discussion of past and future changes, possibly for self-protective reasons, and instead emphasized the value of finding meaning and encouragement from small successes in the present. If anger was expressed, it was more likely to be directed at the lack of involvement from adult children as collaborative caregivers. Caregiver grief inventory scores for this group are likely to be moderate to high on the *personal sacrifice burden* and *heartfelt sadness and longing* subscales, less so on the *worry and felt isolation* subscale.

Severe Dementia

For adult child caregivers at this stage, grief intensity remains high. The grief pattern, however, shifts from dominant anger and frustration to a more pervasive sense of sadness, regret, and resignation. Focus of loss shifts from individual sacrifices to the profound losses of the parent and the losses' impact on the parent-child relationship. With nursing home placement, adult children appear to gain a new perspective on what is lost and experience a true "grief of the soul." A predominant theme is the final and absolute loss of the parent as a parent. One gets the sense that this is not loss in the making, but loss now finalized. Those we interviewed spoke about "defining moments" and "turning points" in their grief as being "additive" in the sense that each experienced loss compounds all previous losses.

Grief now appears associated with lost opportunities (primarily relational) and with regrets over not having maximized experiences while the parent was psychosocially "alive." Some spoke of an appreciation for the parent emerging too late for meaningful interaction. Yet, for others, nursing home placement brought opportunities for new ways of relating and finding meaning in preparing for bodily death.

Scores on the *heartfelt sadness and longing* subscale of our caregiver grief inventory are expected to remain high at this stage, whereas *personal sacrifice burden* and *worry and felt isolation* and scores may decline somewhat due to lifted burden and new opportunities for social interaction outside of the caregiving role.

For spouse caregivers at the severe stage, grief intensity is high and at a peak. Dominant reactions include sadness, uncertainty, a pervasive aloneness, and general emptiness. Focus of loss is now very much on changes for the individual caregiver him/herself. This is a significant focus change.

Although placement has reduced the physical burdens of providing care, it symbolizes for many an end to married life and this brings new emotional struggles. Visits to the nursing home may bring comfort at times, but there's a larger sense that the marital relationship has ended and a new relationship has taken its place. The togetherness of the past has given way to an uneasy individuality for the caregiver.

Unlike adult children at this stage, spouse caregivers appear less interested in trying to "figure out" or otherwise find meaning in what has happened. They are simply tired and wanting of relief, but they do not see spousal death as the ultimate solution to their problems. There is an expectation that new experiences of grief are coming, especially as implications of the lost marital relationship are realized. The scores on our caregiver grief inventory are likely to be moderate to high in all areas, with a potential peak on the *worry and felt isolation* subscale.

STEPS IN SUPPORTIVE INTERVENTION

Intervention research for caregiver grief is still in its infancy. The literature that does exist addresses intervention for post-death grief. Regarding this literature, it is fair to say that we have learned much about the basic parameters of the grief process (Marwit, 1996; Raphael, 1983; Stroebe, Hansson, Stroebe, & Schut; 2001; and dozens of other excellent publications); the theoretical underpinnings of grief intervention (e.g., *Meaning Reconstruction Theory*, Neimeyer, 2001; *Dual Process Theory*, Stroebe & Schut, 2001; *Worden's Tasks of Mourning*, Worden, 2002); and informal rituals and formal intervention strategies to lessen emotional distress and improve well-being in terms of both clinical and empirical outcomes (Piper, McCallum, Hassan & Azim, 1992; Worden, 2002). However, it remains to be seen whether post-death grief research provides workable models for the shifting grief processes that result from the pre-death losses facing dementia caregivers. Considerable research is needed to further an understanding of the tasks and rituals beneficial for addressing the grief of specific caregiver types at specific stages of dementia progression. Unlike death-related grief, which begins at a single point in time, dementia caregiver grief begins with living circumstances and changes over multiple points in time.

Differentiating post-death grief from the grief that emerges in response to dementia-related losses presents a challenge for social scientists and raises a number of interesting questions. For example, is the early denial experienced by mild stage dementia caregivers equivalent to the early stages of denial often witnessed in death-related grief? Is the nature of severed or continuing bonds the same when the grief object is an individual who is physically alive but psychosocially dead or dying versus one who has already biologically died? Are there advantages or disadvantages to encouraging a dementia caregiver to accept the reality of a pending loss when that final loss may be seven to ten years away? These are just some of the questions that arise when thinking about applying the models of death-related grief to dementia-related grief. Still, the death-related grief literature provides us with a place to start.

In the infancy of our understanding, we do believe that the most important thing that professional and lay counselors can provide to dementia caregivers is normalization of the grief experience. Losses are mounting and caregivers need to know that it is OK to feel sad, angry, guilty, etc., in response. Identifying commonalities in the caregiving experience provides a basis for discussing grief reactions at their appropriate time. Our model of caregiver grief suggests entry points for grief work in the caregiving career. For example, we now know that the typical adult child caregiver is likely to resist loss and grief-related discussion at the mild stage of dementia, yet may welcome it at the moderate stage when feelings are raw and difficult to manage. Similarly, the model demonstrates that adult children often grieve more for personal life changes and sacrifices in the mild to moderate stages, whereas the opposite seems true for spouse caregivers who are much more concerned with changes in the marital relationship. To effectively normalize the grief experience, it is important to know something about caregiver type and dementia stage differences.

We therefore believe that our model of caregiver grief and the resulting scale can be helpful for individualized assessment. The Marwit-Meuser Caregiver Grief Inventory (long and short versions) can provide a basis for assessment in individuals showing some awareness of loss and a willingness to reach out for help. Take, for example, the following hypothetical case example:

Mary is a 76-year-old retired elementary school teacher. She and her husband, John, have two adult children who live in other states and six grandchildren. Mary and John live in a two-bedroom house in a quiet residential community near a major city and they are financially secure. John was diagnosed with Alzheimer's disease six years ago and is in the moderate stage in terms of cognitive and functional impairment. He can still dress, bathe, and feed himself with supervision, and his social behavior is appropriate. He can also follow simple one-step commands and read simple instructions that Mary leaves for him, but his interests are now very restricted and he needs 24-hour supervision for safety. Mary provides 90% of his care, relying on friends from church and occasional visits and telephone consultations with her children for the rest. All household tasks, including lawn care, are now on her shoulders, and she's often tired and irritable. The retirement of travel and visits with grandkids that she and John had planned will never be. She loves John and tries her best to care for him, but the demands are becoming too much. She doesn't want to leave her home and cannot afford in-home help, so nursing home placement will soon become necessary. Her children insist that "Dad isn't that far gone yet" and Mary feels conflicted about what to do. She recently asked her primary care physician for medication "to help me feel and sleep better."

Although hypothetical, this case example includes many elements that would be familiar to spousal caregivers. The word "grief" does not appear, and this was intentional on our part. From our experience, family caregivers do not reach out for grief-related support when first asking for help. Mary is clearly becoming stressed out, and she knows it. She has asked her physician for medication to help her manage better. Mary may be depressed. There are also indicators in her story of significant personal losses, including loss of lifelong patterns of relating with her husband, lost dreams for a retirement of travel and visits with grandkids, and conflict with her children. Mary is doing her best to care for John, mainly alone, and the harsh reality is that her efforts are no longer succeeding. His needs will soon surpass her ability to provide effective care. She is at risk for negative physical and emotional outcomes, as is he.

Mary's request for help from her physician is an excellent opening for grief-related assessment and intervention. Normalizing the grief experience in this case would not be difficult; Mary is facing a number of significant and impending losses which are shared by other caregivers. Clinical depression is a possibility and we agree that medication may be worth a try. She also needs significant emotional support and opportunities to process what is happening to her. This is where grief counseling from someone familiar with Alzheimer's disease and caregiving would be beneficial.

Let's suppose that Mary's physician responded to her request for medication by assessing her mood, coping resources, and support needs. Her physician decided to prescribe an anti-depressant, but also included a referral to the Alzheimer's Association for supportive counseling. Mary called and was referred to a lay counselor, June, a former caregiver herself, for assistance. June arranged for John to attend an adult daycare center for the day with respite funds available through the Association and met with Mary alone in her home. She administered our caregiver grief inventory as part of this interview. Mary scored at the high end of the average range on all subscales, indicating significant but not necessarily unusual distress. June reviewed these scores with Mary, and this precipitated a lengthy discussion of the sadness and loneliness Mary has experienced in recent months. Mary felt safe enough to cry and express feelings that she had bottled up for some time.

Let's also assume that Mary's subscale scores on the caregiver grief inventory are typical of spouses confronted with a moderately demented husband or wife (i.e., moderately elevated scores on the *personal sacrifice burden* and *heartfelt sadness and longing* subscales, yet lower scores on *worry and felt isolation*. This would instruct June (the individual offering support in this case) to focus her interview and intervention targets on current, meaningful, and case-specific areas. Exploration of the intensity of *personal sacrifice burden* might lead to permanent arrangements for John to attend adult daycare, thereby giving Mary much needed respite. It might also involve strategizing to see who else might provide caregiving help. Exploration of the elements contributing to *heartfelt sadness and longing* might lead to a recommendation for professional grief counseling. If the pattern were different, with *worry and felt isolation* being high, there might be recommendations for support group attendance or other interpersonal activity, but given the relatively low score, this might not be a target here. Reassessment with the caregiver grief inventory in the future may reveal differential needs for intervention based on score profile. This is how we see the Marwit-Meuser Caregiver Grief Inventory being used.

SUMMARY AND FUTURE DIRECTIONS

The literature on caregiver grief and intervention strategies is sparse, but growing. In this chapter, we have tried to sensitize the would-be counselor (professional and lay) to the importance of grief-related assessment and supportive intervention for family caregivers of persons with progressive dementia. The Marwit-Meuser Caregiver Grief Inventory is a tool to facilitate this process. How this tool may be understood and applied is still an open question. More research is needed on grief and associated inter-vention strategies based on age, gender, caregiver type (e.g., when other relatives or friends play this role), and stage of dementia. We intend to pursue work in these areas and invite others to do the same. ▪

Thomas M. Meuser is Clinical Psychologist and Research Assistant Professor of Neurology at Washington University School of Medicine in St. Louis. He serves as a research investigator and Director of Education and Rural Outreach for the Washington University Alzheimer's Disease Research Center, one of 30 centers funded through the Alzheimer's Disease Centers Program, National Institute on Aging. Dr. Meuser earned his bachelors degree in psychology in 1986 from the College of the Holy Cross in Worcester, Massachusetts, and his Ph.D. in clinical psychology in 1996 from the University of Missouri–St. Louis. His research interests include grief, coping and communication issues in dementia caregiving, educational program evaluation, and psychotherapeutic intervention. Dr. Meuser has received grant funding from the Alzheimer's Association, the National Institute on Aging, and the State of Missouri's Alzheimer's Disease and Related Disorders Research Program.

Samuel J. Marwit received his Ph.D. from the State University of New York at Buffalo in 1968. He is currently Professor of Psychology at the University of Missouri–St. Louis where he supervises bereavement-related research and teaches graduate and undergraduate courses in end-of-life issues. He is a diplomate in clinical psychology and a fellow in the Academy of Clinical Psychology; American Board of Professional Psychology (ABPP). He presently serves on the editorial boards of Death Studies and Omega: Journal of Death and Dying.

Sara Sanders is an assistant professor at the University of Iowa. She obtained her Master of Social Work degree from the George Warren Brown School of Social Work at Washington University in 1995 and her Ph.D. from the University of Maryland in 2002. Her research interests pertain to grief and loss reactions in caregivers of individuals with Alzheimer's disease, male caregiver issues, and the impact of client suicide on social workers. Dr. Sanders has worked as a clinical social worker in hospice settings and with Alzheimer's patients and their families.

REFERENCES

Almberg, B.E. (2000). Caregivers of relatives with dementia: Experiences encompassing social support and bereavement. *Aging and Mental Health, 4*, 82.

Beck, A.T., Ward, C. H., Mendelson, M., Mock, J., & Erbaugh, J. (1961). An inventory for measuring depression. *Archives of General Psychiatry, 4*, 561-571.

Bass, D.M., & Bowman, K. (1990). The transition from caregiving to bereavement: The relationship of care-related strain and adjustment to death. *The Gerontologist, 30*, 35-42.

Bass, D.M., Bowman, K., & Noelker, L.S. (1991). The influence of caregiving and bereavement support on adjusting to an older relative's death. *The Gerontologist, 31*, 32-46.

Blieszner, R., & Shifflett, P.A. (1999). The effects of Alzheimer's disease on close relationships between patients and caregivers. *Family Relations, 39*, 57-63.

Bodnar, J.C., & Kiecolt-Glaser, J.K. (1994). Caregiver depression after bereavement: Chronic stress isn't over when it's over. *Psychology and Aging, 3,* 372-380.

Boss, P. (1999). *Ambiguous loss: Learning to live with unresolved grief.* Cambridge, MA: Harvard University Press.

Bowlby, J. (1977). The making and breaking of affectional bonds, I & II. *British Journal of Psychiatry, 130,* 201-210; 421-431.

Burke, M.L., & Eakes, G.G. (1999). Milestones of chronic sorrow: Perspectives of chronically ill and bereaved personals and family caregivers. *Journal of Family Nursing, 5,* 374-389.

Collins, C., Liken, M., King, S., & Kokinakis, C. (1993). Loss and grief among family caregivers of relatives with dementia. *Qualitative Health Research, 3,* 236-253.

Connell, C.M., Janevic, M.R., & Gallant, M.P. (2001). The costs of caring: Impact of dementia on family caregivers. *Journal of Geriatric Psychiatry & Neurology, 14(4),* 179-187.

Davies, H., Priddy, J.M., & Tinklenberg, J.R. (1986). Support groups for male caregivers of Alzheimer's patients. *Clinical Gerontology, 5,* 385-395.

Doka, K.J. (2000). Mourning psychosocial loss: Anticipatory mourning in Alzheimer's, ALS, and irreversible coma. In T.A. Rando (Ed.), *Clinical dimensions of anticipatory mourning: Theory, and practice in working with the dying, their loved ones, and their caregivers* (pp. 477-492). Champaign, IL: Research Press.

Dubois, S.L. (2002). Understanding ambiguous loss in the context of dementia care: Adult children's perspectives. *Journal of Gerontological Social Work, 37,* 93.

Gilhooly, M.L.M., Sweeting, H.N., Whittick, J.E., & McKee, K. (1994). Family care of the dementing elderly. *International Review of Psychiatry, 6,* 29-40.

Gilliland, G., & Fleming, S. (1998). A comparison of spousal anticipatory grief and conventional grief. *Death Studies, 22,* 541-570.

Gwyther, L.P. (1998). Social issues of the Alzheimer's patient and family. *American Journal of Medicine, 104(4A),* 17S-21S.

Haugse, J.E. (1999). *Heavy snow—My father's disappearance into Alzheimer's.* Health Communications; Illustrated edition.

Jones, P.S., & Martin, I.M. (1992). The experience of bereavement in caregivers of family members with Alzheimer's disease. *Image: Journal of Nursing Scholarship, 24,* 172-176.

Liken, M.A., & Collins, C.E. (1993). Grieving: Facilitating the process for dementia caregivers. *Journal of Psychosocial Nursing & Mental Health Services, 1,* 21-26.

Lindgren, C.L., Connelly, C.T., & Gaspar, H.L. (1999). Grief in spouse and children caregivers of dementia patients. *Western Journal of Nursing Research, 21(4),* 521-537.

Loos, C., & Bowd, A. (1997). Caregivers of persons with Alzheimer's disease: Some neglected implications of the experience of personal loss and grief. *Death Studies, 21,* 501-515.

Mace, N.I., & Rabins, P.V. (1981). *The 36-hour day.* Baltimore, MD: The Johns Hopkins University Press.

Marwit, S. (1996). Reliability of diagnosing complicated grief: A preliminary investigation. *Journal of Consulting & Clinical Psychology, 64(3),* 563-568.

Marwit, S.J., & Meuser, T.M. (2002). Development & initial validation of an inventory to measure grief in caregivers of persons with Alzheimer's disease. *The Gerontologist, 42(6),* 51-65.

Maxwell, J.A. (1996). *Qualitative research design: An interactive approach.* Thousand Oaks, CA: Sage Publications.

Meuser, T. M., & Marwit, S. J. (2001). A comprehensive, stage-sensitive model of grief in dementia caregiving. *The Gerontologist, 41(5),* 658-670.

Meuser, T.M., & Marwit, S.J. (2000). An integrative model of personality, coping & appraisal for the prediction of grief involvement in adults. *OMEGA: Journal of Death & Dying, 40(2),* 375-393.

Meuser, T.M., Davies, R.M., & Marwit, S.J. (1995). Personality and conjugal bereavement in older widow(er)s. *OMEGA: Journal of Death & Dying, 30(3),* 223-235.

Morgan, D.G., & Laing, G.P. (1991). The diagnosis of Alzheimer's disease: Spouse's perspective. *Qualitative Health Research, 1,* 370.

Morris, J.C. (1993). The Clinical Dementia Rating (CDR): Current version and scoring rules. *Neurology, 43(11),* 2412.

Neimeyer, R.A., & Hogan, N. (2001). Quantitative or qualitative? Measurement issues in the study of bereavement. In Margaret S. Stroebe, Robert O. Hansson, Wolfgang Stroebe, & Henk Schut (Eds.), *Handbook of bereavement research: Consequences, coping, and care* (pp. 89-118). Washington, DC: American Psychological Association.

Neimeyer, R.A. (2000). *Meaning reconstruction & the experience of loss.* Washington, DC: American Psychological Association.

Padgett, D. (1998). *Qualitative methods in social work research.* Thousand Oaks, CA: Sage Publications.

Parkes, C.M. (1992). Bereavement and mental health in the elderly. *Reviews in Clinical Gerontology, 2,* 45-51.

Peterson, B. (in press). *Voices of Alzheimer's.* New York, NY: Perseus/DaCapo Publishers.

Pinquart, M., & Sorensen, S. (2003). Differences between caregivers and non-caregivers in psychological health and physical health: A meta-analysis. *Psychology and Aging, 18(2),* 250-267.

Piper, W.E., McCallum, M., & Azim, H.F.A. (1992). *Adaptation to loss through short-term group psychotherapy.* NY: Guilford Press.

Ponder, R.J., & Pomeroy, E.C. (1996). The grief of caregivers: How pervasive is it? *Journal of Gerontological Social Work, 27,* 3-21.

Rabins P.V. (1984). Management of dementia in the family context. *Psychosomatics, 25(5),* 369-71; 374-5.

Rando, T.A. (2000). The six dimensions of anticipatory mourning. In T.A. Rando (Ed.), *Clinical dimensions of anticipatory mourning: Theory, and practice in working with the dying, their loved ones, and their caregivers* (pp. 51-101). Champaign, IL: Research Press.

Raphael, B. (1983). *The anatomy of bereavement.* New York: Basic Books.

Rudd, M.G., Viney, L.L., & Preston, C.A. (1999). The grief experienced by spousal caregivers of dementia patients: The role of place of care of patient and gender of caregiver. *International Journal of Aging and Human Development, 48,* 217-240.

Sanders, S., & Corely, C.S. (2003). Are they grieving? A qualitative analysis examining grief in caregivers of individuals with Alzheimer's disease. *Social Work in Health Care, 37,* 35-53.

Sanders, S., Morano, C., & Corely, C.S. (2002). The expression of loss and grief among male caregivers of individuals with Alzheimer's disease. *Journal of Gerontological Social Work, 39*, 3-18.

Sorensen, S., Pinquart, M., & Duberstein, P. (2002). How effective are interventions with caregivers? An updated meta-analysis. *The Gerontologist, 42(3)*, 356-372.

Stolley, J.M., Buckwalter, K.C., & Koenig, H.G. (1999). Prayer and religious coping for caregivers of persons with Alzheimer's disease and related disorders. *American Journal of Alzheimer's Disease, 14*, 181-191.

Stroebe, M.S., & Schut, H. (2001). Models of coping with bereavement: A review. In Margaret S. Stroebe, Robert O. Hansson, Wolfgang Stroebe, & Henk Schut (Eds.), *Handbook of bereavement research: Consequences, coping, and care* (pp. 89-118). Washington, DC: American Psychological Association.

Stroebe, M.S., Hansson, R.O., Stroebe, W., & Schut, H. (Eds.). (2001). *Handbook of bereavement research: Consequences, coping, and care.* Washington, DC: American Psychological Association.

Walker, R. J., & Pomeroy, E.C. (1996). Depression or grief? The experience of caregivers of people with dementia. *Health and Social Work, 96*, 247-254.

Walker, R.J., Pomeroy, E.C., McNeil, J.S., & Franklin, C. (1994). Anticipatory grief and Alzheimer's disease: Strategies for interventions. *Journal of Gerontological Social Work, 22*, 21-39.

Wasow, M., & Coons, D. (1987). Widows and widowers of Alzheimer's victims. Their survival after spouse death. *Journal of Independent Social Work, 2(2)*, 21-32.

Whitlatch, A.M., Meddaugh, D.I., & Langhout, K.J. (1992). Religiosity among Alzheimer's disease caregivers. *The American Journal of Alzheimer's Disease and Related Disorders and Research, 7*, 11-20.

Williams, C., & Moretta, B. (1997). Systematic understanding of loss and grief related to Alzheimer's disease. In K.J. Doka (Ed.), *Living with grief: When illness is prolonged.* Washington, DC: Hospice Foundation of America.

Worden, J.W. (2002). *Grief counseling & grief therapy: A handbook for the mental health practitioner.* New York: Springer Publisher.

■ CHAPTER 13 ■

Styles and Strategies of Caregiving Spouses

Mary A. Corcoran

INTRODUCTION

Despite all that is known about caregiving for individuals with dementia, the actual processes by which caregivers conceptualize and enact their role remain poorly described. Yet there are many indicators that a range of culturally influenced thinking and action processes exist. Caregiving has been described as a cultural activity that is both defined and carried out according to shared beliefs and values of the caregiver and his or her family network (Albert, 1990; Able, 1991; Lyman, 1993).

Ethnic and cultural differences in caregiving are well documented—one example being the tendency for black caregivers to use quasi-kin networks for care provision while white caregivers may purchase help or rely on spouses or adult children (McCann et al., 2000; Haley et al., in press). Gender roles also appear to play a part in how caregiving is approached and experienced, as well as in the consequences reported by men and women who provide informal care in the home (Corcoran, 1992; Kramer & Thompson, 2002). These culturally related trends suggest underlying patterns in how care is defined and implemented.

This chapter will describe thinking and action processes, or caregiving styles, of 68 spouses who provide in-home care to a husband or wife with Alzheimer's disease. Describing caregiving styles can be useful in a number of ways. For one, it can assist caregivers and service providers in assessing the caregiver's style, which can lead to more structured, effective, and meaningful intervention strategies.

WHAT IS A CAREGIVING STYLE?

A caregiving style is a pattern in the thinking processes and actions of caregivers (Corcoran, 2000). The concept of style in other venues is familiar. Most of us intuitively understand the notion of personality, coping, fashion, and parenting styles. Caregiving depends on many different styles, such as coping and personality, but it may be most similar to parenting styles in which decisions are made about the well-being of another person. One example of a stylistic difference: a caregiver who is largely focused on the physical aspects of care may act to address the nutrition, exercise, and medical needs of the care recipient. In contrast, a caregiver who focuses on the emotional aspects of care may prioritize the quality and level of activities and psychosocial well-being of the care recipient.

The information about caregiving styles presented in this chapter is taken from the Caregiving Style study (NIA R29-AG13019) conducted by Corcoran and Gitlin. This five-year, qualitative study involved 68 spouses who provided care to a husband or wife with dementia.

CAREGIVER BELIEFS

Caregiving requires a person to define the nature and symptoms of the health condition(s) involved in a particular care situation. In the Caregiving Styles study, spouses talked about dementia as being primarily a brain disease and many of them claimed that the symptoms of the disease could be at least partially controlled by the care recipient.

In other words, while most caregivers understood the basic pathology of dementia in the brain, many did not understand how those changes were manifested in behaviors, level of dependence, and emotional responses. Thus, when the care recipient engaged in typical behaviors related to dementia, such as refusing care or acting agitated, many caregivers regarded those behaviors as deliberate, instead of as a symptom of the disease. As an illustration of this belief, Mrs. C said on several occasions that her husband was intentionally trying to "work me to death" and "get on my last nerve."

In summary, variation in beliefs about dementia was most notable in the ways that the symptoms of dementia were described, including: childlike behavior, embarrassing behavior, change of personality, and helplessness.

Admittedly, the whole story cannot be known from a snippet of information or a single observation. However, the decisions that caregivers make may be based primarily on how they define key concepts, such as sickness, health, and disability.

CAREGIVER MEANINGS

Caregivers can cite various aspects of their role that have significance or meaning to them. These meanings often are expressed when a caregiver talks about what is important, rules for care, and how a difficult decision was made. The meanings given by informants in this study are reflected in the gerontological literature and include a sense of responsibility, implications for self-image, consequences of care (positive and negative), and conflicts with family members and professionals (Cohen et al., 2002; Farran, 1997; Hinrichsen et al., 1992; Noonan & Tennstedt, 1997; Ory et al., 2000; Schulz et al., 1995; Skaff & Pearlin, 1992). Participating caregivers described their role as presenting the following issues:

Responsibilities

Women, especially, cited their increased responsibilities as a significant aspect of caregiving. Not only do caregivers retain their own workload, but that load increases with care. In addition, they now must assume the responsibilities of the care recipient. One caregiver described this phenomenon as "two people living in one body." Several caregivers talked about how helpful it would be just to have another person to talk with when decisions must be made.

Self-Image

Again, women seemed to define their self-image through their caregiving. This occurs to a lesser degree among men. Some caregivers talked about being "lifers," meaning that they had always been involved in some aspect of caregiving (such as choosing a helping profession or having extensive experience with child care). Women talked about caregiving as being consistent with the role of a woman as nurturer, parent, and homemaker. Both men and women talked about how caregiving fit or did not fit their personalities, e.g., (strong, independent, patient, etc.) and how their personalities may have changed as a result of performing the role ("I don't have such a quick temper"). Caregivers also talked about their self-image as spiritual beings, which often became clearer through the caregiving role. These caregivers found spiritual renewal through their selfless acts.

Conflicts

All caregivers talked about conflicts, especially with the care recipient, professionals, and family members. These usually occurred due to a difference of opinion, anger at specific actions (or inaction), and lack of responsibility. Some caregivers even talked of internal conflicts in which they experienced conflicting feelings or beliefs (such as the need to have respite in conflict with intense worry about how things would go while they were away).

Costs and Losses

These are well documented in the literature and include anger, resentment, stress, and sadness, as well as loss of companionship, former interests, and privacy (Ory et al, 1999; Ory et al., 2000; Schulz et al., 1995). Caregivers in the study discussed a particular type of loss that is typical of caregiving: anticipatory grief. The experience of grief, whether anticipatory or reactive to loss, is a significant aspect of all caregiving.

Rewards

According to the caregivers in the study, and in keeping with the literature, many rewards also came with the role, including a sense of accomplishment, doing the right thing, satisfaction, personal growth, and even joy at being able to meet the needs of a loved one.

Changing Relationships

Many aspects of life change when a spouse becomes a full-time caregiver. Friends and family either become closer and more helpful or more distant. Caregivers themselves sometimes were a factor in those decisions, such as mothers who would protect adult children from understanding the daily work of care because "they have their own lives to live." Caregivers also found that more formal relationships changed.

CAREGIVER ACTIONS: MANAGING AND ORGANIZING

The Caregiver Style Study was designed to collect information about how caregivers carry out the daily tasks associated with care, or caregiver actions. Interviewers asked caregivers to describe in detail their daily routines and methods for dealing with atypical occurrences, such as a fall or other accident in the house. Three main categories of caregiver actions emerged from the data: managing and organizing, taking care, and getting help.

The first clue that caregivers considered themselves to be managers and organizers came from a woman who, in describing her role as a caregiver, said, "I am the CEO of a small but busy organization." By far the most detail offered by spouse caregivers in the study had to do with how they managed and organized a number of different physical, temporal, and emotional aspects of care, including the need to manage and organize time, space, self, and others.

Managing and Organizing Time

Informants in the study talked most often about the need to manage and organize their time, using some of the strategies that follow:

Making trade-offs. In making a trade-off, or giving up one thing to assure another, caregivers are making decisions that reflect their priorities. Sometimes these decisions are not so hard, as in the case of a caregiver who gave up elaborate meal preparation in order to coordinate her husband's network of friends for a weekly golf game. Another caregiver kept odd hours, sleeping in catnaps so that he could be up during the night when his wife was asleep. This free and quiet time was more restful than sleep, he said. More often, trade-off decisions are difficult and have consequences. Many caregivers talked about giving up meaningful aspects of their lives in order to make room for caregiving.

Planning. This is a familiar approach for many of us. Making "to-do" lists, mentally ticking off what needs to be accomplished, or simply resolving to get that one big chore done today are all aspects of planning. No matter how it's accomplished, many caregivers talked about the need to plan. Planning can be frustrating if stymied due to a chaotic situation, which is why some caregivers recommend a more general scheme for the day.

Creating and maintaining a routine. Some service providers in dementia care would point to the establishment of a routine as a critical caregiving strategy. The reason for a routine is to create a calming environment for the care recipient, including rest breaks, pacing, and balancing quiet activities with more active ones such as an outing or social visit.

Managing and Organizing Physical Space

Caregivers talked about managing and organizing space through the use of four different types of strategies.

Making physical changes to the home. Caregivers as a group appear to be well-informed consumers of adaptive equipment (such as grab bars or tub benches) that can make things easier or safer (Olsen et al., 1993; Corcoran & Gitlin, 2001). They also tend to use visual cues such as signs, pictures, and bright colors that provide information about where things are and what to do. Many caregivers in the study talked about the importance of making their home safe for the care recipient to move about freely.

Moving to be closer to family and services. Perhaps related to the problem of needing to manage time, especially on days when the care recipient has an appointment, caregivers talked about consolidating their services to an area closer to home or easier to access. Many caregivers even changed their doctor to avoid a difficult drive or problematic parking. Some caregivers did the opposite, selling their homes and moving to an area that was closer to family or to needed services.

Creating barriers or distractions. Caregivers attempted to limit the care recipient's access to certain areas of the home (kitchen, basement) or items (sweets, medications) in order to make caring for him or her easier and safer. This was done by installing locks, changing the existing lock to an odd position on the door, camouflaging the door with a curtain or wallpaper, or providing an interesting distraction. For example, one caregiver knew how much her husband liked playing with several little puzzles, so she set them up in the entrance to the kitchen when she needed to prepare meals. On his way to the kitchen, he noticed the puzzles and was distracted from getting in his wife's way. Other caregivers used stuffed animals, dolls, photograph albums, activities, or pets to quickly divert attention when needed.

Hiding or getting rid of things. Too many items can make it difficult to find what you need quickly and may introduce other problems. Caregivers talked about the need to avoid problems such as wearing dirty, torn, or inappropriate clothing, and safety hazards such as cooking or driving. Many caregivers placed out-of-season clothing in a different closet so that spouses with limited energy or attention span could easily make choices of what to wear. Caregivers often disabled the stove or the car by removing key parts such as stove knobs or spark plugs.

Managing Self

In a functional, loving, interdependent relationship between adults, one expects to modulate behavior somewhat, but the need to manage oneself may come as a surprise. At least that's how many of the spouses in our study talked about their realization that self-management involved taking control of their emotions and learning skills that they otherwise would not have considered.

Handling one's emotions. The striking aspect of caregivers talking about learning to handle their emotions is found in the context of this experience. Many spouses began the narrative with information about how they "used to" respond to certain behaviors. Those previous responses were perfectly reasonable in an interdependent relationship. The following quotes illustrate the realization that emotions must be managed:

> Mrs. A: I was showing off my paintings to my daughter. I had just finished them the week before in a watercolor class. Art came in the room and set a cup of coffee right on one of my paintings! I began crying and shouting at him "How could you do something like that? I worked so hard and you act like it's a useless piece of paper!" Art and I were both upset for the rest of the evening. He didn't know what he had done and couldn't focus. He slept in his clothes that night and I cried myself to sleep in the guestroom. The next day, my daughter told me that Art didn't mean it and that my reaction, although understandable, only made things bad for both of us. Now I try to keep my things out of reach and never let Art see me upset.

Mr. B: I was feeling so cooped up in the house all day with Olive. She followed me around like a puppy. I thought, "She's a grown woman and she's letting herself be helpless." I figured that if I left for awhile, she'd have to do for herself, so I went out for an hour. When I got home, I found Olive on her side, stuck between the wall and the table in front of the window. I think Olive stood there looking out the window the whole time I was gone and, who knows, maybe she fell asleep on her feet. I never got angry with her again for following me around. She is helpless, but it's not her fault.

Mrs. C: You really can't reason with them like you used to. Forget everything you used to know. I realize now that if I talk sweet to him, it saves a lot of problems later on. They just don't understand if you yell or get upset.

These quotes illustrate three different types of strategies caregivers talked about using to handle their emotions. They are to:

Let it out. This strategy seems to come from the notion that keeping things bottled up inside will cause problems ("If I don't let it out, I'll have a stroke or heart attack"). Sometimes letting it out is manifested by shouting; other times more like firm voice tones.

Handle it in your head. This was a very common strategy and involved decisions to just ignore certain behaviors, decide that some things are just not important enough to get excited about, or looking at the situation differently in order to change the outcome ("I decided he really wasn't asking for help, he just wanted to be close to me. I held his hand and after awhile he got dressed by himself").

Get away. This strategy involved getting out of the home, either physically or mentally. Methods used for getting away mentally were innovative, such as wearing earphones and listening to music or a book on tape. Many caregivers talked about using the Internet as an escape as well as a source of information.

Learning New Skills

Caregivers talked about the need to change themselves, often in ways that may not have been attempted if not for being a caregiver. These new skills required them to:

Develop patience. This was mentioned frequently by men and women. Those who considered themselves to be naturally impatient talked about having great difficulty learning patience. Although several caregivers testified to the need for patience, and some even stated that they were successful in this effort, not one said specifically how this skill could be developed.

Get a feel for things. Mothers talk about knowing their children so well that they can just look at them and understand their mood. In a similar way, caregivers talked about developing a sense of how the day would go by certain actions that occurred or did not occur. For example, one caregiver said, "If he sleeps late and is groggy, then doesn't eat much breakfast, I usually know that I won't get much out of him today." It may take some reflection and comparisons of day-to-day behaviors to develop the sense of how things could go.

Set goals. Some caregivers talked about setting goals as a helpful way to be efficient and effective. Others, however, regarded goal-setting as useless and frustrating because they usually could not achieve the goals they established. One caregiver said that instead she strives to create directed tendencies, which means establishing general goals (such as "trying to be affectionate today") and avoiding specific ones.

Learn to do household chores. This skill seemed to relate to the spouse's need to absorb the work that could no longer be performed by the spouse. The experience of learning these skills was described not as interesting or satisfying but rather as a dreaded chore. One man captured this attitude toward learning to cook when he said, "I didn't know what pre-heating the oven meant. I turned the oven on and when it got to 350, I put the TV dinner in and turned it off. I didn't appreciate how my neighbor laughed at that. Let him come over and cook. I hate it!"

Managing and Organizing Others

Caregivers seek out the help of others to varying degrees. Gender differences in the type and amount of help requested, as well as the sources of help, are well documented (Corcoran, 1992; 2000; Kramer & Thompson,

2000; Ory et al., 2000; Schulz et al., 1995). The Caregiving Style study revealed the following strategies for managing other helpers, regardless of who the helpers are or what they are helping with.

Establish rules. Caregivers talked about the types of actions, attitudes, and behaviors that were minimum requirements for helpers. Often mentioned were rules such as: "Don't just watch TV when you have free time; read or talk to him." Other rules at the top of the list included compassion, an interest in the care recipient and his or her welfare, reliability, and honesty. Reliability was a particular issue, judging by the frequency of reports regarding helpers who didn't show up on a scheduled date or were late so as to ruin the caregiver's plans. These rules were used to guide the caregivers in hiring helpers and in evaluations thereafter.

Make a list of what needs to be done. This was mentioned less often than expected, but a few respondents felt empowered to create detailed lists of expectations for helpers. This was particularly necessary if the caregiver did not directly interact with a helper or when multiple helpers were involved.

Taking Care

This category of caregiving actions focused on taking care of oneself as a caregiver as well as taking care of one's spouse, the patient.

Taking Care of Oneself

Although caregivers talked about managing their emotions, this was considered by the investigators to be different than the types of actions described for the purposes of taking care of self. Controlling emotions (part of managing and organizing) was often initiated to reduce the consequences of care while taking care of self included staying connected, making things simple, getting healthy, and doing something important.

Staying connected. Caregivers spoke of the need to stay connected to family, friends, enjoyable pastimes, and sources of emotional support. These connections were maintained with or without the care recipient, as long as the quality of the experience was undiminished. Caregivers used email and telephone for connections, as well as visits at home or in a restaurant and social groups formed for recreational purposes. Emotional support was found in these contacts, but primarily caregivers talked about emotional support from groups, such as support groups and religious gatherings.

Making things simple. This strategy overlapped somewhat with making trade-offs, but went beyond to include decisions about how to remove complications from the daily routine that required focus and concentration. For example, one caregiver kept things simple at dinner by always serving her husband the same food since, "He doesn't know if we have chicken every night." In doing so, she avoided having to even consider what he would eat and could shop ahead in bulk. Another caregiver simplified his life by purchasing all elastic-waist pants and loose blouses, so that his wife "could just grab something and put it on."

Getting healthy. Caregivers realized the need to attend to their own health to varying degrees. Although some put off regular visits to the doctor unless something seemed amiss, others became diligent about their own health. A number of caregivers began or increased their physical exercise, sometimes taking the care recipient along on trips to the gym or on walks. It was apparent that getting and staying healthy had the added benefit of giving couples something to do together.

Doing something important. This strategy surprised the investigators. Caregivers explained that they could not reduce their self-image to one of a caregiver only. They needed to do other things that they considered to make a difference in the community. Several types of volunteer opportunities filled this need. Other caregivers talked about doing important work by staying active in support groups long after they could still learn any new information for the purposes of imparting their own knowledge to more novice caregivers. In fact, several caregivers reported their intention to remain in these support groups after the death of the care recipient, as they had noticed other caregivers do.

Many of the strategies for taking care of self could be carried out with the spouse, therefore allowing the caregiver to engage in the next type of caregiver action discussed, taking care of the care recipient.

Taking Care of One's Spouse

Taking care of one's spouse proceeded on many different levels, reflected in the following six categories, which range from physical to emotional health.

Being Siamese twins. This term refers to working so closely with the care recipient that the caregiver is able to quickly compensate for any cognitive or physical deficits of the spouse with dementia. Caregivers using this strategy tended to choose activities that were interactive and cooperative. Home chores were particularly well-suited to performing as a team since the caregiver could choose the types of tasks that the care recipient could partially or fully complete alone, thereby setting up a situation where the two seemed to be working as equals. This strategy seemed to have at least three purposes. First, the caregiver could use the strategy as the basis for other types of care-taking strategies (such as maintaining an identity or staying active, discussed below). Second, the caregiver could supervise the care recipient while completing other necessary tasks, such as cooking. Third, the caregiver could enjoy the companionship of the care recipient in a way that may have been similar to their interactions before the onset of dementia.

Maintaining identity. Caregivers talked often of the need to help the care recipient continue to feel like a productive adult or a loving spouse. This was accomplished through demonstrations of affection or by the types of activities the care recipient was asked to complete. For example, one caregiver illustrated this strategy by describing how she "gave him all the junk mail to open and go through. It makes him feel like he is still an important part of our home."

Breaking things down. This strategy was used to help the care recipient avoid confusion. Instructions were provided in very simple terms and a job was broken down into its smallest steps so the spouse could complete one step at a time.

Staying active and stimulated. Caregivers were often distraught if their spouse was inactive or slept much of the day. For this reason, care recipients were given small chores by the caregiver or enticed to take walks. Other decisions were made for the purposes of keeping the care recipient active, which was cited as a main reason for using adult day care or visiting regularly with grandchildren.

Keeping calm and reassured. Dementia can be a frightening experience and the caregivers in the study seemed to realize a connection between confusion and fear. They often talked of the need to reassure the care recipient that everything was fine and to avoid upsetting experiences like news coverage or other television programs with graphic scenes. Caregivers also used humor, calm voices, and facial expressions to reduce fear and general anxiety.

Keeping physically healthy. Caregivers used regular preventive medical visits, multivitamins and herbal supplements, and exercise, to keep their spouses healthy. This strategy also included the elaborate systems sometimes observed for making sure that the care recipient ingested medications correctly.

GETTING HELP

Although some caregivers are determined to assume full responsibility for the majority of their spouse's care, all talked about their need for help in two areas: emergencies and ideas or information.

Emergencies. Caregivers typically had an arrangement with a family member, friend, or neighbor to lend a hand in an emergency. Those individuals could be counted on for transportation or emotional support. Several caregivers had identified neighbors who were health professionals and would be willing to provide an opinion in a potential medical crisis.

Ideas or information. A person with inside information about the quality of services available in the community, or who is a wealth of information about how to address care issues, was a valuable asset to caregivers. Such individuals may be a health professional who takes a personal interest in the caregiver or a knowledgeable friend or family member.

CONCLUSION

In this chapter, a framework for the way caregivers think about and enact care is presented. The caregiving style framework, comprised of beliefs, meanings, and actions, emerged from data gathered as part of the Caregiving Style study. This chapter seeks to introduce the caregiving style framework as the basis for a more nuanced understanding of the caregiving process. Caregivers themselves may benefit from identifying and understanding their own styles and their underlying value structures. ■

*Mary A. Corcoran, Ph.D., OTR/L, FAOTA, is a Research Professor in
the Department of Health Care Sciences, George Washington University,
Washington, DC. She has degrees in occupational therapy, social gerontology,
and health planning for the elderly. Dr. Corcoran has a long history as an
author, researcher, and educator. She has published and presented widely on
the topics of environmental modifications, management of Alzheimer's
disease, family caregiving, and collaboration. Dr. Corcoran has served as
both principal investigator and co-principal investigator on several projects
funded by the National Institute on Aging. Her experience includes use of
qualitative and quantitative, as well as mixed, methodologies.*

REFERENCES

Able, E. (1991). *Who cares for the elderly? Public policy and the experiences of adult daughters.* Philadelphia: Temple University Press.

Albert, S. (1990). Caregiving as a cultural system: Conceptions of filial obligation and parental dependency in urban America. *American Anthropologist, 92*(2), 319-331.

Cohen, A., Colantonio, A., & Vernich, L. (2002). Positive aspects of caregiving: Rounding out the caregiver experience. *International Journal of Geriatric Psychiatry, 17,* 184-188.

Corcoran, M.A. (1992). Gender differences in dementia management plans of spousal caregivers: Implications for occupational therapy. *American Journal of Occupational Therapy, 46,* 1006-1012.

Corcoran, M.A. (2000). Caregivers. In Burke, M.M., & Laramie, J.A. (Eds.), *Primary care of the older adult: A multidisciplinary approach* (pp. 578-588). Philadelphia: Mosby.

Corcoran, M.A., & Gitlin, L.N. (2001). Family acceptance and use of environmental strategies provided in an occupational therapy intervention. *Occupational and Physical Therapy in Geriatrics, 19*(1), 1-20.

Farran, C. (1997). Theoretical perspectives concerning positive aspects of caring for elderly per-sons with dementia: Stress/adaptation and existentialism. *The Gerontologist, 37*(2), 250-256.

Haley, W.E., Gitlin, L.N., Wiszniewski, S., Mahoney, D.R., Coon, D.W., Winger, L., Corcoran, M.A., Schinfeld, S., & Ory, M (in press). Well-being, appraisal, and coping in African-American and Caucasian dementia caregivers: The REACH study. *Aging and Mental Health.*

Hinrichsen, G.A., Hernandez, N.A., & Pollack, S. (1992). Difficulties and rewards in family care of the depressed older adult. *The Gerontologist, 32*(4), 486-492.

Kramer, B.J., & Thompson, E.H. (2002). *Men as caregivers: Theory, research, and service implications.* Springer series: Focus on men. New York: Springer Publishing.

Lyman, K. (1993). *Day in, day out with Alzheimer's stress in caregiving relationships.* Philadelphia: Temple University Press.

McCann, J.J., Herbert, L.E, Beckett, L.A., Morris, M.C., Scherr, P.A., & Evans, D.A. (2000). Comparison of informal caregiving by black and white older adults in a community population. *Journal of the American Geriatrics Society, 48,* 1612-1617.

Noonan, A.E., & Tennstedt, S.L. (1997). Meaning in caregiving and its contributions to caregiver well-being. *The Gerontologist, 37,* 785-794.

Olsen, R.V., Ehrenkrantz, E., & Hutchings, B. (1993). *Homes that help: Advice from caregivers for creating a supportive home.* Newark, NJ: New Jersey Institute of Technology Press.

Ory, M.G., Hoffman, R.R., Yee, J., Tennstedt, S.L., & Schulz, R. (1999). Prevalence and impact of caregiving: A detailed comparison between dementia and non-dementia caregivers. *The Gerontologist, 39*(2), 177-186.

Ory, M.G., Lee, J., Tennstedt, S.L., & Schulz, R. (2000). The extent and impact of dementia care: Unique challenges experienced by family caregivers. In R. Schulz (Ed.), *Handbook on dementia caregiving* (pp. 1-32). New York: Springer.

Schulz, R., O'Brien, A.T., Bookwala, J., & Fleissner, K. (1995). Psychiatric and physical morbidity effects of dementia caregiving: Prevalence, correlates, and causes. *The Gerontologist, 35,* 771-791.

Skaff, M.M., & Pearlin, L.I. (1992). Caregiving: Role engulfment and the loss of self. *The Gerontologist, 32,* 656-664.

CHAPTER 14

Spirituality and Alzheimer's Disease

Earl A. Grollman

*A person reacts in three directions. Inwards to oneself,
out to others, and up to God. The miracle of life is that
in truly reaching up in one direction, one embraces three.*
—Hassidic master Rabbi Nachman of Bratslav (1772-1810)

Many cultures consider the elder years as a gift. Lives that conclude without that final chapter, without the time to grow old and gain perspective, often seem bitterly incomplete. But the greatest loss, the greatest dehumanization, is to grow old without possession of the mind. That is Alzheimer's disease.

It is a difficult and sobering task for individuals with Alzheimer's to accept the tragedy of their disease and to face the future with courage and resourcefulness. For the Alzheimer's caregivers, too, the journey is long and rough, its path winding and arduous. Caregiving is a risky business. Watching the disintegration of loved ones is stressful, often resulting in depression and feelings of hopelessness.

There are no instant solutions to the challenges they face. Caregivers must make decisions based on their own needs and resources, as well as on the needs of their loved ones. At the same time, they must consider not only practical needs, but emotional and spiritual needs as well. It is my hope that this chapter will assist you, the professionals, in helping those afflicted with

Alzheimer's and their caregivers on their difficult journey by assisting them to move in three necessary directions: up, in, and out. You can help them move from helplessness to hope, from fear to action.

REACHING UP

Perhaps more than any event, having a loved one with Alzheimer's disease raises the most urgent issues about spiritual concerns—the search for higher meanings and purposes. Many secular therapists are uncomfortable with matters of faith. They may fear imposing their own values or extending themselves beyond their professional competence. Spiritual concerns may thus be overlooked, despite the influences of holistic models that demand that the client should be viewed not only as a biological and physical entity, but also as a whole person with spiritual needs.

In the 20th century, modern medicine had, for the most part, separated health and spirituality into separate realms. But before the 20th century, the two were interlinked and often intertwined. (In some societies, spiritual leaders not only dispensed prayers, but also administered medicinal herbs. Their followers believed these holy people had a transcendental ability to heal.) However, health and spirituality grew apart as scientific methods and discoveries revolutionized medicine. Spirituality became solely the province of theologians.

Until recently, mental health professionals often thought of spiritual concerns as non-scientific and sometimes even as indications of a mental illness. Renewed interest in the writings of people such as Carl Jung and Viktor Frankl, Benson's mind-body connection, and the 12-step program of Alcoholics Anonymous has fostered greater openness of the offices of secular counselors. When some of their clients incorporated faith, worship, and prayer into their treatment, they attained not only a sense of community, tradition, and spiritual satisfaction, but also an enhancement of physical and mental health as well. Prestigious professional journals began publishing articles suggesting that:

- Prayer and meditation slowed the heart and breathing rate of stressed caregivers;
- Attendance at worship reduced hypertension;

- In the quest for wrestling with such profound issues of God and good and evil, some people were able to release feelings of hopelessness and guilt by finding a sense of belonging and hope.

One need not be a clergyperson or a religious therapist to gather information about the religious or spiritual beliefs of the Alzheimer's patient and his or her caregivers. In fact, a recent article in the American Medical Association magazine (Lo, Ruston, Kates, Arnold, Cohen, Faber-Langendoen, et al., 2002) urges physicians to clarify patients' concerns and beliefs about religious or spiritual issues in order to mobilize the optimum sources of support. A spiritual needs assessment has served as a useful tool for addressing both the caregivers' and patient's spiritual needs. During the early stages of the disease, such an assessment could be invaluable, helping both caregivers and patients reconnect with familiar age-hallowed traditions of religious symbols, attachments, and memories.

What follows is a sample spiritual needs assessment that counselors might consider. Start with non-threatening questions to help ease caregivers' fears and concerns, asking in reference to both the patient and caregivers.

I. Childhood Memories

- As a youngster, did the Alzheimer's patient as well as the caregiver attend church, synagogue, mosque, etc.?
- Were there special prayers and rituals that were valued in the home or place of worship?
- How were religious holidays commemorated? What were their emotional and spiritual responses to these ceremonies?
- How have their emotional and spiritual responses changed as they grew older and matured?

II. Current Religious Attachments

- Are they now a member of a religious/spiritual group?
- What is the frequency of attendance at services, social activities, study groups? (never/seldom/occasionally/often)
- What is the level of practice and observance?

III. Religious Symbols

- Are there particular rites, sacraments, symbols, or rituals that feed the mind and calm the spirit? For example, a favorite religious hymn might soothe the frightened, hostile Alzheimer's patient. Or a Star of David might help a Jewish patient feel more comfortable in a Catholic hospital.

- Are there favorite hymns, Bible readings, daily devotions, or other traditions that offer both patients and caregivers a source of serenity in the midst of turbulent times?

IV. Clergy

- How do they relate to their pastor, priest, rabbi, elder, or religious leader?

- In what way might that person be involved (e.g., counseling, visits, prayers, etc.)?

V. Perceptions of Spiritual Self

- Do they consider themselves as believers, non-believers, agnostics, alienated?

- Do they feel that God is punishing them?

- Do they feel that they need forgiveness?

- What principles do they attempt to live by?

A spiritual needs assessment can help counselors better understand their clients: their beliefs, their needs, and their sources of support. Such insights can guide clients to reach up to find comfort and consolation during this painful time.

As you assist the caregivers in their struggle to accept the unacceptable, you may hear the same questions again and again. These questions, which have seemingly spiritual overtones, can be addressed in a helpful, therapeutic manner.

Q: "Why?" "Why?" may not involve a theological response. For those afflicted with Alzheimer's and those who love them, it is a torturous journey of grief. "Why?" could be more than a question. It could be an agonizing cry for the devastating disease that so radically has altered their lives. It is an expression of shock, denial, panic, guilt, anger, and depression.

You, as counselors, can remind the clients that as children they may have believed that life was fair, or at least, ought to be fair. As adults, they now know that they have to live in an unfair world. Of course, it is natural in our scientific milieu to seek explanations. But no one, not even the greatest philosophers and theologians, knows why good people suffer.

You might ask them even if the questions were answerable, would their despair be less agonizing? There is no simple response that bridges the chasm of "irreparable separation." There is no satisfactory answer for an unresolvable dilemma.

Not all questions have complete answers. Unanswered "whys" are part of life. The search may continue but the real question may be, "How best can you help each other to live as meaningfully as possible?"

Q: How could God do this to us? Reverend Larry Yeagley of Charlotte, Michigan (2003), reminds us that anger at God does not beg for the counselor's immediate response. Again, it may be a cry of desperation that calls for quiet restraint and acknowledgment of their sadness and bitterness. He tells of lying in a hospital with a diagnosis of lymphoma, filled with anger at God and a sense of bewilderment. The hospital chaplain's theological pronouncements and Biblical quotations did not assuage his despair. He was helped by someone who later came to his room, sat close to him, and held his hand. She didn't rebuke him for his feelings of doubt; she quietly acknowledged his panic and despair. That's all he needed at the time.

Professionals understand that anger is a part of grief. Blaming God is a natural, normal response to anguish. Many of the greatest spiritual leaders have felt this way, including the Psalmist who cried, "My God, my God, why hast thou forsaken me?" (Psalm 22:2) Many in the faith community have acknowledged this anger and have said: "It's okay. God can take it."

These religious leaders understand that honest anger can be a form of prayer. To be furious at God could indicate that there is still a "God-Force" in them. No one can hurt like those closest to them and those they trust. Their wrath may be evidence that God was present in their life and may be again. This is not the time to argue theology. It is the time to work through the consequences of this lingering, crippling disease.

Q: Is God punishing me? As families endure the distressing behaviors of their loved one and the groundless suspicions, they ask the same question over and over again: "What did I do wrong?" They may feel that this is a kind of Divine chastisement for their sins and misdeeds.

You might ask: "Do you think that faith is an insurance policy offering protection against the cruel blows of sickness?" Help them to understand that religion does not preclude grief nor inoculate against suffering. Highlight again and again that Alzheimer's disease has nothing to do with rewards and punishments. They and their loved ones are not being disciplined. They are not responsible for the illness. Bad things do happen to good people. As theologian Mordechai Kaplan said, "Expecting nothing bad to happen to you because you're a good person is like expecting the bull not to charge you because you're a vegetarian."

Please understand that spirituality should never be viewed as a replacement for medical treatment. At the same time, therapists should not be viewed as ersatz theologians. As clients pose difficult questions, you might consult with the clergy, as it is no longer clergy versus secular counselor. Counselors and clergy can form a collaborative partnership for each has unique contributions with diverse perspectives. Consider hospice as a model in which clergy and counselors function as a team to better serve patients and their families: not only their practical needs, but their emotional and spiritual needs as well.

The importance of a holistic approach is emphasized by Dr. Rachel Naomi Remen (1996). In reflecting on her work, she says life often defies science, and that life is best defined by mystery. Many scholars recognize the spiritual quality of staying connected in a disconnected world.

Just as you can help clients reach up to find hope, you can also help them to reach in and come to terms with their profound emotional reactions.

REACHING IN

Alzheimer's disease destroys the mind, eroding and gradually destroying the qualities which embodied the individual. Families mourn the loss of the person they once knew—an adventuresome partner, a loving parent, a quick-witted friend. Their loved one is replaced by a patient who may no longer recognize them, who may be suspicious, irritable, and aggressive. Loved ones grieve as they struggle to meet the new responsibilities and challenges that present themselves each day.

Denial, panic, guilt, anger, depression, bodily distress: these emotions are not neat, sequential stages leading family members through the process of grief. They are recurring themes of anguish as patients and their families confront an unfair fate. At different times, different emotions will predominate. By helping clients and caregivers to learn about the various facets of grief, you can help them to accept their own barrage of feelings as they journey through this sad and difficult time. Consistently remind clients that there is no right way or wrong way to grieve, no prescribed time for them to adjust. Each person experiences grief in his or her own way. They may be seized by panic: "Will she forget who I am?" "Will he wander away and get lost?" "How can I take care of him?" "What about the rest of my family? What about my job?" "Who's going to pay for all this?" Or they may be trapped in guilt: "I should have spent more time with my loved one, done the things I promised, taken the trips we always planned." "I should have taken the time to appreciate the one I love."

They may also be consumed with anger: "Why me?" "Why my spouse, lover, sibling, parent, friend?" "What did I do to deserve this?" They may feel fury toward God for being unjust and capricious; fury toward their loved one whose illness has plunged the family into this hell; fury toward the doctors and nurses for not doing more, for not trying harder; fury against their own inability to help their loved one to solve the problem; fury toward their family and friends for their unreasonable suggestions and their criticism of the way they are handing the situation; and fury toward themselves for succumbing to rage.

They may also experience bodily distress: "I can't remember the last time I felt good." Their head throbs, their stomach aches, their mouth feels dry. Exhaustion and lack of concentration make it impossible for them to complete necessary tasks. They may begin to worry that they too are starting to experience the symptoms of Alzheimer's.

Help them to understand that they are overloaded emotionally, spiritually, and physically. Help them to find ways to collect themselves by finding constructive ways to release their grief so that their despair does not cost them too dearly in terms of inner stress, fractured relationships, and their own health and strength. Help them to acknowledge and express their painful feelings and to recognize each step they have taken. As a Chinese proverb teaches us, "The journey of a thousand miles starts with a single step." And every small step is a victory. Rabbi Harold Kushner (Raub, 2003) expressed this sentiment eloquently when he was asked what the most memorable experience of his life was. His response was not the many books he has written or his worldwide acclaim. Rather, he said, "I want it to be remembered that when my son was dying and in pain, I could make him laugh."

So as you help your clients to search within themselves, it is also essential that you help them reach out to others.

Reaching Out

The philosopher, Martin Buber, highlighted the importance of others: "One person is no person. The solitary heart has to throb with the hearts of others." Reaching out is especially critical during the ongoing mourning of a person whose life changes are so conspicuous. The daughter and caregiver of an Alzheimer's victim explains, "My father was a shell of himself. The man that he had been, my father whom I had loved and who had loved me was not there. I grieved for my father, and missed him terribly, long before he was physically gone and afterward as well."

Help caregivers to accept that they do not have the power to control the disease or make it go away, but that there are still some things they can do to reach out to their loved one. If the patient is in the early stages of the disease there is probably still time to fulfill some dreams and goals. Alzheimer's disease does not cripple a person overnight. They may still share the pleasures that brought them so much delight. Get together with small groups of close friends and family members. Strengthen bonds with those they love.

At the same time, encourage caregivers to reach out to family and friends. Your clients might say: "But I have so much on my mind. Just doing those things that need to be done consumes my every moment. I can't think of being with anyone else." Acknowledge that they are tired and weary, but emphasize that they need other people like never before.

Sharing their thoughts and fears with trusted friends is crucial; emotions that are denied expression grow in isolation. Encourage them to carefully choose those who will accept and understand, who will not fault them or deny their feelings. Feeling the outstretched hand of a kindred spirit, whether it is a friend or family member, can ease their burdens.

The tragedy of Alzheimer's disease can bring family members together. Alzheimer's disease can also drive a family apart. Just as reactions in the family have differed at other times and in other situations, so will responses to this disease. Each person's relationship with the afflicted family member is unique and different. No one can write a script for the other members of a family to follow. The families that cope most effectively with Alzheimer's disease are those who share their feelings and discuss their problems clearly and openly without hostility. It is very important that caregiving responsibilities and roles are discussed, agreed upon, and honestly acknowledged by all family members.

Reaching out in Alzheimer's support groups has also served as a lifeline for many caregivers. Alzheimer's support groups, whether they are regular meetings, buddy systems, crisis phone lines, or special groups for children, can help caregivers travel a difficult path in the company of others whose circumstances are similar to their own. Each person has reached different points along the route, and can share the road map of his or her journey.

Alzheimer's support group members understand when someone asks, "Why me?" They understand when someone says, "I don't think I can make it." In an Alzheimer's support group, one can weep without feeling embarrassed, laugh without feeling guilty. For many, Alzheimer's support groups provide the compassionate network of a "second family."

WHAT PROFESSIONALS CAN LEARN

As you work with Alzheimer's patients and their families, you discover new ways to help your clients reach up, in, and out. At the same time, you gain insights about the meaning of your own life. "All persons are mortal. I am a person. Therefore, I am mortal...My God, it could happen to me and members of my family."

You begin to realize that good health may not always be permanent. The slogan, "Today is the first day of the rest of your life" is but a half-truth. Now you know the other half. "Today may also be the last day you'll ever get." No one knows about tomorrow, not even professionals.

Now that you are actually aware of the fragility of life you realize that the two least important details are usually inscribed upon the tombstone: dates of birth and death. You will not be remembered for the length of your years, but for the breadth of your sympathy for others, the depth of your appreciation for beauty, the height of your love for your clients and your family.

Being an Alzheimer's disease caregiver forces you to ask hard questions. Through the trials of witnessing the devastation of the illness, you may begin to rethink priorities, refine your goals, and redefine your future. As you reach up, in, and out, may you discover how best to live the rest of your days. L'Chayim—To Life! ■

(This chapter is lovingly dedicated to the memory of my brother-in-law and sister-in-law, Aaron and Sonia Levinson, who recently died of Alzheimer's disease.)

Dr. Earl A. Grollman is a writer, lecturer, and rabbi whose books on coping with loss number over more than 750,000 copies in print. A pioneer in the field of crisis intervention, he appears on many national television programs and his writings have appeared in virtually every American daily. His volume, When Someone You Love Has Alzheimer's: The Caregiver's Journey, *was written with Professor Kenneth S. Kosik of Harvard Medical School. He writes a monthly "Because You Asked" column for* Journeys: A Newsletter to Help in Bereavement *(Hospice Foundation of America).*

REFERENCES

Brenner, D.S., Blanchard, T., & Fins, J.T. Hirschfeld (2002). *Embracing life and facing death.* New York: CLAL Press.

Buber, M. (1991). *Tales of the Hassidim.* New York: Schocken Books.

Coon, D.W., Gallagher-Thompson, D., & Thompson, L.W. (Eds.). (2003). *Innovative interventions for reduced dementia caregiver distress.* New York: Springer Press.

Elderly caregivers face stress toll. (2003, July 1). *Wall Street Journal,* p. 7.

Fitzsimmons, S., & Buettner, L. (2003). Health promotion for mind, body, and spirit. *American Journal of Alzheimer's Disease and Other Dementias, 18*(4).

Grollman, E.A. (1995). *Caring and coping when your loved one is seriously ill.* Boston: Beacon Press.

Grollman, E.A., & Kosik, K. (1996). *When someone you love has Alzheimer's: The caregiver's journey.* Boston: Beacon Press.

Harris, P.H. (Ed.). (2002). *The person with Alzheimer's disease: Pathways to understanding the experience.* Baltimore: Johns Hopkins Press.

Knittweis, J., & Harch, J. (2002). *Alzheimer's solutions: Personal guide for caregivers.* Sausalito, CA: Lucid Press.

Lo, B., Ruston, D., Kates, L.W., Arnold, R.M., Cohen, C.B., Faber-Langendoen, K., et al. (2002). Discussing religious and spiritual issues at the end of life: A practical guide for physicians. *JAMA, 287,* 749-754.

Mace, N.L., & Rabins, P.V. (1991). *The thirty-six hour day.* Baltimore: Johns Hopkins Press.

Mykoff, M. (1994). *The empty chair: Finding hope and joy—Timeless wisdom from a Hassidic master, Rabbi Nachman of Bratslav.* Woodstock, VT: Jewish Lights.

Raub, D.F. (October 2003). Profile: Harold Kushner. *Hadassah Magazine, 85*(2).

Remen, R.N. (1996). *Kitchen table wisdom.* New York: Riverhead Books.

Schutz, R. (Ed.). (2000). *Handbook of dementia caregiving.* New York: Springer Press.

Yeagley, L. (2003, September). Ministering to families of the terminally ill III (part 2). *Ministry Magazine,* 24-29.

■ PART IV ■

Facing the Future

It is a theme of this book that as the baby boom generation ages, dementia will become an even more significant issue, leaving few areas untouched. This will clearly be a problem for end-of-life care. It will certainly be an issue for hospice. The promise of hospice care—holistic, palliative, family-oriented care—may be difficult to fulfill in dementia. Charles Corr and his co-authors discuss the defining characteristics of hospice in their chapter and analyze factors that make it difficult to offer such care in dementia. This is further elucidated in Leslie Fried's chapter. Both chapters acknowledge structural barriers to offering such care, particularly in the Medicare benefit, which so narrowly define hospice care. Both also note other barriers, attitudinal ones, as hospice has to adjust to new problems of patient care. However, both chapters reaffirm the value of good hospice care and are confident that hospices can rise to this new challenge.

Some of these problems are ethical. As Jennifer Kapo and Jason Karlawish clearly demonstrate in their chapter, the rise of dementia creates new ethical issues in end-of-life care. They note as well the uncertainty of prognosis, the difficulty of indirect decisions, and the difficulty of symptom management with uncommunicative patients. Bruce Jennings also raises a critical ethical issue: how does one define the quality of life? In many ways this is the essential issue in end-of-life ethics. Jennings provocatively challenges us to broaden that definition.

Presently, hospices are responding to the challenge of dementia. There are exciting and innovative programs to better serve the needs of individuals with dementia and their families. For example, San Francisco's ONE Generation program actively involves children in the care of persons with Alzheimer's disease. Such programs offer mutual benefits. They help children and their parents become more sensitive of the illness, while offering older persons stimulation and a sense that they still have a contribution to make. Other programs have trained hospice staff to deal with persons with Alzheimer's disease, seeking to surmount attitudinal barriers to care. One Phoenix-based program, "Providing Palliative Care to Person with Alzheimer's Disease," formed a coalition made up of hospices, the southwest chapter of the Alzheimer's Association, assisted living facilities, and nursing homes, to offer training that will promote quality of life in persons with dementia. The program not only emphasizes pain management but also nutrition, meaningful activities, and orientation to patients' life histories.

Programs such as these provide a path for the future—one that might assist programs at any stage of care. Successful treatment is holistic. It should include not only medication but also programs that utilize multiple modalities. For example, in the earlier stages of dementia, medication that slows the onset of disease and alleviates symptoms might be included with other activities such as exercises that continue to stimulate and challenge the patient. Care should, following the hospice model, view the family as the unit of care. Constant assessments of caregiver coping, health, and stress are as critical as understanding the progression of disease in the patient.

The book's final chapter on resources can help family members and other caregivers face the immediate future. Barring some dramatic medical breakthrough, we as a society face a future rise in dementia. We can start preparing now for that certainty. ■

CHAPTER 15

Alzheimer's Disease and the Challenge for Hospice

Charles A. Corr, Karen M. Corr, and Susan M. Ramsey

Many years ago, a wise nurse told us: "Hospice is a philosophy, not a facility." She meant that the central point about hospice is the outlook, attitude, or approach it represents, not the building or structure in which it may be housed. That view of hospice has been confirmed by the fact that the vast majority of hospice care is delivered in the homes of patients and their family members. Hospice care is also delivered in hospitals, long-term care facilities, assisted living facilities, and other locations, but only a very small percent of that care occurs in specially-designed buildings or designated hospice facilities.

In this chapter, we view "hospice" not as a noun to designate a specific facility, but as an adjective that is best used in two ways: (1) to single out a particular philosophy of care, and (2) to identify the organized programs that seek to implement or deliver that care. Our argument in this chapter is that while the hospice philosophy of care is very well suited in principal to Alzheimer's disease, hospice programs of care face practical challenges in applying that philosophy to the actual delivery of services. In fact, we believe that hospice programs of care can have much to offer in relationship to Alzheimer's disease, but they need to reckon with some of the challenges that we will examine. Although we focus here on Alzheimer's disease, much of our argument is equally applicable to other forms of dementia.

HOSPICE AS A PHILOSOPHY OF CARE

As a philosophy of care, hospice is:

- An outlook on care that affirms life;

- A way of thinking about care that links together efforts to minimize sources of discomfort, maximize present quality in living, and provide opportunities for personal growth and resolution wherever possible;

- A viewpoint that recognizes human beings as persons with physical, psychological, social, and spiritual dimensions in their lives;

- An approach to care that is focused on the needs, values, and decisions of the person-and-family unit from diagnosis through bereavement, as well as the concerns of all who are providing care to the ill person and/or his or her family members, and the needs those providers may have for support in this work.

Perhaps the most important thing about the hospice philosophy of care is found in its single-minded focus on upholding the value and dignity of life embodied in every human being. According to the hospice philosophy, care is provided to everyone who is to be served because they are alive and because they are unique and valuable. This is true even when death is near or persons are burdened with dementia and other significant challenges, handicaps, and disabilities.

The hospice philosophy advocates for minimizing sources of suffering and distress, even when their underlying causes cannot be removed. Even when the progression of disease cannot be reversed, halted, or slowed, the hospice philosophy argues that much can be done to modify the negative and distressing influence on quality of life, and to foster opportunities for personal growth. In this way, the hospice philosophy rejects the view that "there is nothing more we can do." It also insists that professional skills and simple human presence can have much to offer even when there is no longer any reasonable prospect of cure or prolonging life and death is near.

The hospice philosophy argues that care should not be limited to one or two aspects of the lives of the persons it serves. Instead, this philosophy champions holistic care that is sensitive to the needs, tasks, goals, and desires in all aspects of a person's life. As such, the hospice philosophy approaches persons both as individuals and as members of family units, however "family" may be defined by those involved in any individual case. This outlook recognizes the proper roles of all who are legitimately caught up in making important decisions about care, as well as in the giving and receiving of care. In each instance, the hospice philosophy is sensitive to the values of the individuals and family members being served, as well as to the ethnic, religious, and cultural principles that are important to them. The hospice philosophy also appreciates that it is appropriate to initiate hospice-type interventions as early as the point of diagnosis of a life-limiting or life-threatening condition and to continue care for bereaved survivors after the death of someone they love.

As a philosophy of care, hospice is essentially a form of palliative care. The adjective "palliative," together with its verb form "to palliate" and its noun "palliation," all derive from a Latin root for the English word "pall," which means a cloth or cloak. In its relevant meaning here, palliative care seeks to cover over, cloak, or mitigate suffering from a disease. The relevant sense of "covering" in palliative care is not one of "concealing" or "disguising," but rather one of "caressing" and "comforting." By alleviating distressing symptoms, palliation moderates the effects of a disease even when its underlying cause cannot be affected. Thus, the World Health Organization (1990, p. 11) has defined palliative care as:

> ... the active total care of patients whose disease is not responsive to curative treatment. Control of pain, of other symptoms, and psychological, social and spiritual problems, is paramount. The goal of palliative care is achievement of the best quality of life for patients and their families.

As a philosophy of care, palliation need not be limited to end-of-life care nor to situations in which there is no reasonable prospect of cure. In fact, far more of modern medical and health care than we often realize is really a form of palliation. For example, there is no cure for the common cold. Even so, aspirin, decongestants, antiexpectorants, antihistamines, medications to dry up unwanted secretions, and many other interventions of various types (including rest and good nutrition), as well as simple medical acknowledgment of the condition, are typically employed to improve quality of life when individuals have a cold and cough. As a result, symptoms are palliated. In the meantime, for most individuals, the body's immune system and other resources rally to repel the invader and restore the person to a healthier condition. Even though cure is not offered for the common cold, we are all grateful when our distress is relieved.

Alzheimer's Disease

Here, we consider some typical features of Alzheimer's disease and contrast them briefly with selected examples of the features of other advanced diseases that are well known in themselves and/or in relationship to hospice care. This allows us to comment on the relevance of the hospice philosophy of palliative care to Alzheimer's disease.

To begin, we know that each advanced disease has its own unique trajectory and symptoms. For example, there are many forms of cancer, each with its own processes and with distressing symptoms such as pain, breathlessness, and mutilation. By contrast, the trajectory of Acquired Immunodeficiency Syndrome (AIDS), the end stage of infection by the Human Immunodeficiency Virus (HIV), is often said to be like a roller coaster ride, with symptoms that vary according to the direct effects of the virus, the indirect effects of opportunistic infections arising from either internal or external sources when one's immune system is severely compromised, and the side effects of various interventions designed to halt, slow down, or reverse the progress of the infection.

By contrast with cancer or AIDS, motor neuron disease, such as amyotrophic lateral sclerosis (ALS; commonly called "Lou Gehrig's disease" by most Americans), is another advanced disease that more closely resembles Alzheimer's disease in certain ways. Like Alzheimer's disease, ALS is a chronic disease with a slow and lengthy progression. However, the primary symptoms of ALS arise from degeneration of motor neurons of the spinal cord, medulla, and cortex, leading to loss of muscle control that most often results in loss of speech and swallowing abilities in its end stages.

On its own, Alzheimer's disease does not involve symptoms that are characteristic of many types of advanced cancers. It also does not normally follow the pattern of remission, relapse, and further remissions often seen in AIDS and some advanced cancers. Alzheimer's disease is more like motor neuron disease since both have a characteristic pattern of slow progression measured in many months or years rather than a matter of days or weeks. Like motor neuron disease, Alzheimer's disease is most often experienced in its late-onset form where it is commonly first identified in individuals who are 65 years of age and older. Alzheimer's disease is also similar to motor neuron disease in that problems with speech and swallowing often characterize its end stages.

As a form of senile dementia, however, Alzheimer's disease is a brain disorder resulting from atrophy of the frontal and occipital lobes of the brain. Thus, Alzheimer's disease most often first presents itself in problems of short-term memory and cognitive disorders. Unlike the mental alertness that usually endures throughout ALS, Alzheimer's disease displays a progressive, irreversible loss of memory, deterioration of cognitive and intellectual functions (e.g., those involving reasoning and judgment, orientation, speech, and communication), alterations in personality, deficits in the ability to recognize persons and objects, and problems in carrying out activities of daily living. As a result, Alzheimer's disease usually imposes heavy burdens and challenges over a long period of time on family and professional caregivers. As many family members have said, "I lost the person I loved many years before that individual finally died."

HOSPICE PHILOSOPHY OF CARE AND ALZHEIMER'S DISEASE

We believe that the hospice philosophy of care is relevant to Alzheimer's disease in several ways:

- The hospice philosophy of care affirms the value of the life of the individual with Alzheimer's disease whatever the stage of his or her dementia and the problems that may be associated with it;

- The hospice philosophy can help to mitigate or ease dementia-related and other problems, minimize sources of distress, support abilities that remain, promote quality in living that is still present, and provide opportunities for personal growth and resolution whether an individual is in the early stages of Alzheimer's disease in which he or she may only be experiencing minor problems in cognitive functioning through the end stage of the disease when that same individual may be experiencing major physical decline, weight loss, multiple co-morbidities, and dependence in most activities of daily living;

■ The hospice philosophy does not limit itself to one or two dimensions of a human life; rather it recognizes all of the dimensions in the lives of individuals with Alzheimer's disease, whether they be physical, psychological, social, or spiritual;

■ The hospice philosophy takes into account the needs of both the ill person and his or her family members, as well as their values and their participation in decision making from diagnosis through bereavement;

■ The hospice philosophy is also sensitive and responsive to the needs of all who join in the care of the ill person and his or her family members, whether at home or in a long-term care facility, often over a long period of time.

At present, cure is not an option for Alzheimer's disease. Science and medicine can only attempt to mitigate the effects of this disease, i.e., to offer a form of palliative care. As a result, there is a clear role for the hospice philosophy in the care and treatment of Alzheimer's patients and their family members.

This does not mean that the hospice philosophy is sufficient in itself to provide comprehensive care for an individual with Alzheimer's disease and his or her family members. Specific expertise related to dementia in general and Alzheimer's disease in particular is also required, along with proficiency in the challenging work of home care and long-term care. Expertise in caring for individuals and family members encountering Alzheimer's disease must take into account state-of-the-art diagnostic and therapeutic techniques that currently exist or may be developed. Palliative care needs to work hand in hand with disease-related expertise in terms of assessment, intervention, education, and research. The balance between palliation and other perspectives must be carefully established and can be expected to change as the disease progresses.

HOSPICE AS A PROGRAM OF CARE

As a program of care, hospice is:

- A type of end-of-life care that affirms life and active living, wherever possible, not death;

- A means of offering holistic care to everyone it serves, including patients, their family members, and their caregivers;

- A way of bringing together through an interdisciplinary team the skills, experiences, and abilities of the patient, family members, professional staff members, and volunteers; the team may include the staff of a hospice program, a home health agency, a long-term care facility, or other relevant care providers;

- A method of insuring coordination and continuity of care in whatever setting is desirable and/or appropriate to the needs of the patient-and-family unit, including care at home, in a long-term care facility, or in a hospice facility;

- A system that makes services available on a 24-hour-a-day, 7-day-a-week basis;

- A service that offers continuing care and ongoing support to bereaved survivors, including family members after the death of someone they love, as well as individuals who may have provided care over many months and years at home or in a long-term care facility and who may have come to have close, loving relationships with the person who died of Alzheimer's disease;

- A practice that offers both formal and informal programs of support to staff members and volunteers in hospice programs, long-term care facilities, home health agencies, and other institutions who may have taken part in caring for the person with Alzheimer's disease.

Since its introduction to the United States in the mid-1970s, the hospice philosophy has been implemented in a wide variety of programs that suit the needs and circumstances of local communities. In all of those forms, hospice has come to be known as a skilled and compassionate type of end-of-life care. As a result, in the United States in the year 2002 over 3,200 hospice providers served an estimated 885,000 patients. According to the National Hospice and Palliative Care Organization (2003), that represented an increase of almost 15 percent over the number of patients served in 2001. Although hospice programs in the United States initially gave their principal attention to advanced cancer patients, in 2001 approximately 47 percent of all patients served by hospice providers had diagnoses other than cancer.

For all of these patients, the services offered by American hospice programs were distinguished by their emphasis on holistic care to patients and family members alike, as well as to their caregivers. This was accomplished by providing care through an interdisciplinary team. The multidisciplinary approaches of traditional American health care have great strengths in the range and depth of specialized medical and health care skills they command especially in the hierarchical settings of our best teaching hospitals and medical research centers. What those approaches often lack, however, is the shared input, coordination, and cooperation of hospice interdisciplinary teams. These interdisciplinary teams seek out the input of team members in developing and implementing joint plans of care. Hospice interdisciplinary teams do not confine themselves only to professional expertise. When they function in an optimal form, they also take into account the experiences, abilities, and contributions of patients, family members, caregivers in various settings, and volunteers.

Interdisciplinary teams in hospice programs are essential not only for providing holistic care to patients and family members, but also for insuring coordination and continuity of care in whatever setting that care is delivered and as individuals are transferred from one setting to another to meet their changing needs. Patients and family members who must tell and retell their stories innumerable times as they confront what seems to be a never-ending series of new care providers, as staff change from shift to shift, and as they are moved from one care setting to another, know all too well how that adds to their burdens and creates opportunities for mistakes and deficiencies in care. An effective hospice program of care will take pains to see that at least one member of its team is in charge of insuring that the care being provided is harmonious and seamless.

An effective hospice program of care also recognizes that what patients and family members perceive as a crisis or an urgent need for assistance does not merely occur at times when care providers and care systems are maximally available. For this reason, as well as to insure security and support for those it serves, an effective hospice program of care will have in place a system to guarantee that someone representing the interdisciplinary team is available 24 hours a day, 7 days a week to respond to inquiries and calls for help. That representative or someone acting on his or her behalf will need to have the authority to insure that effective, timely care is carried out.

Finally, an effective hospice program of care does not limit its services solely to ill or dying persons. Instead, hospice programs of care are sensitive to the needs of family members and others who are closely associated with the ill person. Hospice programs of care are also attentive to the needs of their own staff members, volunteers, and others who may have been involved in providing care before, during, and after the death of a patient. Therefore, hospice programs offer continuing care to family members before their loved one dies and ongoing support for a reasonable period of time (usually 12-13 months) after that point. And hospice programs also respond to the needs of other care providers who may have taken part in caring for the individual with Alzheimer's disease. Finally, hospice programs develop and implement careful programs of selection, training, and mentoring, along with both formal and informal programs of support, for their own staff members and volunteers.

Hospice Programs of Care and Alzheimer's Disease

Hospice programs have extensive experience in caring for patients with far-advanced disease who are nearing the end of their lives, as well as for their family members. This experience can and already has been applied to individuals with Alzheimer's disease. Thus, the National Hospice and Palliative Care Organization (2003) has estimated that approximately 7 percent of all individuals admitted to hospice care in 2002 had Alzheimer's disease as their primary diagnosis.

Admission for these individuals is normally based on Functional Assessment Staging (FAST; Reisberg, 1988). According to the FAST criteria, an individual with Alzheimer's disease is usually judged to be appropriate for admission when that individual is rated no higher than Stage 7b. This means that the individual's "speech ability is limited to the use of a single intelligible word in an average day or in the course of an intensive interview (the person may repeat the word over and over)." Such an individual would ordinarily have a score of 0 on a Mini Mental State Exam and would be diagnosed as having a life expectancy of six months or less. For an individual in these circumstances, the question that hospice staff members might ask family members or other persons is: "Would you be surprised by this patient's death within the next year?"

A good example of a hospice program that admits Alzheimer's patients can be found in Hospice of the Florida Suncoast (HFS) in Pinellas County, Florida (encompassing St. Petersburg, Clearwater, Largo, and several other cities located between the western side of Tampa Bay and the Gulf of Mexico). Hospice of the Florida Suncoast is the largest community-based hospice program in the world with an average census in September 2003 of 1,700 patients per day. Approximately 6-8 percent of these patients have advanced Alzheimer's disease. Like many hospice programs that have accepted Alzheimer's patients, HFS looks to core and disease-specific indicators such as the following on which to base its admission decisions:

Core Indicators	Disease-Specific Indicators for Dementia
Physical decline	Unable to walk without assistance
Weight loss	Urinary and fecal incontinence
Multiple comorbidities	Complications: aspiration pneumonia, urinary tract infection, sepsis, decubiti
Serum albumin <2.5 gm/dl	Speech limited to <= 6 words/day
Dependence in most ADL's	Unable to dress without assistance Unable to sit up or hold head up Difficulty swallowing/eating
Karnofsky Score <= 50%	Reduced nutritional status

Patients who can be described by indicators like these often face multiple health challenges, are clearly quite far advanced in their disease, and are nearing death.

Like all hospice programs, Hospice of the Florida Suncoast offers comprehensive care for the Alzheimer's patients that it admits. In this case, those services might be delivered in residential facilities that are part of the HFS system, as well as in nursing homes and assisted living facilities that have cooperative arrangements with the hospice program. HFS is also able to offer services to Alzheimer's patients under its (non-hospice) license as a home care provider. This can help establish productive relationships with Alzheimer's families well ahead of the time for traditional hospice care. In every setting services offered by HFS address issues related to all of the core and disease-specific indicators noted above, as well as other issues that might arise such as previously unrecognized or untreated depression or pain in Alzheimer's patients who are incapable of verbal communication.

In addition to services for the patient, hospice programs that offer services to an individual with Alzheimer's disease must also be attentive to the needs of his or her family members and other care providers who have been involved with that individual and family. Family members, in particular, typically need many things:

- Support in their roles as family care providers, whether some or all of the family members live with, near, or at a distance from the person with Alzheimer's disease;

- Education that will explain and help family care providers to understand the behaviors of the person they love who may have changed so much because of his or her disease;

- Guidance as to how family members can respond most effectively to those behaviors and changes;

- Encouragement for family members to find appropriate ways to address their own personal life demands, including physical handicaps and individual health care burdens, even in the midst of caring for their loved one with Alzheimer's disease;

- Opportunities to share their burdens with members of the hospice team and others;

- Permission to take respite from their obligations as family care providers, especially when responding to those obligations may risk wearing them out;

- Assistance in coping with the loss to this disease of the "person" whom they love, adapting to the new individual who remains biologically alive, and then coping with new types of loss and grief when that individual dies.

Other caregivers are likely to have been involved in providing care for the individual with Alzheimer's disease, for example, at home or in a long-term care facility. Hospice programs must strive not to discount or push aside the knowledge and skills of these familiar caregivers. Instead, family members, traditional caregivers, and hospice staff must learn to work together as a team in planning and delivering care.

Many of these familiar caregivers may have formed special relationships with the individual with Alzheimer's disease. Sometimes, they may be a kind of surrogate family to that individual, at least until death nears and traditional families appear on the scene. Hospice programs must strive to help all of these familiar caregivers, as well as family members, cope with the losses they are currently experiencing as the person with Alzheimer's disease approaches his or her death. Hospice programs can also try to prepare these persons, insofar as that is possible, for the death of the individual in question and to support them in coping with their bereavement following that death. One small contribution to this work might be when a hospice chaplain or staff member returns to a long-term care facility after an individual with Alzheimer's disease has died and provides some form of memorial service for the staff, family, and interested residents.

Hospice programs of care can offer specific expertise in relation to particular issues that frequently arise in the course of Alzheimer's disease, such as:

- Respite care or day care, which can provide the Alzheimer's patient with a change of scenery and a context in which he or she can be closely monitored and evaluated for a relatively short period of time, as well as an opportunity for family members to find some relief from the burdens they experience over long periods of time in providing care for their loved one;

- End-of-life decision making in situations such as: when the individual with Alzheimer's disease is still sufficiently competent to formulate and give consent to advance directives about future care issues and other matters; when family members are challenged by having to uphold an individual's previously-established decisions about end of life; or when family members have to act on their own best judgment because there is no existing advance directive and there have been no prior detailed conversations with the individual on these matters;

- Treating infections that may arise in the course of the disease, especially when the individual with Alzheimer's disease is bed bound and limited in his or her ability to perform activities of daily living;

- Choosing to use or decline restraints, an issue that involves balancing concerns for safety with those of individual freedom and family perspectives;

- Providing resources and information as needed or appropriate to help reduce the fears, apprehensions, and isolation of family members;

- Using tube feedings, as well as foregoing (withholding or withdrawing) nutrition and hydration, related issues that are difficult for family members to consider but are likely to arise in far-advanced Alzheimer's disease (Such questions might include: Is it right to start our loved one on regimes of artificial feeding in his or her present condition and in light of a death that seems both near and inevitable? Does withholding or withdrawal of such regimes amount to starving our loved one or causing death?);

- Helping family members identify their proper roles in providing care to their loved one, roles that do not overwhelm their capacities and that respect the losses they, too, are experiencing during the progression of the disease and at the death of their loved one.

ALZHEIMER'S AND HOSPICE: SOME ONGOING CHALLENGES

Although we believe that hospice programs have many resources and competencies to offer to situations involving Alzheimer's disease, we also believe that hospice programs need to be judicious and deliberate about their decision to accept such patients. All hospice programs need to work within the limits and requirements of hospice Medicare legislation (which is often a model for private health insurance, as well), unless they can develop other sources of reimbursement or funding to support their services. When they are restricted to serving individuals who have been certified as having a prognosis of six months or less to live, hospice programs may do their best work by sharing with other caregivers the principles of palliative care that they represent and serving as a model for what that care has to offer in advanced Alzheimer's disease.

That is one reason why, before entering into this work, hospice programs should first determine whether or not there really is a need in their community for hospice services for Alzheimer's patients. Perhaps any supposed need is already being met in appropriate ways by other community health services.

At the same time, before taking on Alzheimer's patients, hospice programs need to identify available resources that can be directed to this purpose. Such resources may be found within their own programs or within the community at large. In particular, it is likely that hospice programs will need to establish close partnerships with community resources through cooperative arrangements with home care agencies, assisted living facilities, and long-term care facilities to provide optimal care for Alzheimer's patients.

Hospices will need to apply sensitively and sensibly their own goals as they deal with other organizations. Sometimes poorly trained staff can misinterpret the mission of hospice. For example, we know of one hospice program that was working with a long-term care facility to care for an Alzheimer's patient. When that patient developed problems in swallowing and the facility's rehab director proposed a non-invasive intervention to alleviate those problems, a hospice staff member commented, "You know this person is dying, don't you?" We certainly agree that every intervention proposed for a hospice patient should be evaluated to determine the person's desire for such intervention (which may, in many cases of advanced Alzheimer's disease, be expressed by a surrogate decision maker), its relevance to the needs of the individual patient, the likelihood that it will improve that individual's quality of life, and its appropriateness in relation to the hospice interdisciplinary team's plan of care. Nevertheless, handicaps in swallowing can significantly impair an individual's quality of life. For that reason, to reject an intervention for a hospice patient solely on the grounds that the individual is dying is to undercut the whole point of hospice services.

In addition, hospice staff need to recognize that some of their special strengths such as pain control may not be applicable in every situation. We have had personal experience of a hospice nurse who visited one of our own family members who had been recently admitted to a hospice program. That nurse delivered a lengthy explanation of the abilities that she and her hospice team had to manage pain. Sadly, the relevance of that explanation was shown to be questionable when the patient finally asked: "This pain that you are speaking of, when will it begin?"

In approaching individuals with Alzheimer's disease, as in approaching all other individuals whom they are to serve, hospice programs need to insure that their staff members *listen carefully* to the needs and concerns of the ill person, his or her family members, and everyone else who is or has been involved in caring for this person and family. If members of hospice interdisciplinary teams can do that and can develop timely and effective interventions that are relevant to all of those needs and concerns, then they certainly do have much to contribute to meeting the challenges posed by Alzheimer's disease to hospice programs and the hospice philosophy of care. ■

We dedicate this chapter to the memory of James J. Sands, our Uncle Jim, who died of Alzheimer's disease on March 24, 1991.

Charles A. Corr, PhD, is Professor emeritus, Southern Illinois University Edwardsville, and a member of the following organizations: the Executive Committee of the National Kidney Foundation's transAction Council; the Board of Directors of the Hospice Institute of the Florida Suncoast; the ChiPPS (Children's Project on Palliative/Hospice Services) Executive Committee of the National Hospice and Palliative Care Organization; and the International Work Group on Death, Dying, and Bereavement (Chairperson, 1989-93). Dr. Corr's publications include 25 books and booklets, along with more than 75 articles and chapters, in the field of death, dying, and bereavement. His most recent publication is the fourth edition of Death and Dying, Life and Living (Wadsworth, 2003), co-authored with Clyde M. Nabe and Donna M. Corr.

Karen M. Corr, RN, MSN, ARNP, is a gerontological nurse practitioner in a shared geriatric practice and a consultant in local skilled nursing facilities in Tacoma, Washington. Her article, "Taking the Gloves Off: Caring for Confused Patients without Using Restraints" (co-authored with Donna M. Corr, RN, MS), was published in Nursing94.

Susan M. Ramsey, MS, CCC-SLP, is a speech-language pathologist and Regional Rehab Director for CPL in Tacoma, Washington. She has practiced in a geriatric setting since 1991 and has presented at the local and state level on the topics of swallowing, its disorders, and management strategies.

REFERENCES

Mace, N.L., & Rabins, P.V. (1999). *The 36-hour day: A family guide to caring for persons with Alzheimer disease, related dementing illnesses, and memory loss in later life* (3rd ed.). Baltimore: Johns Hopkins University Press.

National Hospice and Palliative Care Organization. (2003). *NHPCO facts and figures.* Alexandria, VA: Author.

Reisberg, B. (1988). Functional assessment staging (FAST). *Psychopharmacology Bulletin, 24,* 653-659.

World Health Organization [WHO]. (1990). *Cancer pain relief and palliative care.* WHO Technical Report Series 804. Geneva, Switzerland: Author.

■ CHAPTER 16 ■

Alzheimer's and the (Underused) Medicare Hospice Benefit

Leslie Fried

Calling Hospice to qualify a loved one with Alzheimer's disease or related dementia can be a difficult step for a caregiver to take… Many times for a caregiver to admit to herself that their loved one is on the final leg of the journey, can be scary…Many caregivers do not realize that they can use hospice for end stage Alzheimer's disease and other related dementias, not just cancer or AIDS.
—Edyth Ann Knox, author of
Hospice and Alzheimer's Disease: One Family's Story

THE PROMISE OF THE MEDICARE HOSPICE BENEFIT

Hospice is a special way of caring for people who are terminally ill, and for their family. This care includes physical care and counseling. Hospice provides palliative or comfort care for an individual at the end-of-life. The primary purpose of hospice care is to manage the pain and other symptoms of the terminal illness, rather than to provide treatment for the illness. Through hospice, families and caregivers receive almost daily assistance and support to provide the difficult care for their family member from professionals trained in end-of-life care. For many caregivers, hospice provides substantial reinforcement in the challenging task of caring for their family member.

Although the hospice benefit provides integrated care services, prescription medications and counseling for the beneficiary and family members, it is an under-utilized benefit by Medicare beneficiaries with Alzheimer's disease. Not surprisingly, cancer is the prominent diagnosis of individuals in hospice, accounting for 63 percent of the hospice population. As individuals with Alzheimer's near the end stages of the disease, they are enrolling in hospice in greater numbers. In 1996, only 2.3 percent of the hospice population had a primary diagnosis of Alzheimer's disease (Gage & Dao, 2000). Yet, in 2000, approximately six percent of the hospice population had a primary diagnosis of dementia (U.S. Department of Health and Human Services, 2003).

THE MEDICARE HOSPICE BENEFIT: ELIGIBILITY AND MEDICAL NECESSITY

Most individuals with Alzheimer's disease depend on Medicare as their primary health insurance. In order for Medicare to cover hospice services, beneficiaries must meet the following criteria:

- The individual is entitled to Medicare Part A benefits;

- The individual's treating physician and a hospice medical director certify that the individual is terminally ill, that is, his or her life expectancy is six months or less, if the illness runs its normal course; and

- The individual chooses or elects to receive hospice care and gives up (waives) the right for Medicare to pay for any other services to treat the terminal illness. Instead, Medicare pays the hospice and any related physician expenses. Medicare will continue to pay for any services not related to the terminal illness. (Center for Medicare and Medicaid Services, 2000)

Determining when an individual with Alzheimer's disease is terminally ill, that is, has a life expectancy of six months or less, can be problematic for physicians. Physicians are often poor prognosticators with regard to when their patients have a life expectancy of six months or less (Christakis, 2000). Unlike cancer, Alzheimer's disease does not progress in the same way in all individuals, making it difficult for physicians to determine when the individual is terminally ill for purposes of eligibility for the Medicare benefit. In a recent program memorandum, the Centers for Medicare and Medicaid Services (CMS) explained that the six month test is a general one: "CMS recognizes that medical prognostication is not an exact science" (CMS, 2003).

In order to assist physicians with prognosis, hospice organizations have published guidelines to help identify which dementia patients are likely to have a prognosis of six months or less, if the disease runs its normal course (National Hospice Organization, 1996). These guidelines were only developed to facilitate doctors in their clinical decisions as to whether hospice care may be appropriate for a patient. Private insurance companies that contract with CMS to process Medicare hospice claims (called fiscal intermediaries) have modified these guidelines to determine appropriateness of payment. Fiscal intermediaries have significant latitude to develop rules as to when an individual is "terminally ill" and therefore, medically eligible for hospice. These local rules, called Local Coverage Determinations or Local Medical Review Policies, may be overly restrictive and limit access to hospice for a non-cancer diagnosis, such as Alzheimer's disease or dementia.

For example, currently most Medicare contractors require that in order for an Alzheimer's beneficiary to be eligible for hospice, the patient must show all of the following characteristics:

I. 1. Stage seven or beyond according to the Functional Assessment Staging (FAST) Scale;
2. Unable to ambulate without assistance;
3. Unable to dress without assistance;
4. Unable to bathe without assistance;
5. Urinary and fecal incontinence, intermittent or constant; and
6. No meaningful verbal communication; stereotypical phrases only or ability to speak is limited to six or fewer intelligible words.

II. In addition, the patients must have had one of the following
within the past 12 months:
1. Aspiration pneumonia;
2. Pyelonephritis or other upper urinary tract infection;
3. Septicemia;
4. Decubitus ulcers, multiple, stage 3-4;
5. Fever, recurrent after antibiotics; or
6. Inability to maintain sufficient fluid and calorie intake with
10 percent weight loss during the previous six months or
serum albumin < 2.5 gm/dl.

(Palmetto Government Benefits Administrators, 1998)

The substantial reliance on the Functional Assessment Staging Test
(FAST) scale to ascertain life expectancy is controversial. Its overuse has
been questioned by, among others, Barry Riesberg, who developed it. In a
long-term study of dementia patients published in 1996, Dr. Riesberg and
his co-authors found that the use of the FAST scale is limited to patients
whose disease progresses in an ordinal fashion throughout the stages of the
scale, and does not skip stages. In addition, Dr. Riesberg noted that functional loss according to the FAST scale might not be valid for patients with
dementia other than Alzheimer's disease.

Geriatricians and hospice providers have expressed concern that these
criteria will decrease access and length of stay in hospice for some dementia patients. In a recent commentary, one bioethicist whose mother died
from Alzheimer's disease without the benefit of hospice care observed that
the current criteria for Medicare coverage of Alzheimer's disease "do not
reflect a state-of-the-art understanding of late stage Alzheimer's disease"
(Jennings, 2003).

Although Medicare is a federal program with the same benefits provided to all beneficiaries regardless of geographic location, Medicare contractors that process its claims have considerable discretion to determine when
services are medically reasonable or necessary for a given diagnosis. For
example, the local coverage policy for determining terminal illness for
dementia patients in the New England states is similar to the criteria listed
above. However, the Medicare contractor requires that the individual show

only four of the criteria listed in section I above, not all of them. Consequently, a beneficiary who lives in Massachusetts and is in the end stage of Alzheimer's disease will be eligible for hospice care services earlier than the same beneficiary who lives across the border in New York or Ohio due to the local coverage policies in effect in those states. These variations in local coverage policies that determine the terminal status of beneficiaries with dementia often result in inequitable restrictions on access to treatment based on the beneficiaries' place of residence.

Once an individual decides to enroll in hospice, the individual may receive benefits for two periods of 90 days each, and an unlimited number of periods of 60 days each. At the beginning of each period, the patient has to be certified as terminally ill, in accordance with the guidelines implemented by the Medicare contractor. The recertification process can be very stressful for the family and caregivers. Once they have acknowledged that their family member is dying, and have accepted hospice into their home and lives, the family learns to depend on the hospice staff for their care and comfort. A family member describes the angst she experienced during the recertification process as follows:

> I found the requalifying (especially the frequency with which
> it occurred) the most stressful. In order for your loved one to
> requalify for hospice and for Medicare to cover the cost you must
> show that the loved one has declined since the last evaluation
> of hospice. This can be very difficult to do with those with
> Alzheimer's disease and related dementias. To me, the requalifi-
> cation process brought great stress. The fear that hospice would
> drop Milly from their program was intense. (Knox, 2000)

Some hospice patients, or their families, may decide that hospice is not what they expected or may be averse to a home death. If at any time the individual changes his or her mind, the individual can decide to stop receiving hospice care and immediately begin to receive the other Medicare benefits.

HOSPICE: A WEALTH OF SERVICES

Once an individual elects to participate in a hospice program, the hospice agency must establish a plan of care for the palliation and management of the terminal condition. This integrated and interdisciplinary approach to care, coupled with the provision of a broad array of hospice services, is rare in the Medicare program. Some of these services are not currently covered in the non-hospice traditional fee-for-service program. The following hospice services, provided by qualified personnel, are included in this benefit: nursing services, nurse practitioner services, physician services, physical, occupational and speech therapy, medical social services, home health aide and homemaker services, counseling services for the individual and family members, short-term inpatient care, respite care, outpatient prescription drugs and medical appliances, and supplies. In addition, Medicare will continue to pay for services provided by the beneficiary's treating physician.

Hospice care is most often provided in the beneficiary's home. However, hospice can also be provided in a freestanding hospice facility or in a hospital or nursing facility. If an individual is a resident of a nursing facility, Medicare will only pay for the hospice services provided, not for the nursing facility's room and board expenses (Center for Medicare and Medicaid Services, 2000).

There are generally four levels of hospice care, which correlate with four different payment rates to the hospice agency. Most hospice patients remain in their home and receive less than eight hours of care a day. This is considered routine home care. In some circumstances, during periods of crisis in order to allow the patient to stay at home, the hospice can provide "continuous home care" during which the hospice would provide more than eight hours of care a day, which would principally be provided by nursing staff. The other levels of care are provided as an inpatient in the hospital. Inpatient respite care is provided in order to afford short-term relief to the individual's caregivers and general inpatient care is provided when necessary to control pain or manage symptoms.

Unlike most Medicare benefits, there are no deductibles and only limited coinsurance payments for hospice services. A beneficiary is responsible for five percent of the cost of a drug or biological, not to exceed $5.00.

For respite care, there is a coinsurance payment of five percent of the Medicare payment for each respite care day.

AN UNFULFILLED PROMISE: BARRIERS TO CARE

The primary barrier to hospice care for Alzheimer's patients is the six-month life expectancy rule and the criteria for enrollment utilized by some fiscal intermediaries. Use of these criteria results in delayed referral to hospice or no referral at all. From 1992-1998, there was significant growth in the number of Alzheimer's beneficiaries who elected to enroll in a hospice program. Yet during that same period, the average number of days used in hospice declined significantly. In 1992, beneficiaries with a primary diagnosis of Alzheimer's disease averaged almost 180 days of hospice. In 1998, the average days of use for this population declined to 100 (General Accounting Office, 2000).

There are multiple reasons, other than the restrictive Medicare rules, that impact the decision to and the timing of enrollment in hospice. As individuals near the end-stages of Alzheimer's disease, they usually have lost their capacity to make decisions about their health care. Family members or close friends usually become the individual's agent or surrogate to make health care decisions. It is strongly recommended that treating physicians and other health care providers encourage their patients and families to discuss the patients' wishes and preferences for end-of-life health care prior to loss of capacity. It is best when patients' preferences are known and can guide the decision maker when end-of-life decisions are required. Thus, it is the patients' wishes regarding end-of-life-care that are being followed when difficult choices must be considered.

To enroll someone in hospice, families will have to accept and acknowledge that the beneficiary's death is on the horizon. As Alzheimer's research has dramatically increased over the past decade, some families may be hopeful that a treatment may be developed to slow or arrest the progression of the disease. In October 2003, the United States Federal Drug Administration approved the first drug, memantine, for treatment of moderate to severe Alzheimer's disease. In several clinical trials, memantine demonstrated that it could benefit cognition, as well as overall function of the Alzheimer's patients. Families will have to surrender hope of improvement and acknowledge that their family member will succumb to the disease before accepting hospice and palliative care as an alternative to aggressive treatment.

Physicians and family members are often not well informed about the availability of hospice or the range of services provided. In a recent study, caregivers of individuals with dementia expressed a willingness to consider hospice enrollment after a detailed discussion of the goals and service provided by hospice agencies (Casarett, 2002). The study authors recommend that clinicians initiate discussions about hospice and emphasize the potential benefits for the caregivers as well. Yet, given that physicians are particularly poor prognosticators of life expectancy for their patients with Alzheimer's disease, they fail to inform family members about hospice or refer their patients for hospice care in a timely manner. Some physicians find it particularly difficult discussing end-of-life for their Alzheimer's patients since they often die from other complications or infections (Hurley, 2002). Generally, in order for a patient to have maximum benefit of the services provided by hospice, the care should be provided for a minimum of 30 days. In 2000, less than nine percent of dementia patients in hospice were enrolled in hospice for 30 days or more. The average length of hospice care for this population was 12.9 days (U.S. Department of Health and Human Services, 2003). The first few weeks of hospice care is the most time extensive and expensive for the provider, given the need to assess the patient and develop a care plan to meet those needs. It is clinically beneficial for the patient and fiscally most advantageous for the hospice provider for the individual to be enrolled promptly upon the determination that the patient is terminally ill.

Finally, once a caregiver acknowledges the benefits of hospice, it is important for caregivers to investigate the hospice agencies that service their community to determine if they accept patients with dementia. One physician recounted how once his patient's family accepted hospice as an appropriate alternative, it was difficult to locate a hospice willing to enroll the individual with dementia (Hurley, 2002).

THE HOSPICE PROMISE: WORTH ITS WEIGHT IN GOLD

For Alzheimer's individuals and their families, hospice provides the greatest breadth of services and assistance at the end of a difficult journey. It provides support for the physical and emotional needs of terminally ill individuals and their families. Receiving the full benefit often requires advocacy by the treating physician, the family or caregiver, and the hospice provider to overcome barriers to care and to Medicare coverage. With hospice, Alzheimer's patients can receive quality end-of-life care in their home and their family members can receive essential support. The teamwork and advocacy effort to remove impediments to access hospice is a worthwhile endeavor, for the benefits received are worth their weight in gold. ■

Leslie Freid, J.D., is an associate staff director with the American Bar Association Commission on Law and Aging. She joined the ABA in September 1998, as the Medicare Advocacy Project attorney, a collaborative project with the Alzheimer's Association. She specializes in Medicare issues and responds to Alzheimer's-related Medicare inquiries from local Alzheimer's Association chapters. From 2001-2003, Ms. Fried was a member of the National Academy of Social Insurance Study Panel on Medicare and Chronic Care in the 21st Century. In 2003, she was selected to be a member of the National Academy of Social Insurance, a nonpartisan organization made up of the nation's leading experts on social insurance.

REFERENCES

Casarett, D., Takesaka, J., Karlawish, J., Hirschman, K., & Clark, C. (2002). How should clinicians discuss hospice for patients with dementia? Anticipating caregivers' preconceptions and meeting their needs. *Alzheimer's Disease and Associated Disorders, 16*(2), 116-122.

Center for Medicare and Medicaid Services [CMS]. (2000). *Medicare Hospice Manual,* 42 CFR: §418.20-.24; §200; §204. Washington, DC: Author.

CMS. (2003, March). *Hospice care enhances dignity and peace as life nears its end.* Program Transmittal AB-03-040.

Christakis, N. (2000, September). *Barriers to the use of hospice care at the end of life.* Presented before the U.S. Senate Special Committee on Aging, Washington, DC.

Gage, B., & Dao, T. (2000). *Medicare's hospice benefit: Use and expenditures—1996 Cohort.* Washington, DC: U.S. Department of Health and Human Services.

General Accounting Office. (2000). *Medicare: More beneficiaries use hospice, yet many factors contribute to shorter stays.* (GAO/HEHS-00-201). Washington, DC: author

Hurley, A., & Volicer, L. (2002). It's okay, mam, if you want to go, it's okay. *JAMA, 266*(18).

Jennings, B. (2003). Hospice and Alzheimer's disease: A study in access and simple justice. *Hastings Center Report* (Suppl. 33, No. 2), S24-S26.

Knox, E. (2003). *Hospice and Alzheimer's disease: One family's story.* Retrieved December 23, 2003, from http://www.ec-online.net/Knowledge/Articles/hospiceknox.html

National Hospice Organization. (1996). *Medical guidelines for determining prognosis in selected non-cancer diseases* (2nd ed.). Arlington, VA: Author.

Palmetto Government Benefits Administrators. (2003). *LMRP for hospice-dementia (L285), original policy effective date January 29, 1998.* Washington, DC: American Medical Association.

Reisberg, B., Ferris, S.H., Franssen, E.H., et al. (1996). Mortality and temporal course of probable Alzheimer's disease: A five-year prospective study. *International Psychogeriatrics, 8*(2), 291-311.

U.S. Department of Health and Human Services. (2003). *Characteristics of hospice care discharges and their length of service: United States, 2000* (NCHS Series report 13, No. 154). Hyattsville, MD: Author.

CHAPTER 17

Ethical Challenges of End-of-Life Care for Dementia Patients

Jennifer Kapo and Jason Karlawish

Hospice is a successful model for providing holistic palliative care to patients with advanced stages of chronic diseases as well as to their families. A key feature of this model is that it is patient-centered and driven. Until the very last days or weeks of their illness, patients direct their care. When, in the final days of life, they become too ill to do this, their previously expressed preferences speak for them. These preferences guide both hospice providers and families in making day-to-day decisions for the patient. The knowledge of these preferences gives them the confidence that they have a good sense that they are doing what the person would want.

The hospice model is also successful because the standard of care for the typical hospice patient with cancer is reasonably well understood. Clinicians are fairly comfortable determining when a patient with metastatic cancer meets criteria for hospice placement because they have guidance from studies and practical experience in predicting the illness trajectory and the prognosis of metastatic cancer. They are also comfortable with treatment decisions. Clinicians understand how to assess cancer patients' symptoms and how to alleviate them. There are abundant scientific studies examining the effects of pain in cancer and the treatments that are most effective to guide physicians.

But hospice care for persons with dementia presents four unique challenges. First, demented patients have lost the ability to direct their care long before they have reached the terminal stage. Any preferences for care they did make were spoken or written several years before their dementia progressed to terminal stage. Second, the person who is responsible for making decisions for them—typically called a caregiver—is not simply a decision maker but also suffers from symptoms in need of palliation, especially depression and anxiety. Third, the standard of care for symptom assessment and management is not well defined. Finally, the ability to determine prognosis and the judgment that a patient is terminal is laced with uncertainty.

The failure of the health care system to meet these unique challenges has substantial costs for persons with dementia and their families. Their final months of life may be marked by unnecessary interventions such as tube feeding and repeated hospitalizations. Demented patients may fail to receive needed interventions such as satisfactory pain control due to inadequate assessment. This also has costs for society. An estimated 4 million persons have dementia and the growth of the aged population means the projected prevalence could be as many as 15 million by 2030. Not only will the care of these patients be costly, but also the accumulated experience of patients receiving less than optimal palliative care offends our society's expectations that all persons are treated with dignity and respect.

Clinicians, policy makers, and families can meet these challenges. Below we describe these challenges in detail and propose strategies for clinicians and caregivers to approach these obstacles aiming to achieve the ultimate goal of providing superior end-of-life care for all patients with dementia.

THE CHALLENGE OF THE LOSS OF SELF-CONTROL

One of the paramount ethical principles of modern medicine is respect for patient's autonomous choice. This principle is fulfilled through the practice of informed consent. A patient makes medical decisions after the clinician explains the risks, benefits, and alternatives of a treatment and the patient shows adequate ability to think about this information. These abilities include understanding, appreciation, and reasoning. For each decision, the clinician's responsibility as a teacher is to assure that the patient has enough ability to make the decision.

In most illnesses, patients retain enough cognitive function that they are able to make their own medical decisions or direct other people, such as a trusted family member to make decisions for them. But in the care of persons with a neurodegenerative dementia, decision-making is markedly different. Early in the course of the illness, the patient has impairments in the ability to make decisions. By the moderate stage of the disease, these impairments are substantial. A family member is typically making decisions for the patient.

This stereotypical pattern has substantial consequences over the decision to enroll in hospice. Autonomy and the respect for the desires of the patient are particularly important when considering decisions about end-of-life care. The choice between aggressive curative treatments versus treatments that maximize comfort is often based on a person's previous life experiences, values, fears, and hopes. Quite literally, it is a matter of life and death. But in the care of persons with dementia, years before it is time to make the decision to enroll in hospice, the patient is unable to decide whether he or she wants to be in hospice.

A set of ethical norms and practices has developed around deciding for others. Clinicians and families can rely on the written documents or statements the patients made when they could reason and communicate clearly. These advance directives are a means of expressing wishes about end-of-life care when patients can no longer speak for themselves. These are usually divided into two kinds: a living will and a durable power of attorney for medical decision-making. A living will describes a patient's wishes regarding treatments such as intubation and feeding tube. A durable power of attorney identifies an individual who the patient chooses to act as a surrogate decision maker once he is unable to speak for himself because of illness and disease progression.

But how useful are advance directives in the care of persons with dementia? Patients with terminal dementia completed the advance directive many years prior to the occasion when the document is needed. Clinicians and family members must interpret documents written when the patient had little if any experience of the illness that may cause their death.

This raises legitimate concerns about the relevance of the document to guide decisions about the patient's present circumstances.

These concerns center on the validity of advance directives to represent the patient's preferences. Family members or clinicians may feel that the demented patient would make different choices if she could see her current state. They may also find that the document does not address the possibility of living with dementia. Could the person writing the advanced directive anticipate what it would be like to live with dementia? If she could not, does that alter the validity of the advanced directive?

At the core of these questions is a problem of personal identity. Ethicists argue two opposing views of personal identity in a person with dementia. Those that follow Derek Parfit's position, the Parfitians, believe that a person with end stage dementia is so completely different from the person they were prior to the development of dementia given the severity of their impairment that, in fact, they are a different person. The competent, non-demented person who wrote the advanced directive is a different person than the incompetent, demented patient (Dresser & Whitehouse, 1994). Therefore, the advanced directive is not valid, and decisions about end-of-life treatment should be based on the benefits and risks to the person who the patient is at present.

A common example used to describe this theory is of a patient who wrote a detailed advanced directive indicating that she did not want life-sustaining treatment of any kind if she were to develop significant cognitive impairment. As she aged, she developed dementia and lost the capacity to make medical decisions. Although vastly different from her previous self, she appears happy, has no pain, and exhibits no signs of suffering in any sense. Parfitians would argue that the competent person who wrote the initial advanced directive has no semblance to the demented and incompetent, but content person. A Parfitian would advise that medical decisions be made based on the patient's current best interest.

Richard Dworkin advances an opposing viewpoint (Dworkin, 1993; Rich, 1998). He argues that the competent patient who transformed into the incompetent patient as the dementia progressed is still the same person. The competent person may have envisioned the progression of dementia with significant cognitive and functional impairment to be a life not worth living. Therefore any advanced directive stating her wishes should be honored. The competent and non-competent persons are the same person, and therefore the advance directive is valid.

Dworkin further clarifies personal identity as having two types of interests that shape it: experiential and critical. Experiential interests are valued for the pleasure they provide but have no essential value. An example could be the sensory pleasure of eating an ice cream cone. Critical interests have an enduring value for the identity of the person. Examples are the pursuit of a career and the raising of a family. He suggests that the progression of dementia involves the loss of critical interests, replaced almost exclusively by experiential interests. The recognition of this eventual loss of meaningful experiences may guide patients to desire the limitation of medical treatments in advanced directives (Rich, 1998). Parfitians may focus on the experiential interests and aim to maximize positive interests, or what is in the best interest of the persons in the state in which they currently exist.

What do these two opposing ethical views have to do with the day-to-day care of persons with dementia? They are not simply an armchair dilemma. They are the foundation of the sharp disagreements over decisions for patients. Imagine the discord among family members who have opposing views on personal identify in a person with dementia! There is a possible solution to these dilemmas. One approach reinvents the context of the debate between warring schools of personal identity. Instead of a clash of the then self versus the now self, it asks who is this self here before us? The answer to these questions seeks a narrative consensus (Karlawish & Casarett, 1999) regarding the best treatment plan for an individual who cannot make medical decisions.

Narrative consensus recognizes that all lives are a story that will end. It demands of the family and the clinicians to discuss how that ending will come to pass. The clinical and ethical facts of treatment decisions including the medical necessity of different approaches, and stories about the patient's life, her values and goals that in total describe and define who the patient is are the materials to generate a narrative portraying the patient's final months of life. By merging these ideas, a consensus can be reached as to the best care plan for the patient.

This alternative theory has empirical support. When patients are asked to execute an advance directive about how they would want to be cared for if they had dementia, many will grant their proxy freedom or leeway to do the opposite of the advance directive. In other words, they are granting family the authority to tell a story that is different than how the patient thinks it should be told. This approach describes an ethic grounded in trust in the family. Clinicians can help a family member who is struggling with whether to do what the patient wants or what is in the patient's best interests by prompting the family member to think about how much leeway or freedom the patient would have granted the family member in making this decision.

The Challenge of the Patient as Part of a Dyad

Hospice workers, as well as other practitioners who care for patients at the end of their lives recognize that the family becomes the unit of care, rather than the terminally ill patient alone. In fact, all Medicare certified hospice programs view the patient and her family as a care unit, and provide bereavement services for families up to a year after their loved one has died. Care of demented patients raises unique issues. Caregivers experience substantial morbidity including depression as well as physical ailments including infections and sleep disorders. Caregiver strain has been studied, and scales have been developed that describe the particular stresses that are placed on caregivers.

This focus on the family as the unit of care poses distinctive dilemmas. Caregivers may request treatments of unproven efficacy if they fear the patient is suffering. A common example of this is the request for tube feeding for a patient with end stage dementia who has lost the ability to swallow properly. Although tube feeding has not be shown to have any survival or palliative benefit for patients with end stage dementia, clinicians may feel compelled to place the tube to alleviate the psychological suffering of the family faced with believing they are starving the patient, despite the fact that when hand fed, the patient takes in little food and does not experience suffering from starvation.

Other treatment decisions may be based on the caregiver interpreting signs and utterances by the patient as meaning they are experiencing discomfort. In some situations, it is unlikely that these signs correlate to patient's suffering; however, it is virtually impossible to determine with confidence what "the truth" is. This situation is often encountered during the last hours to days of a person's life. During this time, patients frequently make a gurgling noise as secretions pool in their throat. To eliminate this noise and thereby alleviate concerns of the family, a medicine can be administered to dry the secretions. However, this medicine has the adverse effect of causing urinary retention and dry mouth, potentially uncomfortable symptoms. Since the clinician is unable to ask the patient if she is having trouble breathing, it remains a treatment dilemma, and focus turns to the suffering of the family who is present, and their distress. Should the family's needs ever take precedence other the patient's needs? When assessment of the patient is difficult, should clinicians focus on the family's distress?

An approach to these questions uses two strategies. First, clinicians have a clear responsibility to evaluate and treat the family members for depression and anxiety. There is copious evidence of increased risks of depression and anxiety. There are even case reports of caregivers who have committed suicide or have killed their demented relative. A reasonable approach is to screen the caregivers for depression and caregiver strain, and to have a means to contact their primary physician if concerns arise. Referrals to support groups for caregivers of Alzheimer's disease patients are also recommended. Caring for the caregiver will not only benefit the caregiver, but will allow them to continue to care for the demented patient. Second, clinicians need to keep the focus on maximizing the patient and the caregiver's dignity and quality of life.

The Challenge of Deciding That the Patient is Dying

Implicit in the discussion above is the idea that patients with dementia reach a definable stage when it is widely recognized they are dying. But estimates that a patient is terminal are frequently inaccurate. Physicians tend to overestimate prognosis (Christakis & Lamont, 2000). These errors are substantially increased in prognosis for patients with dementia. There is considerable variability in illness trajectory seen among individuals with dementia.

In the early stages of the disease, decline is noted in the patient's memory and her ability to perform usual and everyday instrumental activities of daily living, such as managing money, cleaning, and shopping. As the disease progresses to the severe stage, patients lose the ability to perform their basic activities of daily living. But a patient in this stage still retains abilities to ambulate and eat. They may live for many more years. Behavioral problems such as agitation and aggression, that lead families and clinicians to identify the patient as "severely demented," typically wax and wane and may peak in the moderate stages of the disease, when the patient has many more years to live.

Although most staging criteria do not address stages beyond the severe stage, validated staging systems can aid in estimating prognosis in persons with dementia that is at least in the severe stage. The Functional Assessment Staging (FAST) model describes the progression of dementia through a series of seven stages (Reisburg, 1988). In Stage 1, patients have no observable symptoms while patients in Stage 7 are significantly impaired. Stage 7 identifies patients who have a median survival of six months or less. These patients are dependent on their caregivers for feeding, toileting, and dressing. Their ability to speak is severely limited to less than six words, and they lose the ability to walk and to hold their head up while sitting. Other predictors of poor prognosis include medical complications associated with dementia such as the development of skin ulcers, pneumonia, and urinary tract infections (Luchins, 1997).

Clinicians can use this tool to predict prognosis. However, they must recognize that the tool does not provide an exact estimate of each patient's survival. Patients have unique characteristics that affect their survival, such as other illnesses and caregivers who are more or less devoted and capable of round-the-clock care. Consequently, clinicians have a responsibility to communicate this uncertainty to the family making the decision for the patient. This discussion needs to address the cost of taking a "wait and see" approach to hospice. The patient and family are deprived of services they may benefit from.

ELUSIVENESS OF STANDARD OF CARE FOR DEMENTIA PATIENTS AT THE END OF LIFE

In the care of the typical patient in hospice, there is a reasonably well-established evidence base. But in the case of patients with dementia, there is a substantial gap in the quality of the evidence to support an intervention. An intervention that is widely used and highly controversial is enteral feeding. This is commonly prescribed for patients who have repeated episodes of aspiration. The logic of the procedure is that bypassing the oral route of eating will eliminate or substantially reduce the frequency of aspiration episodes. As appealing as this mechanism of action is, there is little evidence that supports it and no study has compared its efficacy and safety to oral feeding (Finucane et al, 1999). The variability of enteral feeding across the United States suggests that much of its use is largely driven by regional factors.

Assessment of a demented person's pain is another challenge for clinicians. Patients with severe dementia lose the ability to communicate. They can no longer express the need for pain medications or name the part of their body that hurts. Instead, demented patients may exhibit changes in behavior such as restlessness, irritability, or moaning that may or may not be related to pain. More subtle changes, such as decreased appetite or decreased alertness may also indicate that the patient is in pain.

Researchers have developed pain rating scales to guide those caring for demented patients in interpreting signs that could indicate the patients is in pain (Feldt, 2000). Although these scales can give clues that the patient is experiencing pain, it cannot determine this definitively. Caregivers are faced with treating pain empirically for conditions known to be associated with pain such as open wounds, or relying on criteria in scales that are likely too vague to distinguish between the presence and absence of pain. Complicating these decisions further is the knowledge that the administration of pain medicines is not completely benign. Pain medicines are associated with adverse effects such as constipation and mental status deterioration.

Although no clear standard of practice exists for the care of persons with end stage dementia, decisions must be made. Clinicians need to rely on information from the caregivers describing the status of the patient, their own observational evidence, and a weighing of the risks and potential benefits of treatment options. In each case, the decision to intervene or not to intervene should be viewed as an empirical exercise. There should be consensus between the health care practitioner and family on clear and measurable endpoints to define success and a willingness to change course if success is not achieved.

CONCLUSION

People do die of dementia. But ethical challenges may inhibit many people with dementia from benefiting from the hospice model for providing holistic palliative care to both patients and their families. These ethical challenges include deciding for others, failing to recognize the unique needs of the patient-caregiver dyad, prognostic uncertainty and an elusive standard of care. Clinicians need to recognize these challenges and adopt sensible approaches to address them. ■

Jennifer M. Kapo, MD is an Instructor in the Department of Medicine, Division of Geriatrics, and an Associate Fellow of the Center for Bioethics at the University of Pennsylvania. She is geriatrician at the Ralston House Geriatrics clinic at the University of Pennsylvania and teaches at the medical school. She is a recipient of the Hartford Academic Fellowship Award and the Geriatric Academic Career Award. Her research interests include the needs of patients who are discharged from hospice and the medical treatment of patients with non-cancer diagnoses at the end of their lives.

Jason H. T. Karlawish, MD is an Assistant Professor in the Department of Medicine, Division of Geriatrics, and a Fellow of the Center for Bioethics at the University of Pennsylvania. He is the Associate Director of the Memory Disorders Clinic and the Director of the Alzheimer's Disease Center's Education and Information Transfer Core. He is a recipient of a Brookdale National Fellowship, Paul Beeson Fellowship, Greenwall Faculty Scholar in Bioethics, and the Lancet's Wakley prize.

REFERENCES

Christakis, N., & Lamont, E.B. (2000). Extent and determinants of error in doctor's prognoses in terminally ill patients. *British Medical Journal, 320,* 469-472.

Dresser, R., & Whitehouse, P.J. (1994). The incompetent patient on the slippery slope. *Hastings Center Report, 24,* 6-12.

Dworkin, R. (1993). *Life's dominion: An argument about abortion, euthanasia, and individual freedom.* New York: Knofp.

Feldt, K.S. (2000). The checklist of nonverbal pain indicators (CNPI). *Pain Management Nursing, 1,* 13-21.

Finucane, T.E., et al. (1999). Tube feeding in patients with advanced dementia: A review of the evidence. *JAMA, 282,* 1365-1370.

Karlawish, J.H., & Casarett, D. (1999). Working in the dark: The state of palliative care for patients with severe dementia. *Generations, 23,* 18-23.

Luchins, D.J. (1997). Criteria for enrolling dementia patients in hospice. *JAGS, 45,* 1054-1059.

Reisburg, R. (1988). Validation of the FAST staging model. *Psychopharmacology Bulletin, 24,* 653-659.

Rich, B.A. (1998). Personhood, patienthood, and clinical practice: Reassessing advance directives. *Psychology, Public Policy and Law, 4,* 610-628.

CHAPTER 18

Alzheimer's Disease and the Quality of Life

Bruce Jennings

The concept of quality of life plays a controversial role in the care of patients with Alzheimer's disease. In general, the notion of one's quality of life is something that should be defined by the person to whom it applies. When others make a judgment of quality of life they are exercising power (because quality of life judgments have consequences for caregiving services), and they may be imposing a value or set of values that the patient does not share. Hence, improper or inappropriate quality of life assessments may both harm and wrong a person. To harm is to hurt or to violate a person's interests. To wrong a person is to treat that person like an object or a thing; it is to fail to recognize and acknowledge the humanity of the person.

In the case of dementia (and many other disabling impairments as well), the person is particularly vulnerable to both harm and wrong. Unfortunately, the misuse of the notion of quality of life is probably quite widespread in situations of Alzheimer's disease, because dementing illness undermines precisely those qualities that in American culture are seen as making an individual distinctively human—coherent communication, memory, social orientation, and behavioral self-control. And yet, as dangerous as it is, we cannot entirely avoid using the notion of quality of life when talking about Alzheimer's. We may avoid using the words, but we cannot avoid the idea. It is particularly important that we get this idea straight and use it appropriately. In this chapter I sort through the various meanings of the notion of quality of life, and discuss how to use it ethically and appropriately for the benefit, not the detriment, of Alzheimer's patients, caregivers, and families.

FOUR MEANINGS OF QUALITY OF LIFE

Some people refuse to use the term quality of life at all because to them it means that we are trying to evaluate something that is presumptuous or wrong for us to evaluate. Another version of this worry is that the idea of quality of life necessarily turns into a judgment about the value human life. (This mistaken line of reasoning goes something like this: "A life of very poor quality is not worth living. If a life is not worth living, then it has no value.") The term quality of life seems to suggest that life is not intrinsically worthy of respect, but can have greater or lesser value according to its circumstances. (Cohen, 1983)

These are powerful and plausible worries, but I think there is a way that the concept of quality of life can be used to enhance, rather than detract from, ethics. It is not only possible but essential to distinguish quality of life from the value or worth of life. Properly understood, the notion of quality of life can be used to enhance respect for them as human beings, as members of our common moral community. And it can be used to strengthen the case for social reform and improvements in Alzheimer's disease caregiving systems on the basis of social justice and equity. In order to use the notion of quality of life appropriately and for these ends rather than inappropriately, we need to become more precise about what the concept means. I think there are four different senses in which the term is used.

Quality of Life as a Property of the Individual

First, the notion of quality of life is used to refer to some characteristic or state of being of the individual person. A quality of life (whether good or poor) is something one has or possesses, much as one has a physical characteristic or a personality trait. Moreover, it is a temporary characteristic that can change over time, or it is a characteristic that can be compensated for or ameliorated by some artificial device or by special training—and for this reason quality of life is not an essential component of one's identity or self-esteem. As such it has no straightforward moral significance. A poor quality of life (due to ill health, loss of a job, breakdown of personal relationships, or the like) is not necessarily a sign of a person's moral failing, and it says nothing about the intrinsic value of life as such, or even about the moral value of that particular life at that particular time. Those who suffer are not generally thought to be less deserving on that account of others' care and concern. On the contrary, morality teaches that they are more deserving.

Quality of Life as a Goal of Care

A second common meaning of quality of life defines it as a goal of care. The moral point of our dealings with another (whether the situation be health care or some other form of relationship) is to sustain and improve the quality of life. In this sense, quality of life becomes a benchmark to guide human activity and a concept of assessment and evaluation, not of the person, but of the care he or she receives. Notice that the evaluation here is directed primarily at the caregiver and the caregiving process, not at the recipient of care, who partakes of the quality of life achieved but is not judged by it. Moreover, the quality of life that the person enjoys may be thought of as an interaction, so to speak, between the person and her surrounding circumstances, including other people. Thus understood as a goal or outcome of care, an improved quality of life may be a change (for the better) in the person's symptoms or perceptions; or it may be a change in the person's relationship with his environment. Medical cure, symptom relief, psychological happiness, or social empowerment may all be goals of care as comprehended by the concept of quality of life.

Quality of Life as a Social Situation

Next, quality of life refers to the quality of the interaction between an individual and his social and physical environment. Here a certain quality of life is not a property of the individual per se, but a function of that individual's form of life, his way of being in the world. Once again, a low assessment of a person's quality of life in this sense does not suggest a negative evaluation of the person or his worth; only a negative evaluation of his circumstances. Instead it implies a critical evaluation of the person's environment and can be used to find ways in which that environment could be enhanced or improved. There are some kinds of cognitive function that persons with Alzheimer's disease can no longer perform, but the capacities for stimulation, response, and enjoyment that they do still have can be enriched by a good environment or can be starved by a poor one. Quality of life is less about what the person with Alzheimer's has lost and more about how to make the environment support the capabilities he or she still has. Far from rejecting human dignity as a moral touchstone, the concept of quality of life in this sense can be used as a critical champion of dignity, attacking circumstances that undermine it and supporting change in the person's surrounding conditions that will respect it. Quality of life, high or low, does not reside in people, but in the space of interactions between and among people.

Quality of Life as the Moral Worth of a Life

Finally, it must be acknowledged that the term quality of life is sometimes, perhaps often, used to refer to the moral worth or value of a person and his or her life. Pushed to its logical extreme, this understanding of the quality of life takes us to the infamous Nazi concept of "life unworthy of life," (*lebensunwertes Leben*), which was used to rationalize everything from active euthanasia of those with disabilities to the genocidal death camps. (Lifton, 1986)

It is this last sense of the concept of quality of life, and this last sense only, that makes the concept prone to abuse and morally dangerous. How can a life of very poor quality possibly be respected or judged to have moral value? If the notion of "quality" refers to the moral worth of life, then the notion would seem incompatible with the idea of life's intrinsic value, and it would lead us, perhaps illicitly and improperly, into the realm of instrumental value only. But the notion of quality can be understood differently, and the implications are then reversed. The notion of quality may mark the gap between the *actual* circumstances and the *possible* circumstances of an intrinsically valuable life. I need not say that Beethoven is merely a means to the end of making great music (and thus value him only instrumentally) in order to say that he would be better off with access to a piano than he would be without access to one. Nor do I have to deny his intrinsic worth (or indeed make any judgment about his moral worth whatever) if I were to make the (admittedly much more controversial) quality of life judgment that Beethoven was better off when he could hear than he was after he became deaf.

An account of moral worth is based on an underlying account of humanness or the human person; an account, that is, of what it is to be human. The concept of quality of life, on the other hand, is based on an account of a person's inherent capacities and external circumstances. Quality of life may tell us something about the experience, but not the moral worth of humanness, or it may tell us something about *becoming (more fully) human*, but never about the value of *being human*.

In the end, the concept of quality of life must be judged by how it is used. In the hands of those who want to deny services or rights of individuals who purportedly experience a life of low quality, the concept is dangerous. However, the concept may also be used by those who seek a way to assess individual need and the quality of care and services so that more effective and humane care can be provided, and so that more human benefit will result from these services.

PHILOSOPHICAL THEORIES OF QUALITY OF LIFE

Philosophical discussions of the meaning of quality of life fall into three main types: (1) sensation (or "hedonic") theories, (2) reasonable preference theories, and (3) theories of human flourishing. (Brock, 1993; McCormick, 1978; Scanlon, 1993)

Sensation Theories

This version identifies quality of life with states of awareness, consciousness, or experience of the individual. Happiness or pleasure are the constituents of a good quality of life; pain and unhappiness define a poor quality of life. This allows for considerable individual variation in assessing good quality of life because different things make different people happy, but it also allows for some kind of common measuring rod because there are seemingly universal negative states of pain or suffering or unhappiness that all (normal) persons avoid.

The trouble with this theory seems simple once you think of it. Imagine a person locked in a cell with an electrode implanted in a pleasure center of the brain. All he does is press a button and experiences pleasure all the time. No freedom, no friends, just pleasant sensation. This theory holds that such a person would be experiencing the highest quality of life. Most of us, I imagine, would see this as a stunted, pathetic way to live.

An interesting question, when applying this type of theory to the case of Alzheimer's disease, is whether it is necessary for the person to realize he is happy in order to be happy. If the pleasure or happiness in question requires some form of self-awareness (not only being happy, but being happy to be happy), then at some point in the course of Alzheimer's, when that capacity is lost, this theory will provide only a negative assessment of the patient's quality of life. It will load the dice against Alzheimer's disease. But surely we want that to remain an open question, subject to empirical research, and not a closed question settled in advance by the very definition we give to the notion of quality of life.

Reasonable Preference Theories

The second type of theory defines quality of life in terms of the actual satisfaction or realization of a person's rational desires or preferences. This is a much more objective theory than the sensation account in that a person need not be aware that his preferences are being fulfilled (or need not take pleasure in that knowledge) in order for the quality of his life to be good, it just must be the case that they are. For example, if I arrive in Chicago during a snowstorm to attend a political meeting that furthers the cause of justice, my quality of life is enhanced (because my rational desire for justice is furthered) even though subjectively I may feel cold, miserable, homesick, and bored by longwinded speeches. If I skip the meeting and go to a beach in the Virgin Islands instead, my pleasurable experience may be enhanced, but my quality of life will be diminished. The underlying appeal of theories of this type is the notion that individuals have a good life when the objective state of the world conforms to what they rationally desire.

Theories of Human Flourishing

This type of philosophical theory attempts to base our understanding of the good life on an account of those functions, capacities, and excellences that are most fully and constitutively human. To the extent that we attain and master those capacities, and to the extent that we negate those conditions that would stunt or undermine those capacities, we flourish as human beings. Theories of this type also usually have a developmental component built into them, for those most fully human capacities are ones that are not mastered at birth or automatically expressed by instinct, but must be developed and nurtured by education, interaction with others, and practice over the course of a life time. To the extent, then, that the individual continues to grow and develop throughout her life, the quality of life is enhanced thereby.

This account emphasizes the human capacity to express and to experience meaning in social relationships of intimacy, friendship, and cooperation; the capacity to use reason and to develop and follow a life-plan of self-fulfillment and self-realization; the capacity for independence and self-reliance; and the human need for an appropriate social and cultural environment that provides the individual with various types of resources—material, symbolic, spiritual—necessary to live a developmentally human life and to meet both basic and secondary needs.

These brief sketches scarcely do justice to theories that are in fact very elaborate and complex. But perhaps enough of a flavor of these three common approaches to the concept of quality of life comes through to draw a few conclusions.

For understandable reasons perhaps, in the literature on quality of life and dementia the most commonly adopted philosophical perspective is the sensation or hedonic account. It may seem that only this type of theory is compatible with the radically diminished cognitive capacity in Alzheimer's disease and other dementias. Or it may be that this type of theory seems most congenial to the value relativism and the subjective approach Americans are most comfortable with in dealing with such a sensitive and potentially discriminatory concept as the quality of life, especially when applied to this most vulnerable population.

I believe that we should not limit ourselves to this understanding of quality of life in Alzheimer's disease or other dementias. The main problem with this theory is its tacit conceptual bias. In discussions of quality of life in dementia, the relative strengths and weaknesses of these three types of philosophical theory have not been explicitly discussed, and the sensation approach has been adopted without sufficient critical analysis.

The concept of quality of life is misused, in my judgment, when it becomes a floor below which no significant societal expenditure of resources is required, and below which personal caregiving efforts may be reduced to the decent minimum. A much better way to think about quality of life is to see it as a ceiling, a potential level of functional capacity and capacity for relationship, toward which caregiving efforts should be designed to strive. The height of this ceiling will not be the same for everyone, and quality of life is not a test that you fail if you do not reach a certain height. But the important point is that quality of life should be used as a teleological concept—setting a goal to reach and a process to reach it, rather than as a prioritizing concept—setting a rank ordering for the allocation of scarce resources. In discussions of Alzheimer's disease, when we focus too much on the hedonic elements of pleasant sensation and immediate experience, this very point about how quality of life notions are used in policy analysis tends not to be raised at all. Since we assume the ceiling is inevitably going to be so low, we turn our attention to not "wasting" resources on those who have already fallen below the floor.

Future work on the quality of life with dementia needs to adopt a more synthetic and eclectic conceptual approach, drawing on the resources offered by each of the main types of philosophical theory of quality of life. Life lived with dementia, even well into its later stages, can be explicated by drawing on conceptions of rational desire and even human flourishing, and it need not be assessed only in the most directly sensate, hedonic terms. If we try to work with broader and richer notions of quality of life, as Lawton, for example, has done, we will in fact be rewarded with more insightful findings that will be helpful in guiding public policy and clinical practice. (Lawton, 1991; Lawton, 1995; Burgener, 1998; Albert et al, 1996; Russell, 1996) But I also argue for this broader approach because I believe the consequences of adhering to the sensation approach exclusively, are unacceptable.

A Life Greater than Its Sensations

When we use only hedonic notions of quality of life as our lens to view life lived with dementia, we run the risk of too quickly closing off aspects of meaning making ("semantic agency") and moral personhood from persons with Alzheimer's disease. Alzheimer's does not, until perhaps very, very late, close off the possibility of meaning-making activity by a person supported by the right types of interpersonal relationships and caring systems. This activity cannot be reduced to feelings or sensations alone; it taps a circuit of two-way communication and experience between human beings that goes beyond unilateral sensation or sensate experience. Of course, communication here does not mean verbal or even semiotic communication, for the capacity to manipulate previously learned semiotic systems may be lost with Alzheimer's patients. But touch, gesture, facial expression, posture, eye contact, even control of body movements to permit prolonged physical closeness, like sitting together, can conceivably be media of semantic agency, and these are much slower to be lost than memory, speech, functional capacities for activities of daily living and self-care, and the rest.

By "moral personhood" I mean that respect and acknowledgment of the individual as a member of the human moral community is ethically required. Each moral person (the caregiver, say) has an obligation to maintain and sustain relationships with other moral persons (the Alzheimer's patient). If I am a moral person, I cannot rightfully be ignored, abandoned, exiled from the space of connection between selves that we call the moral community. If we come to the too-easy conclusion that Alzheimer's patients have lost moral personhood—have lost this status, this claim on our attention and response—then it will be all the easier to turn aside from these connections and all the easier to tolerate institutions and caregiving systems that fail to fashion, mend, and create those connections and relationships.

Is this not precisely what we do so often with demented patients now in our health care institutions? Isn't this what our lack of social support to Alzheimer's families makes so difficult to achieve even in the home setting? In asking these rhetorical questions, I do not mean to say that when Alzheimer's patients are seen as lacking in moral personhood they are necessarily neglected, abused, or abandoned. But I do claim that the moral basis of our care giving changes. It is one thing to give care and protection out of a sense of pity, or charity, or professional duty, or even love; it is another to maintain a relationship and connection with the other for as long as possible out of a sense of the moral importance of that connection per se.

Caring and caregiving, after all, are not only about meeting an individual's needs or making him comfortable; they are about the recognition of the person of the other, the one being cared for, and they are about the recognition of the caregiver's own personhood therein also. I have just said the recognition of the person of the other; I should also say that caregiving and quality of life are about the preserving, conserving, sustaining, nurturing, and eliciting of that personhood as well.

We can now return to our discussion of quality of life. When we define quality of life in exclusively hedonic terms—especially when we conceptualize happiness or pleasure in terms of direct sensation rather than the secondary interpretation or mediation of first order sensation— we effectively leave no room for semantic agency and moral personhood, whereas these ideas are at work to some extent in rational desire theories and figure very largely indeed in human flourishing theories. If we thought that an Alzheimer's patient had the capacity for semantic agency or moral personhood, why would we ever be content to say that she has a good quality of life if her pleasurable sensations outnumber her painful ones? Surely we would look at the surrounding conditions that the patient is living in and ask, how can the range of her exercise of (remaining) capacity for semantic agency be enhanced and facilitated? How could caregivers be given a better opportunity to mend and maintain those relationships and interactions appropriate to the recognition and honoring of moral personhood? Pleasant sensations or feelings will come through the exercise of semantic agency and with the recognition of moral personhood, to be sure, but they, not the feelings per se, are the sum and substance of her quality of life. (Tragically, with Alzheimer's disease we may actually have to choose between happiness and agency, for to slow the progress of the disease in its early or middle stages and to extend the period of capacity and agency is also to extend the suffering that accompanies the awareness of ongoing and impending loss. Hedonic conceptions of quality of life would not necessarily view drugs that have this effect as beneficial.)

There is another reason why relying solely on sensation or hedonic conceptions of quality of life is a bad idea. The notion of quality of life is a tool for health policy makers to use in assessing the quality of health services. For Alzheimer's disease, this means mainly long-term care, rehabilitative, and palliative care. The hedonic conception of quality of life sets the bar too low for policy makers. We need more than safe, comfortable warehouses for persons with advanced Alzheimer's. We need to demand caregiving environments that provide some measure of rehabilitation in terms of the human relationships, modes of interaction and communication, and the sustaining of semantic agency and moral personhood (making meaning, and being treated with respect). (Solomon & Jennings, 1998)

As my generation ages into the first few decades of the next century, I do not want to send a message to young policy makers that it is enough merely to provide a shelter where I can be kept pleasantly senile, as important as comfort and safety are. If Alzheimer's disease is destined to be the last chapter in the story of my life, I want those pages to have more of a plot, and more of a character than that. I can't bring that about by myself now, no matter how much I save or how much long-term care insurance I buy; and I won't be able to protect my own quality of life interests then. But the people and the institutions that care for me could do so. Will they have the wherewithal (the resources and the social investment) and the will (the proper understanding of the goals of care) to do so? The answer to that question will determine the quality of life ahead for millions of persons with Alzheimer's disease. ■

Bruce Jennings is Senior Research Scholar at The Hastings Center, a bioethics research institute located in Garrison, New York. Mr. Jennings has been with the Hastings Center since 1980 and served as Executive Director of the Center from 1990-1999. A graduate of Yale University (BA) and Princeton University (MA), he has written widely on end-of-life care, long-term care, and health policy. He serves on the National Ethics Advisory Committee of the Alzheimer's Association. He has written or edited 15 books, the most recent of which is The Perversion of Autonomy: The Uses of Coercion and Constraints in a Liberal Society (2nd. ed. 2003), co-authored with Willard Gaylin. He is currently at work on a book on chronic illness, dementia, and long-term care policy.

REFERENCES

Albert, S.M., Del Castillo-Castaneda, C., Sano, M., Jacobs, D.M., Marder, K., Bell, K., et al. (1996). Quality of Life in patients with Alzheimer's disease as reported by patient proxies. *Journal of the American Geriatrics Society 44*, 1342-1347.

Brock, D. (1993). Quality of life measures in health care and medical ethics. In M.C. Nussbaum and A. Sen (Eds.), *The quality of life* (pp. 95-139). New York: Cambridge University Press.

Burgener, S.C. (1998). Quality of life in late stage dementia. In L. Volicer and A. Hurley (Eds.), *Hospice care for patients with advanced progressive dementia* (pp. 88-113). New York: Springer.

Cohen, C. (1983). 'Quality of Life' and the analogy with the Nazis. *Journal of Medicine and Philosophy 8*, 113-135.

Jennings, B. (1999). A life greater than the sum of its sensations: ethics, dementia, and the quality of life. *Journal of Mental Health and Aging, 5*(1) (Spring), 95-106.

Lawton, M.P. (1991). A multidimensional view of quality of life in frail elders. J. E. Birren et al (Eds.), *The concept and measurement of quality of life in the frail elderly* (pp. 3-27). New York: Academic Press.

Lawton, M.P. (1995). Quality of life in Alzheimer's disease. *Alzheimer's Disease and Associated Disorders, 8* (Suppl. 3), 138-150.

Lifton, R.J. (1986). *Nazi doctors.* New York: Basic Books.

McCormick, R. (1978). The quality of life, the sanctity of life. *Hastings Center Report* (February), 30-36.

Russell, C.K. (1996). Passion and heretics: Meaning in life and quality of life of persons with dementia. *Journal of the American Geriatrics Society, 44*, 1400-1401.

Scanlon, T. (1993). Value, desire, and quality of life. In M.C. Nussbaum and A. Sen (Eds.), *The quality of life* (pp. 185-200). New York: Cambridge University Press.

Solomon, M.Z., & Jennings, B. (1998). Palliative care for Alzheimer patients: Implications for institutions, caregivers, and families. In L. Volicer and A. Hurley (Eds.), *Hospice care for patients with advanced progressive dementia* (pp. 132-154). New York: Springer.

CHAPTER 19

Resources

Lisa McGahey Veglahn

As the Alzheimer's population increases, so does the number of people who face caregiving responsibilities and the issues of loss that inevitably follow. In response, many organizations offer support and resources to meet both personal and professional needs. The following list provides a guide to a wide range of these organizations and the services they offer.

As this book goes to press, the Alzheimer's Association has prepared a supplementary resource list on hospice and Alzheimer's disease. This list will be posted on the Association's Web site at http://www.alz.org in the "Resources" section under "Resource List." Hospice Foundation of America wishes to extend special thanks to JoAnn Ciatto and Mary Ann Urbashich of the Alzheimer's Association for their guidance and collaboration.

■

(U.S.) Administration on Aging
U.S. Department of Health and Human Services
1 Massachusetts Avenue, NW
Washington, DC 20201
Phone: (202) 619-0724
E-mail: AoAInfo@aoa.gov
Web: www.aoa.gov

The U.S. Administration on Aging (AoA) provides a comprehensive overview of a wide variety of topics, programs, and services related to aging. The Alzheimer's Resource Room is where families, caregivers, and professionals can find information about the Alzheimer's Demonstration Program, which includes fact sheets, state contacts, brochures, and links for caregivers, volunteers, clergy members, and support groups. The National Family Caregiver Support Program provides a variety of services to help people who are caring for family members who are chronically ill or who have disabilities. AoA also provides the Eldercare Locator, a national toll-free directory assistance public service that helps people locate aging services in every community throughout the United States. The primary goal of the service is to promote awareness of and improve access to state, area agency, and local community aging programs and services. This service can be accessed at www.eldercare.gov or by calling (800) 677-1116.

Alzheimer's Association
National Office
225 North Michigan Avenue, Floor 17
Chicago, IL 60601-7633
Phone: (800) 272-3900 or (312) 335-8700
TDD Access: (312) 335-8882
Fax: (312) 335-1110
E-mail: Info@alz.org
Web: www.alz.org

The Alzheimer's Association, a national network of chapters, is the largest national voluntary health organization dedicated to advancing Alzheimer's research and helping those affected by the disease. Having awarded nearly $150 million in research grants, the Association ranks as the top private funder of research into the causes, treatments, and prevention of Alzheimer's disease. The Association also provides education and support for people diagnosed with the condition, their families, and caregivers. The Association's Web site includes a Resource Center, which contains fact sheets, downloadable documents, and links to associations and other available community and Internet resources on treatment, caregiving, training, and special programs. The Alzheimer's Association is an authority on the issues that affect people with Alzheimer's disease and their families, serving as a voice for them in the capitals of every state, hundreds of U.S. congressional offices, and even the White House. The Benjamin B. Green-Field National Alzheimer's Library and Resource Center, the nation's first privately funded resource facility focusing on Alzheimer's disease, is housed in the national offices of the Alzheimer's Association. (See also Benjamin B. Green-Field National Alzheimer's Library and Resource Center.)

Alzheimer's Disease and Education Referral (ADEAR) Center
P.O. Box 8250
Silver Spring, MD 20907-8250
Phone: (800) 438-4380
Fax: (301) 495-3334
E-mail: adear@alzheimers.org
Web: www.alzheimers.org

The U.S. Congress created the Alzheimer's Disease Education and Referral (ADEAR) Center in 1990 to compile, archive, and disseminate information concerning Alzheimer's disease for health professionals, people with Alzheimer's disease and their families, and the public. The ADEAR Center is operated as a service of the National Institute on Aging (NIA), one of the federal government's National Institutes of Health and part of the U.S. Department of Health and Human Services. The NIA conducts and supports research about health issues for older people, and is the primary federal agency for Alzheimer's disease research. As a public, U.S. government-funded resource, the ADEAR Center strives to be a current, comprehensive, unbiased source of information about Alzheimer's disease. The Center offers free publications, referrals, Spanish language resources, clinical trials information, and a literature database search.

Alzheimer's Information Site
c/o Fisher Center for Alzheimer's Research Foundation
One Intrepid Square
West 46th Street & 12th Avenue
New York, NY 10036
Phone: (800) ALZINFO (800-259-4636)
E-mail: info@alzinfo.org
Web: www.alzinfo.org

Alzinfo.org is for caregivers, family members, and people living with Alzheimer's, and provides a single point of entry for comprehensive information and resources on Alzheimer's disease. The site includes information about warning signs and symptoms, diagnosis and treatment, the latest medical breakthroughs, caregiving information and tips, financial and legal assistance, continuing care facilities, and hospice and end-of-life services. The site also includes a searchable database of senior care services and resources.

Alzheimer Research Forum

Web: www.alzforum.org

The Alzheimer Research Forum was founded in 1996 to create an online scientific community dedicated to developing treatments and preventions for Alzheimer's disease. The Web site creates and maintains Web-based resources for researchers and produces discussion forums to promote debate, speed the dissemination of new ideas, and break down barriers across the numerous disciplines that can contribute to the global effort to cure Alzheimer's disease. The Web site also has resources for consumers.

American Association for Geriatric Psychiatry

7910 Woodmont Avenue, Suite 1050
Bethesda, MD 20814-3004
Phone: (301) 654-7850
Fax: (301) 654-4137
E-mail: main@aagponline.org
Web: www.aagpgpa.org

The American Association for Geriatric Psychiatry is a national association representing and serving its members and the field of geriatric psychiatry. It is dedicated to promoting the mental health and well being of older people and improving the care of those with late-life mental disorders. AAGP's mission is to enhance the knowledge base and standard of practice in geriatric psychiatry through education and research and to advocate for meeting the mental health needs of older Americans.

**Benjamin B. Green-Field National Alzheimer's Library
and Resource Center**
c/o The Alzheimer's Association
National Office
225 North Michigan Avenue, Floor 17
Chicago, IL 60601-7633
Phone: (800) 272-3900 or (312) 335-9602
Fax: (312) 335-0214
E-mail: greenfield@alz.org
Web: www.alz.org/ResourceCenter/Programs/LibraryServices.htm

The Benjamin B. Green-Field National Alzheimer's Library and Resource Center is housed in the national offices of the Alzheimer's Association. The library is the nation's first privately funded resource facility focusing on Alzheimer's disease, established through a generous grant from the Benjamin B. Green-Field Foundation. The Resource Center's mission is to help increase knowledge of the medical, clinical, and social aspects of Alzheimer's disease and related disorders. The center is a source of accurate information for those involved in patient care, policy development, research, or those who simply want to know more about the disease.

Ethnic Elders Care
Phone: (925) 372-2105
E-mail: Ecarenet@yahoo.com
Web: www.ethnicelderscare.net

Ethnic Elders is a Web site designed specifically for people who are currently or will be caregivers to ethnic elders with Alzheimer's disease and related disorders. Ethnic Elders is dedicated to promoting research, prevention, and treatment of Alzheimer's disease and related disorders and to providing education, support, and assistance to ethnic minority elderly patients, their families, and caregivers.

Family Caregiver Alliance
690 Market Street, Suite 600
San Francisco, CA 94104
Phone: (800) 445-8106 or (415) 434-3388
Fax: (415) 434-3508
E-mail: info@caregiver.org
Web: www.caregiver.org

Family Caregiver Alliance (FCA) was the first community-based nonprofit organization in the country to address the needs of families and friends providing long-term care at home. FCA now offers programs at national, state, and local levels to support and sustain caregivers. FCA offers information on legislation, caregiver resources, and medical information.

Hospice Foundation of America
2001 S Street, NW, Suite 300
Washington, DC 20009
Phone: (800) 854-3402 or (202) 638-5419
Fax: (202) 638-5312
E-mail: info@hospicefoundation.org
Web: www.hospicefoundation.org

Hospice Foundation of America (HFA) is a nonprofit organization that provides leadership in the development and application of hospice and its philosophy of care. HFA produces an annual award-winning national teleconference on grief and publishes the companion book series, *Living With Grief®*. HFA provides continuing education opportunities for caregiving professionals through this teleconference, and also through its new subsidiary branch, Hospice College of America. HFA also provides a variety of other resources and titles, some of which are on audiocassettes. HFA offers a monthly newsletter, *Journeys*, as well as many other brochures that offer guidance on coping with end-of-life issues and bereavement.

John Douglas French Alzheimer's Foundation
11620 Wilshire Boulevard, Suite 270
Los Angeles, CA 90025
Phone: (800) 477-2243 or (310) 445-4650
Fax: (310) 479-0516
E-mail: jdfaf@earthlink.net
Web: www.jdfaf.org

The mission of the Foundation is to generate funds for Alzheimer's research to significantly delay the onset or find a cure for Alzheimer's disease within the next decade. Funding is targeted to areas of research typically not supported by government agencies. The emphasis of research will be in two areas: fellowships and grants for talented young scientists in the early stages of their research careers, encouraging them to use new technological skills of study, including the exploration of less traditional avenues of research; and projects investigating new frontiers of research in which the Foundation is an important catalyst in initiating unique studies of a collaborative nature.

Last Acts
c/o Partnership for Caring, Inc.
1620 Eye Street NW, Suite 202
Washington, DC 20006
Phone: (202) 296-8071
Fax: (202) 296-8352
E-mail: kaplanko@partnershipforcaring.org
Web: www.lastacts.org

Last Acts is a national coalition of more than 1,100 organizations engaged in an education campaign to improve care and support for terminally ill people and their families. Last Acts serves as a national clearinghouse for sharing information and ideas at the national, state, and local levels. Last Acts also provides a forum for discussion, collaboration, and broad dissemination of new information. Last Acts sponsors national and regional conferences, publishes a quarterly print newsletter, and offers a number of e-mail discussion groups and newsletters.

Medline Plus Health Information
Web: www.nlm.nih.gov/medlineplus

MEDLINEplus is a service of U.S. National Library of Medicine and National Institutes of Health. MEDLINEplus has extensive information from the National Institutes of Health and other trusted sources on over 600 diseases and conditions, including Alzheimer's disease. There are also lists of hospitals and physicians, a medical encyclopedia and a medical dictionary, health information in Spanish, extensive information on prescription and non-prescription drugs, health information from the media, and links to thousands of clinical trials.

National Alzheimer's Council

c/o National Emergency Medicine Association
306 W. Joppa Road
Baltimore, MD 21204-4048
Phone: (410) 494-0300
Fax: (410) 494-0725
E-mail: info@nemahealth.org
Web: www.nemahealth.org

The National Alzheimer's Council, a program of the National Emergency Medicine Association, is dedicated to the dissemination of information about progress in understanding and moderating the causes and effects of Alzheimer's disease on individuals, their families, and friends. This is accomplished through applied research and education.

National Family Caregivers Association

10400 Connecticut Avenue, Suite 500
Kensington, MD 20895-3944
Phone: (800) 896-3650
Fax: (301) 942-2302
E-mail: info@nfcacares.org
Web: www.nfcacares.org

The National Family Caregivers Association (NFCA) is a grass roots organization created to educate, support, empower, and speak up for the millions of Americans who care for chronically ill, aged, or disabled loved ones. Through its services in the areas of information and education, support and validation, and public awareness and advocacy, NFCA strives to minimize the disparity between a caregiver's quality of life and that of mainstream Americans. NFCA offers Alzheimer's disease-specific resources for caregivers.

National Hospice and Palliative Care Organization

1700 Diagonal Road, Suite 625
Alexandria, VA 22314
Phone: (703) 837-1500
Fax: (703) 837-1233
Consumer HelpLine: (800) 658-8898
E-mail: nhpco_info@nhpco.org
Web: www.nhpco.org

The National Hospice and Palliative Care Organization (NHPCO) is the largest nonprofit membership organization representing hospice and palliative care programs and professionals in the United States. The organization is committed to improving end-of-life care and expanding access to hospice. NHPCO offers educational programs and materials for professionals and the public.

National Institute of Neurological Disorders and Stroke
NIH Neurological Institute
P.O. Box 5801
Bethesda, MD 20824
Phone: (800) 352-9424 or (301) 496-5751
TTY: (301) 468-5981
Web: www.ninds.nih.gov

The National Institute of Neurological Disorders and Stroke (NINDS) conducts and supports research on brain and nervous system disorders. Created by the U.S. Congress in 1950, NINDS is one of the more than two dozen research institutes and centers that comprise the National Institutes of Health (NIH). The NIH, located in Bethesda, Maryland, is an agency of the Public Health Service within the U.S. Department of Health and Human Services. NINDS has occupied a central position in the world of neuroscience for 50 years.

U.S. Department of Veterans Affairs (VA)
Veterans Affairs Central Office
810 Vermont Avenue NW
Washington, DC 20420
Web: www.va.gov

The U.S. Department of Veterans Affairs (VA) operates the largest direct health care delivery system in the country. Veterans with dementia who receive care from VA's network of health care facilities participate in the full range of health care services, including outpatient, acute care, and long term care programs. In order to advance knowledge about care for veterans with dementia, VA investigators conduct biomedical, clinical, health services, and rehabilitation research. VA conducts the nation's largest coordinated education and training effort for health care professionals. VA also funds specialized geriatric training programs in numerous professional disciplines, including geriatric medicine. Continuing education for staff caring for patients with dementia at VA facilities and in the community is provided through training classes sponsored by VA Geriatric Research, Education, and Clinical Centers (GRECCs) and VA's network of education field units. In addition, VA Central Office has disseminated a variety of dementia patient care educational materials in the form of publications, videotapes, and CD-ROMs to all VA facilities.

UNIVERSITY SITES/RESEARCH PROGRAMS

Alzheimer's Disease Cooperative Study
http://www-alz.ucsd.edu/

The Alzheimer's Disease Cooperative Study is a consortium of leading Alzheimer's disease medical research centers providing collaborative investigational clinical trials research.

Alzheimer's Disease Research Center at Washington University
www.alzheimer.wustl.edu

The ADRC provides an interdisciplinary environment in which diverse scientific and patient-oriented activities are focused. The Center also supports new clinical and basic science research programs and projects and provides educational opportunities for healthcare professionals and lay persons, both at Washington University Medical Center and in the community. The Center oversees an active e-mail discussion list.

Caregiver's SEAD (Support & Education for Alzheimer's Disease)
http://neuro-oas.mgh.harvard.edu/sea/

This site was developed by the Massachusetts General Hospital Memory Disorders Unit for anyone who is facing the challenge of managing Alzheimer's disease. Education plays a vital role in giving caregivers the skills that make coping with Alzheimer's disease easier. This site also includes suggestions for symptom management, accessing community services, and facing some common family challenges.

Cognitive Neurology and Alzheimer's Disease Center at Northwestern University

http://www.brain.northwestern.edu/

The mission of the CNADC is to investigate the neurological basis of cognitive function, to elucidate causes of dementia, and to ensure that the patients and their families are the beneficiaries of resultant discoveries.

Duke Alzheimer's Family Support Program

http://www.geri.duke.edu/service/dfsp/about.htm

Based at the Duke University Center for the Study of Aging and Human Development, this site serves as a source for help with Alzheimer's, memory disorders, and elder care decisions. The Duke Family Support Program serves families and professionals concerned about or caring for persons with memory disorders in North Carolina, and Duke employees seeking help with elder care decisions.

Partners Program in Neurodegenerative Disease

http://fisher.mgh.harvard.edu/alzheimers/

The Partners Program in Neurodegenerative Diseases brings together, in one coordinated program, the basic science and clinical resources of Partners HealthCare Systems, Inc., which includes three of the primary Harvard Medical School teaching hospitals (BWH, MGH, and McLean).

Resources for Enhancing Alzheimer's Caregiver Health (REACH)

http://www.edc.gsph.pitt.edu/REACH/

REACH is an NIH-sponsored collaborative study of caregivers of relatives with Alzheimer's disease or a related dementia. Its primary purpose is to develop and test new ways to help families manage the daily activities and the stresses of caring for people with Alzheimer's disease or a related disorder.

University Memory and Aging Center

http://www.ohioalzcenter.org/resource.html

The University Memory and Aging Center (formerly known as University Alzheimer Center) of Case Western Reserve University and University Hospitals of Cleveland promotes the best possible care for persons with memory problems and assists their families through an integrated program of clinical services, research, and education.

Lisa McGahey Veglahn is a consultant to the Hospice Foundation of America. She oversaw the production of seven national bereavement teleconferences for HFA. Ms. Veglahn served as a member of the Last Acts Workplace Task Force and a reviewer for the Robert Wood Johnson Foundation's Sound Partners program. She is currently a member of the Kansas City Caregiving Coalition. She holds a Master's Degree from the Yale School of Drama.

Date Due

NO 0 6 '03			

BRODART, CO.   Cat. No. 23-233-003   Printed in U.S.A.